Socialism, Democracy
and Human Rights

EDITORIAL NOTE

The book includes, either in full or in part, speeches and articles delivered or written by Leonid Brezhnev, General Secretary of the Central Committee of the Communist Party of the Soviet Union, Chairman of the Presidium of the Supreme Soviet of the USSR, in the period from April 1970 to April 1979, in which he touched upon the most important problems of socialist democracy and human rights.

Other titles of interest by or about President Brezhnev:

BREZHNEV: A SHORT BIOGRAPHY

HOW IT WAS ('Malaya Zemlya', 'Vozrozhdenie')

VIRGIN LANDS: Two Years in Kazakhstan, 1954 – 5 ('Tselina')

VIRGIN LANDS: Two Years in Kazakhstan, 1954 – 5

SELECTED SPEECHES AND WRITINGS ON FOREIGN AFFAIRS

SOCIALISM, DEMOCRACY AND HUMAN RIGHTS

by

L. I. BREZHNEV

PERGAMON PRESS

OXFORD · NEW YORK · TORONTO · SYDNEY · PARIS · FRANKFURT

U.K.	Pergamon Press Ltd., Headington Hill Hall, Oxford OX3 0BW, England
U.S.A.	Pergamon Press Inc., Maxwell House, Fairview Park, Elmsford, New York 10523, U.S.A.
CANADA	Pergamon of Canada, Suite 104, 150 Consumers Road, Willowdale, Ontario M2J 1P9, Canada
AUSTRALIA	Pergamon Press (Aust.) Pty. Ltd., P.O. Box 544, Potts Point, N.S.W. 2011, Australia
FRANCE	Pergamon Press SARL, 24 rue des Ecoles, 75240 Paris, Cedex 05, France
FEDERAL REPUBLIC OF GERMANY	Pergamon Press GmbH, 6242 Kronberg-Taunus, Hammerweg 6, Federal Republic of Germany

First Edition 1980

British Library Cataloguing in Publication Data

Brezhnev, Leonid Il'ich
  Socialism, democracy and human rights.
  1. Political science — Addresses, essays, lectures
  2. Communism — Addresses, essays, lectures
  I. Title
  320'.08   DX275.B7   79-42659
  ISBN   0-08-023605-7

Printed in Great Britain by A. Wheaton & Co. Ltd., Exeter

PREFACE

To my American and British Readers

I hope this book will satisfy the curiosity of those readers who wish to know what Soviet socialist democracy is really like, how we view human rights and how these rights are exercised in the Soviet Union.

Democracy has been a subject of debate since the time of Ancient Greece, and human rights have also been discussed for centuries. Although the concept of human rights is of comparatively recent origin, one could no doubt say that it was in a struggle for their human rights that Spartacus long ago led the slaves of Ancient Rome. The movement of history has always been towards a fuller realisation of democracy and freedom. Already last century Friedrich Engels said: 'In our time democracy means communism.' Today this truth — a theoretical one in Engel's day — has been confirmed by life, by the practical activity of millions upon millions of people. I am aware that in the West ideologists of capitalism are impressing upon the public a different view, extolling the real or imagined merits of bourgeois democracy and playing down, slurring over or sullying the meaning and essence of socialist democracy.

To establish the truth it would be only fair to avoid prejudging the issue and to get first-hand information about Soviet democracy. This book contains a selection of statements made on the subject in question over the past 10 years.

Knowledge makes for better understanding, and for our countries and peoples mutual understanding is especially important — if only because no argument of principle on historical or ideological issues can be settled by a nuclear duel. By destroying each other neither side would prove the merits of its interpretation of democracy or human rights. So let us place first among all human rights the most sacred of them all — the right to life, and, consequently, to a lasting peace.

Our countries have different social and political systems, and so arguments and comparisons are unavoidable. In recent years these arguments and comparisons have centred on problems of democracy and human rights.

The Soviet people have great respect for the American Revolution and for the democratic traditions of Great Britain, and they realise that the concern of the Americans and the British for human rights is backed by their history. Karl Marx, for one, called the American Declaration of Independence 'the first declaration of human rights'. We consider the rights and freedoms proclaimed in it a tremendous achievement for that time, but from the standpoint of today they have become elements of formal bourgeois law, which are restricted by the very nature of bourgeois society in which actual rights and privileges are enjoyed by the propertied classes, and the formally democratic institutions serve to further the interests of these classes. It may be recalled, for instance, that neither the Declaration of Independence nor the Bill of Rights abolished slavery. This is not the ony example of a discrepancy between what is proclaimed and what is practised — and not only in the past either.

When among various rights the 'sacred' right to private property is given priority over all the rest, in actual fact those other rights and freedoms are curtailed or even emasculated. It becomes the old issue of both the poor man and the rich man having equal rights to sleep under the bridge.

When the United Nations Charter was being drafted, it was the Soviet Union which suggested that a clause on respect for basic human rights be included in it. The USSR is a signatory to many international agreements on human rights. However, we believe that with each country concern for human rights should begin at home. And this is where we started. Readers may find it interesting to learn that the aim of the October 1917 Revolution actually was to affirm the most basic human rights for the overwhelming majority of the people in our country.

Soon after the Revolution the Soviet government issued the Declaration of the Rights of the Peoples of Russia, which abolished all privileges and restrictions on grounds of nationality and religion. It was followed by the Declaration of the Rights of the Toiling and Exploited People.

The establishment of socialist public ownership of the land, natural resources and the means of production became the main guarantee of not only the political but also the social and economic rights of man in the USSR.

President Carter once said that there were many injustices in life, and the rich could afford what the poor could not. It is precisely this injustice that we strove to abolish, believing that it was an inherent part not of life in general, but of the character of social life, of the social system. It is for that reason that Soviet people reorganised their society; by making social production serve the interests not of groups of people or individuals but of the whole people, they were able not only to proclaim but also actually to secure every person's right to work, health care, education, material provision in old age and housing. In other words people were given freedom from anxiety for their future, they acquired a sense of security.

Proclaiming and ensuring economic, social and cultural rights, together with denying any person the right to exploit others and to appropriate the fruits of other people's labour, marked the transition from formal equality to real equality and put the political rights and freedoms of citizens on a material foundation.

A distinctive feature of Soviet democracy, and of socialist democracy in general, is the involvement of millions of working people in managing both production and the affairs of state.

From the very first days of Soviet rule an immense role in the building of a new society was played by the direct participation of millions not only in elections but also in everyday management of public and state affairs. And today, at the stage of mature socialism, ever broader and more active participation of working people in running their country has firmly established itself as the main trend in the political development of Soviet society. Thus, over the past 20 years 20 million people have worked directly in state administration as deputies to government bodies at all levels — from the USSR Supreme Soviet to the district or village Soviet; a further 30 million citizens have been giving voluntary assistance to government bodies, taking an active part in their work.

During the more than 60 years that the Soviet state has existed, socialist democracy has been constantly developing, growing deeper and richer, but its essence has remained unchanged — the involvement of masses of people in running public and state affairs. The Soviets are improving the democratic principles and methods of their work, which include accountability to the electorate, open conduct of activities, criticism of shortcomings, and combating bureaucracy; new forms of people's participation in running state affairs have appeared, work collectives — those primary cells of our socialist organisation — have become more active, and the role of public organisations, of which there are many, has increased.

PREFACE

We shall continue to develop and improve our democratic traditions which have grown on socialist soil and have passed the test of time.

In 1977 a new Constitution was adopted in the USSR. For several months prior to its adoption it was thoroughly and extensively discussed by the entire Soviet people. In this book readers will find answers, given in the light of that Constitution, to their questions about the rights, freedoms and duties of Soviet citizens. It is my hope that this will help readers to form a better idea of how the ideals of socialist humanism are being implemented in Soviet society, where the free development of each is the condition of the free development of all.

October 1979   LEONID BREZHNEV

CONTENTS

CONTENTS

CONTENTS

1970 – 2

VICTORY OF SOCIALISM IN THE SOVIET UNION —
A TRIUMPH OF LENINISM

. . . Lenin warned that the road to socialism 'will never be straight; it will be incredibly involved' (*Collected Works*, Vol. 27, p.130). But even in the most difficult conditions, Lenin did not lose faith in the titanic possibilities of the working people, the revolutionary working class and the Communist Party . . .

Lenin's profound ideas about the ways of creating a new society still serve as a reliable guide for the builders of the new world.

Lenin's plan for socialist construction is a model of the scientific, complex and realistic approach to the solution of a task of world historic importance. This plan ranged over all the tiers of the social edifice — the development of the productive forces, the transformation of social relations, and the recasting of man's spiritual world. Needless to say, it was based on the vast creative potential of the Party, the millions of builders of socialism, on the fact that in practice, in vibrant activity fresh possibilities were bound to open up, and new methods and means found for advancing towards the set goals. Lenin believed that the insuperable strength of the new social system lay in the unity of Marxist science, which determines the Party's programme propositions, and the initiative and historical creative endeavour of the masses.

Not everyone understood and accepted Lenin's idea that it was possible to build socialism in an economically backward, predominantly peasant country in a capitalist encirclement. The Right and the 'Left' oppositionists strove to impose either capitulationist or adventurist ideas, and to get the country off the Leninist path. The political struggle, which became especially acute after Lenin's death, was protracted and intense. But Lenin's ideas triumphed.

The cause of socialist construction generated such a tide of revolution-

1

ary enthusiasm and inspired, dedicated labour that it literally swept away all the obstacles on the road to socialism. What was once a plan became reality. That was a world historic victory of the Soviet people, a triumph of Leninism.

In the 1930s, socialism was firmly established in every sphere of life in our country. The world saw a socialist industrial and collective farm power moving forward in a determined, powerful drive. Conditions were being created for the next great stride along the way mapped out by Lenin.

This was prevented by the war. The country was subjected to a piratical attack by the fascist invaders. A mortal danger confronted our country. It was then that the Soviet people's courage, steadfastness and indomitable will to victory, and their cohesion round the Leninist Party were displayed with unprecedented force. In the course of the stern ordeal, the Soviet social and state system demonstrated its unbreakable strength. Those harsh years reaffirmed the profound truth of Lenin's words when he said that a people defending its own power and standing up for its just cause and its future can never be vanquished. At the cost of millions of lives of its sons and daughters the Soviet people safeguarded the gains of socialism . . .

Everyone is aware of the heavy losses and destruction which the war brought us. Many towns and villages, factories and power stations, schools and hospitals had to be built anew. Thwarting the enemies' treacherous plans to weaken our state for a long time, and healing the wounds of war in the shortest possible time, the Soviet people took a great stride forward. The material and spiritual gains achieved in the post-war years are staggering. Socialism has once again demonstrated its strength and viability.

Our Party and the Soviet people have accumulated a vast store of experience in the class struggle and social transformation. The innovatory character of these transformations demanded of the Party political and theoretical maturity, efficient organisation and steadfastness, consistency, and a thorough verification of the ways and means of building the new society . . .

The novelty, singularity, and the unprecedented scale of social change and economic construction, the lack of experience, and the frenzied resistance of the bourgeoisie — all made the struggle for socialism

2

especially difficult, but immeasurably noble and heroic. 'Let . . . the bourgeoisie . . . heap imprecations, abuse and derision upon our heads for our reverses and mistakes in the work of building up *our* Soviet system,' wrote Lenin. 'We do not forget for a moment that we have committed and are committing numerous mistakes and are suffering numerous reverses. How can reverses and mistakes be avoided in a matter so new in the history of the world as the building of an unprecedented *type* of state edifice! We shall work steadfastly to set our reverses and mistakes right and to improve our practical application of Soviet principles, which is still very, very far from being perfect. But we have a right to be and are proud that to us has fallen the good fortune to *begin* the building of a Soviet state, and thereby to *usher in* a new era in world history . . . ' (*Collected Works*, Vol. 33, pp. 54–55).

As we look back on the road we have covered, we can say: indeed, our people and our Party have many things to take pride in. Many difficulties and adversities have fallen to the lot of the Soviet people. On their shoulders they have borne a tremendous historical responsibility. But courageously and steadfastly they have overcome all the trials, fulfilling their noble mission with dignity. Everywhere and always, in times of stern trial and fierce battle, in times of joyous victories and grievous setbacks, our people have remained loyal to the Leninist banner, loyal to their Party and to the cause of the revolution. On this momentous day, comrades, we can say that we have some achievements to report in honouring Lenin's memory. For the first time in the history of world civilisation, socialism has scored a full and final victory, a developed socialist society has been built and the conditions have been created for the successful construction of communism . . .

Soviet society today is friendship and co-operation between all classes and social groups, all nations and nationalities, all generations; it is socialist democracy, which actually assures the working people of a part in the administration of all the affairs of state and society; it is advanced socialist science and culture, which belong to the mass of the people.

Soviet society today is the real embodiment of the ideas of the proletarian, socialist humanism. It has placed the production of material values and the achievements of spiritual culture, the whole system of social relations, at the service of the man of labour. The Soviet people have already come to accept as a fact that the growth of production and the development of culture in our country lead to better conditions of life for the working people, for the whole people. This appears to be quite natural, it is not given too much thought, it is sometimes even forgotten. But, after all, it is, essentially, one of the basic distinctions between our system and capitalism, under which production is expanded to enrich the property owner and not to improve the life of the working man.

One of the greatest achievements of socialism is that every Soviet man is assured of his future. He is aware that his work, his abilities and his energy will always find a fitting use and appreciation. He is sure that his children will be given a free education and the opportunity of developing their talents. He knows that society will never abandon him in misfortune, that in the event of illness he will be given free medical treatment, a pension in the case of permanent disability, and security in old age.

Everything we have, everything we live by and take pride in is the result of the struggle and working endeavour of our working class, peasantry and intelligentsia, of the whole Soviet people.

The entire history of our society bears out the great truth of the Marxist–Leninist teaching about the working class being the leading revolutionary and creative force. The Soviet working class has brilliantly demonstrated its capacity to direct society, and build socialism and communism. It is the working class, above all, that has laboured to create all the country's industrial and defence might, the technical basis for the transformation of agriculture and the other branches of the economy. It has produced from its ranks thousands of statesmen and public leaders, commanders of production, scientists and military leaders, writers and artists. The working class, the most numerous and the best organised class, continues to play the leading role in our society.

Its goal — communism — has become the goal of the whole people.

Its ideology—Marxism–Leninism—has become the dominant ideology.

Its Party — the Communist Party — has become the party of the whole people.

The collective-farm peasantry is a reliable ally of the working class in struggle and in labour. Socialism has put an end once and for all to the poverty, deprivation and ignorance of the peasants, and has helped them to escape from the narrow world of individualism. Collective labour on socialised land has transformed the everyday life and spiritual atmosphere in the countryside. More than 3 million farm-machine operators, hundreds of thousands of agronomists, livestock experts, engineers, teachers and doctors work in the villages. Our collective-farm peasantry is a new socialist class, and an active builder of communist society.

At every stage of the socialist revolution, in the course of socialist construction, and today, when the Soviet people are building communism, the alliance of the working class and the peasantry has always constituted the solid foundation of our system, and the pledge of fresh victories on the way to communism!

Lenin's prediction of a future alliance of the working class and the representatives of science and technology, which 'no dark force can withstand', as Lenin put it, has come true. Today, we pay a great tribute of respect and gratitude to Soviet scientists, whose role is especially great in this age of the most profound social, scientific and technical change. In the ranks of our fine Soviet intelligentsia are millions of engineers, technicians, teachers, workers in public health, workers in the arts, and functionaries of the administrative apparatus. The great intellectual potential which our country has built up is a major source of the progress of Soviet society.

Men of different generations march shoulder to shoulder in the ranks of the builders of communism under a common Leninist banner. Among them are those who laid the first stones in the foundation of the socialist edifice, those who arms in hand fearlessly defended the gains of socialism, those who rebuilt our towns and villages from the ruins and ashes, and those who are still young, and are just setting foot on life's highway.

The older generation of the fighters for socialism has brought up a generation fit to take over, passing on to the latter its experience and knowledge, handing on its victorious Leninist baton. The Party is quite sure that Soviet youth and its vanguard, the Leninist Komsomol, in whose ranks more than 100 million Soviet people have already had a political schooling, will bring glory to their country by fresh remarkable achievements . . .

LENINISM AND THE QUESTION OF COMMUNIST CONSTRUCTION

. . . Since Lenin's death, life has gone a long way forward, much has changed, producing a great number of new phenomena and problems which it was hard even to imagine in his lifetime. But today, too the key to their understanding and solution is provided by the laws of socialist development discovered by Lenin. That is why Lenin continues to be a living participant in our endeavour, and our sage and reliable teacher. . .

The more than half a century of experience in socialist economic endeavour provides convincing confirmation that the direction of the economy is perhaps the most challenging and the most creative task of all those which arise after a revolution. Here, as in other spheres of social life, let us add, there are virtually no cut-and-dried solutions which one could adopt and get rid of all cares. The economy is a complex and dynamic organism whose development in itself continuously produces new problems.

The justice of this truth is especially evident today, when the Soviet economy is entering a new important stage. Our socialist production has grown to vast proportions, the interconnections in our national economy have become more complex, and the scientific and technical revolution is advancing at a headlong pace. In view of all this the Party's Central Committee and the Government have arrived at the conclusion that it is necessary to work out an economic policy, methods of conducting economic operations, and forms of organisation and administration that will meet the present stage of the country's development . . .

Comrades, Lenin saw the construction of a communist economy not only as the concern of economic leaders and the organisers and commanders of production. He said that 'creative activity at the grass roots is the basic factor of the new public life. . . Living, creative socialism is the product of the masses themselves' (*Collected Works*, Vol. 26, p. 288). Accordingly, the Party's course is to ensure the further extension of the working people's participation in running industrial enterprises and state and collective farms, in working for greater efficiency of production, higher labour productivity, the maximum use of the available facilities and the raising of labour discipline . . .

In response to the Party's call, and with the active participation of the trade unions and other social organisations, a country-wide popular movement has now been started to improve the use of reserves in production and tighten the régime of economies in the country. The initiatives of workers, collective farmers, engineers, technicians and administrative personnel and the numerous proposals and concrete obligations being undertaken by the working people are striking evidence of the fact that the working people of town and country, the whole Soviet people are truly aware of being masters of their country, and that they show a personal concern for the interests of production and for the preservation and multiplication of the national wealth . . .

It is well known that for our society the fulfilment of economic tasks is not an end in itself but a means. The main purpose and the main meaning of the policy which our Party has been consistently implementing is to create for the working man the most favourable conditions for work, study, leisure and the development and best application of his abilities.

In the last few years we have achieved a great deal in this sphere and have solved a number of major social problems. In that period special attention was devoted to raising the living standards of working people in the lower- and middle-income brackets in town and country. But we are aware that more big tasks lie ahead of us. Men's needs increase constantly as society and culture develop. Lenin was very well aware of this. He wrote: '. . . When we are showered with new demands from all sides, we say: that is as it should be, that is just what socialism means, when each wants to improve his condition and all want to enjoy the benefits of life' (*Collected Works*, Vol. 27, p. 516).

The task today is not only further to raise remuneration for work but also to expand production of the goods needed by the population, to improve the quality of services, to continue extensive housing construction, and to take fresh measures to protect the health of the working people. Understandably, all these tasks cannot be solved at one go, by the adoption of a resolution, however good. This calls for insistent efforts by the whole Party, by the whole people.

The main thing, comrades, is how much we produce and how, and the attitude we take to work, the main source of our social wealth. There is no need, I think, to argue that one can consume and use only what has been produced, what has been created by man's hands and brain. It is up to the

7

Soviet people themselves to raise their living standards. Today we live as well as we worked yesterday, and tomorrow we shall live as well as we work today.

While devoting maximum attention to economic problems, the Party directs the people's energy to the solution of the whole complex of tasks in communist construction.

We are on the way to gradually overcoming the distinctions between classes and social groups, for which it is necessary, Lenin emphasised, 'to abolish . . . the distinction between town and country, as well as the distinction between manual workers and brain workers' (*Collected Works*, Vol. 29, p. 421). It goes without saying that these tasks will be fully solved only in a communist society. But much is already being done to advance in this direction.

The social policy of the Party and the Soviet state is, on the basis of modern science and technology, to more closely approximate the character of the labour of the peasant to that of the worker, to improve living conditions in the countryside, and to raise the cultural level of village life. All this in practice results in a gradual eradication of the socio-economic and cultural-welfare distinctions between town and country, between the working class and the peasantry.

At the same time we are gradually overcoming the distinction between workers by hand and by brain. This requires many more steps forward in the development of the economy and culture, an improvement of working conditions and a change in the character of labour, and the further raising of the cultural and professional–technical level of the whole people.

Lenin said that anyone who undertakes the great endeavour of communist construction must understand this: 'he can create it only on the basis of modern education, and if he does not acquire this education communism will remain merely a pious wish' (*Collected Works*, Vol. 31, pp. 289–90). We have already done much in the sphere of public education. Almost 80 million people, that is, a third of the population, are studying.

However, life does not stand still. We need to go forward, improving the whole system of education in every way. Within a few short years those who are now at school or college will move into production, into science and culture. The progress of our society in the future largely depends on how and what we teach them today. The ancients used to say that a pupil is not a vessel to be filled but a torch to be lit. The task is to teach the young people to think creatively, to prepare them for life, for practical effort.

Comrades, a great achievement of Lenin's is that he worked out the programme for a socialist solution of the national question. This programme has been implemented. The triumph of Lenin's policy on the national question, the Soviet Union's solution of the problem — one of the most acute and most difficult in social life — is an undertaking of tremendous importance, and a major stride forward in mankind's social development.

Communist construction in our multinational country implies the consistent pursuit of the line of bringing the nations together in every way, and strengthening their co-operation and mutual assistance. The way to this is by further development of the economy and culture in all our Republics, an improvement of mutual exchanges of achievements in material and spiritual culture and, of course, persistent effort to overcome the survivals of nationalism and chauvinism.

Lenin demanded the continuous and tireless education of the working people in the spirit of internationalism, rejecting both great power-chauvinistic and narrowly nationalistic tendencies. He said that 'one must *not* think only of one's own nation, but place *above it* the interests of all nations, their common liberty and equality, . . . fight *against* small-nation narrow-mindedness, seclusion and isolation, consider the whole and the general, subordinate the particular to the general interest' (*Collected Works*, Vol. 22, p. 347). The multinational Soviet state founded by Lenin is this whole and this general. Lenin's precept was that we should protect the Union of Soviet Socialist Republics as the apple of our eye. This great precept of Lenin's is being faithfully followed by the Party and the people.

The Soviet socialist state of the whole people is our main instrument in building communism. That is why there is need to constantly strengthen this state and improve the whole system of social administration.

Lenin considered the possibility of involving the working people in the day-to-day administration of the state the greatest advantage of socialism. He set the task of teaching 'the people the art of administration' (*Collected Works*, Vol. 28, p. 426). For that purpose we are working

9

and shall continue to work to enhance the role of the Soviets, of social organisations and working people's collectives in the life and development of society, and to improve socialist legislation.

In developing the Soviet state system and socialist democracy, the Party and the Government have been persistently following the Leninist line in improving the state apparatus and making it more efficient. Every stage in the development of the productive forces and of culture, wrote Lenin, must be accompanied by an improvement of our Soviet system.

Lenin wrote that 'there can be no victorious socialism that does not practise full democracy' (*Collected Works*, Vol. 22, p. 144). Nor can this be otherwise. The Party has been working steadily and purposefully to develop socialist democracy, which serves above all as a means of drawing millions of working people into the process of conscious historical creative effort and into running the affairs of society and the state.

Our democracy in action is the right of every citizen, every collective and every Republic to take part in deciding questions of social life, combating any departures from the rules and principles of socialist community living, criticising shortcomings and taking an active part in eliminating them. To enable Soviet citizens to enjoy their rights to the fullest, the Party has shown constant concern to improve the forms of popular representation and people's control over the activity of the organs of power and administration.

The broad rights extended by socialist democracy to the working people in various spheres of social life are organically combined with their civic duties. This combination, like the very content of their rights and duties, is determined by the interests of the whole people, the interests of building a communist society.

We regard the development of the Soviet state and socialist democracy above all as a powerful means of attaining our main aim — the building of communism. We shall never agree to the 'development of democracy' which is being strongly urged upon us by bourgeois ideologists and their Right-wing opportunist assistants, who show such zeal in trying to recast socialism in their own, bourgeois mould. We have our own, truly democratic traditions, which have stood the test of time. We shall safeguard, preserve, develop and improve these traditions.

No matter how our adversaries may wring their hands over the 'imperfection' of socialism, no matter what touching concern they may display for its 'improvement' and 'humanisation', we repeat with pride Lenin's words about proletarian, socialist democracy being a million times more democratic than any bourgeois democracy. Our state was, is and will continue to be a state of the working people, a state for the working people, a state which is governed by the working people.

Following Lenin's path, the Soviet people have created a new, socialist way of life, a new socialist civilisation . . .

COMMUNIST PARTY OF THE SOVIET UNION — PARTY OF LENIN

. . . Our great Party, under whose leadership the Soviet people have won historic victories, was created by Vladimir Ilyich Lenin. He taught the Party to serve the working people with unbounded devotion. He put in its hands a mighty weapon — the theory and policy of struggle against capitalism, of struggle for the revolutionary reconstruction of society, for triumph of the socialist revolution, the line towards socialism, the line towards the building of communism — these are the words of the Party, expressed in its three Programmes. The victory of the October Revolution, the triumph of socialism and the successful advance towards the communist morrow — such is the action of the Party, the action of the whole people.

The Party's strength lies in its fidelity to the principles of Marxism–Leninism, to the principles of proletarian internationalism. Its strength lies in its monolithic unity, which was consolidated and unflaggingly upheld by Lenin. Its strength lies in its unbreakable bond with the working class, with the masses, whose collective leader and organiser it is. Its strength lies in its revolutionary spirit, in its ability critically to assess and profoundly understand the results of its work.

Intrinsic to our Party are a sense of lofty responsibility before the people and high principles. During Lenin's lifetime and after his death the Party courageously and openly criticised, as it continues to do to this days, errors and shortcomings. It sternly denounced the personality cult which led to violations of the Leninist norms of Party and state

11

life of socialist legality and democracy. It emphatically rejected subjectivism, which expounds unfounded improvisation in place of a scientific approach to phenomena of social life. The Party tells the people the truth, no matter how stern it may be. '. . . Let us face the truth squarely. . .' Lenin taught the Communists. 'In politics that is always the best and the only correct attitude' (*Collected Works*, Vol. 20, p. 275).

Lenin attached immense significance to developing the political awareness of the masses, which, he wrote, remains 'the basis and chief content of our work' (*Collected Works*, Vol. 11, p. 178). In line with Lenin's precepts the Party is making sure that all Communists consciously master the fundamentals of Marxism–Leninism and that their ideological principles find expression in practical participation in the nationwide work of building communism. The Party educates every Communist and every Soviet citizen as an ardent patriot who devotes all his strength for the benefit of the Motherland and, at the same time, as a convinced internationalist . . .

We live in an age witnessing exceedingly swift development. Rates of growth are mounting and the scale of communist construction is increasing. Science and Marxist–Leninist theory are playing an increasingly more important part. The international role and responsibility of the Soviet state are growing. All this is enhancing the importance of the Communist Party as the leading force of Soviet society.

Tested and confirmed by the experience of the CPSU, Lenin's teaching that the Party is the leader of the revolutionary masses and the leading force of the new society and Lenin's principles of Party construction are the property not only of the CPSU but also of the fraternal Communist Parties. Facts show that Communists triumph where the Party consistently implements its role as vanguard of the working class and other working people, where the Leninist norms of Party life are strictly observed and where the Party safeguards and tirelessly strengthens its political, organisational and ideological unity. Conversely, any diminution of the Party's role and any departure from the Leninist principles of Party development lead to serious setbacks and may create a threat to the socialist gains of the people.

In order to ensure the success of the great work of building communism the Party must pursue a correct Marxist–Leninist policy, and the broad masses of working people, the whole Soviet people must understand and implement this policy. '. . . We can administer', Lenin said, 'only when we express correctly what the people are conscious of. Unless we do this the Communist Party will not lead the proletariat, the proletariat will not lead the masses . . .' (*Collected Works*, Vol. 33, p. 304). The programme of communist construction put forward by the Communist Party has become the vital cause of the whole Soviet people. The Party's unity with the people under the banner of Leninism is the best guarantee that this historic task will be carried out successfully.

Lenin used to say that the Communist Party is the brain, honour and conscience of our epoch. We solemnly declare that Soviet Communists will continue doing everything to make our Party, created and reared by Lenin, always worthy of this lofty appraisal of its founder, teacher and leader.

On the Leninist banner of our Party are inscribed the words: 'Everything in the name of man, for the sake of man!' The Soviet people will carry this banner along uncharted trails and make our country — the birthplace of socialism — the birthplace of communism, the most humane of social systems.

Report at a joint celebration meeting of the Central Committee and the Supreme Soviets of the USSR and the RSFSR to mark the centenary of Lenin's birth. 21 April 1970

The election campaign and the elections proper are an important political event. As they prepare for the elections the citizens of our country, so to speak, sum up the results of the work of the Soviets, generalise the best experience, and concentrate on the vital problems of communist construction. . . .

Comrades, as it carefully analyses the current economic activities, the Party endeavours in good time to discern the unsolved problems and on them to focus the attention of Communists, executives, all working people. Our society is developing at rapid rates. And we are tackling the scientific–technological and production problems with undeviating concern for the steady growth of the welfare of the people. This is what makes us basically different from capitalist society. Herein also lies the distinguishing feature of the problems which we are solving. Naturally, in our progress we often come up against complicated problems. This is a normal process, just as our efforts to detect shortcomings and mistakes ourselves, to speak of them frankly so as to correct them. Criticism and self-criticism are a law of development of our society.

We know, of course, that the enemies of the Soviet Union, the enemies of the CPSU, are trying to use our self-criticism to slander the socialist system. Such was the case 50 years ago. The same is happening today when, for instance, the bourgeois press periodically splashes its pages with sensational headlines about some kind of economic 'crisis' in the Soviet Union. There is nothing new in these statements. The ideologists and politicians of imperialism have many times invented all sorts of 'crises' of the Soviet system. Yet, our country is becoming stronger and stronger. And the fact that the enemies are trying to use our self-criticism for their own ends cannot weaken our determination to eliminate in our path everything that interferes with our normal living and working, everything that impedes our progress.

The Party remembers Lenin's instructions that it does not befit Communists to fear serious and businesslike criticism and self-criticism on the grounds that the enemy may take advantage of it. 'Anyone who is afraid of this is no revolutionary', said Lenin. And we, comrades, were and remain revolutionaries.

The Party is aware of the achievements and shortcomings, of the potentialities and the things to be done. Objectively, taking into account all the pros and cons, it may be definitely said that the people, the Party and the state are on the correct, Lenin's road. The chief result of the country's development in the last 4 years has been that the general line of economic development worked out by the Party is successfully passing the practical test and is yielding positive results . . .

At its December Plenary Meeting last year the CPSU Central Committee paid special attention to the style of work with cadres in the Party. We said that trust and a respectful attitude enable workers to acquire the essential feeling of confidence and open up vistas for initiative, a bold and creative approach to questions. Such a style of work helps us to solve the most complex problems — this has now been proved in practice. And we do not intend to change it, to return to methods of administration that have been vigorously condemned by the Party.

At the same time Lenin's style of work is inseparable from great exactingness, businesslike control and criticism of shortcomings. This criticism presupposes respect for the personality, dignity of the worker and his services, but on no account at the expense of lowering requirements. We would not want our style and attitude to cadres to be understood as a sort of indulgence to poor workers. And if an executive does not draw the proper conclusions from criticism he has no right to expect that respect for him will remain . . .

Comrades, development of socialist society is a complex process which encompasses not only the economy, but all spheres of social life. The task of the leadership of such a society apparently consists in revealing to the utmost the potentialities it possesses for harmonious and even development. Where is the key to the solution of this task? The key lies in the correct functioning of the political system of society, and, primarily, the many-sided scientifically substantiated activities of the Communist Party based on its rich practical experience.

The Party regards the development of socialist democracy as an indispensable condition for the successful advancement to communism. It is precisely this principle that underlies the practical measures of the Party and the government in perfecting the state machinery, and the entire system of organs of power and administration.

In this connection I shall deal with questions of law and order. We are all well aware how important is clearly drawn up legislation for the proper development of the social organism. In a generalised and concentrated form Soviet laws express the will of the people, the main trends of Party and state policy and ensure the advancement of society along the given course.

It should be stressed that in our country legislative work is permeated with profound democratism. Broad circles of specialists, scientists, the Soviet public take part in drafting laws. The most important laws are brought up for nationwide discussion. All this guarantees that Soviet laws really express the requirements of society and serve the interests of the working people.

In the years past the Supreme Soviet drafted and adopted laws that regulate important aspects of social relations and actually affect the interests of all Soviet people. I wish to remind you that these are laws pertaining to health protection, consolidation of the family, land tenure, struggle against crime. Work on improving Soviet legislation must continue so that it does not lag behind life, that our laws, while remaining firm and stable, correctly reflect the processes taking place in society.

We know, however, that it is not enough to elaborate a good law, not enough to adopt it. A law exists and operates only when it is observed. It is obligatory for all, it must be observed by all without exception, irrespective of post and rank. Socialist legality and law and order are the basis of the normal life of society and its citizens. This seems elementary. And if we have to speak of this, it is only because there are, unfortunately, some people who have not developed such an essential quality as conscientious and strict observance of Soviet laws, the rules of socialist society. The Party cannot and will not tolerate such a state of affairs.

It is generally known, comrades, how Lenin regarded the issue. Lenin considered that as long as a law was in force no one had the right to disregard it. Some people in our country lack this Leninist approach to the observance of laws. Soviet law protects socialist property, the interests of society and the state, and the rights of citizens. And any violation of laws, no matter for what reason, is very damaging to society, its citizens and our common cause.

That is why it is essential to greatly propagate Soviet laws, raise their authority, educate everybody in the spirit of respect for the law. That is why it is also essential that the Party and government bodies pay greater attention to the links of our apparatus called upon to directly control the observance of laws, to cut short infringements of the law. Every Soviet citizen must be fully confident that his life and health, his property, his rights, his dignity and peace are reliably protected by the state.

Thus, the strengthening of legality, of socialist law and order, is a task for the entire state, for the entire Party. And the role of the deputies here is especially important. The people's representatives in the organs of state power, Lenin stressed, 'have to work, have to execute their own laws, have themselves to test the results, achieved in reality, and to account directly to their constituents'.

16

That was how Lenin saw the task. And that is how it is seen now by the Party.

The second point I would like to talk about today is the work of the Soviets. Implementing what has been outlined in the Programme of the CPSU and in the decisions of the 23rd Party Congress, we have succeeded in invigorating the Soviets both nationally and locally. Their role in the life of the country has been enhanced.

The solution of the task confronting us obliges all deputies, all Soviets to pay special heed to improving the democratic principles of their activity: reporting back to the electorate, publicity, drawing the masses of working people into direct participation in running public affairs, criticism of shortcomings in the work of one or another department or official, and combating red tape. These tasks, naturally, stand not only for the Soviets, but also for the Party organisations, since everything connected with the Soviets, with Soviet power, has been and remains the concern of the entire Party.

The Soviet is the highest body of state authority in its territory, the master of the city or community and it has to be an efficient, thrifty master. Its duty is to think of and to take care of everything, to do everything in a way that the people could live, work and rest better. And, if the Soviet displays the necessary initiative and businesslike enterprise, the constituents appreciate this. It is a question naturally of healthy, sensible initiative and not that kind when parochialism is manifested in detriment to the interests of the entire state. This apology for 'initiative' is something which we can do without.

In other words, it is important to achieve such a state of affairs when all the Soviets will utilise in full all the rights granted them, will act boldly, independently and with initiative and not wait for directives and instructions from 'above'.

While giving our due to the work of the Soviets and worthily assessing it, it is also necessary for us to see the flaws in their work. Attention was justly drawn to these shortcomings by the constituents who spoke at the rallies of collectives of working people and at election area conferences. It is important to carefully generalise and analyse all the critical remarks, bring them to the attention of the appropriate bodies, and demand that they adopt the necessary measures on them.

And, lastly there is one other question about the deputies. A deputy is an authorised representative of the working people in the organs of state power. He is their trusted person. He should be reckoned with and his voice should be heeded. His interpellations should be answered by all officials and government departments.

Such are his constitutional powers. Two concepts — rights and duties — are linked in the word *powers*. This, comrades, is both a great honour and a great responsibility. They are inseparably bound together. A deputy not only has the right, but is obliged to work for the implementation of the constituents' mandates, to be tactful and attentive towards the people, to tell them how matters are progressing and what difficulties arise and how they are being surmounted . . .

The life and requirements of society prompt the need for an assessment of the work of the Soviets, like all other organisations, on the basis of much higher criteria, from the positions of today, and not of yesterday. The Party and its Central Committee will continue to show constant concern for the role and significance of the Soviets to be enhanced still more, for each deputy always to maintain the level of those great requirements imposed on him by our Soviet system, by our times.

*Speech to the Baumansky District
electorate, Moscow, the traditional
speech made by the candidate to the
USSR Supreme Soviet. 12 June 1970*

The history of every nation knows events which remain in the memory of the people as a precious heritage that is passed on from generation to generation as an ever-living symbol of the people's brightest hopes and greatest achievements. The signing by Vladimir Lenin and Mikhail Kalinin on 26 August 1920 of a Decree 'On the Formation of the Autonomous Kirghiz (Kazakh) Socialist Soviet Republic' has turned out to be such an event for the Kazakh people. The history of Soviet Kazakhstan is a vivid testimony of the Party's firm and consistent implementation of the Leninist nationalities policy, a policy of friendship and fraternity of the peoples.

Within the lifetime of a single generation, the once neglected and backward borderland of tsarist Russia has become an advanced socialist republic.

From squalid nomad settlements in the steppe to prosperous state- and collective-farms, from primitive mines and makeshift looms to first-class industry, from near-starvation subsistence, from backwardness and illiteracy to the remarkable flourishing of a culture which is national and distinctive in form and socialist in content — such is the astonishing path traversed by Soviet Kazakhstan.

The boundless territory of Kazakhstan is now dotted with vast, modern industrial and agricultural enterprises, cities with excellent facilities and villages with schools, hospitals and cultural centres. From the Altai mountains to the Caspian sea people are leading an active and happy life.

United by indissoluble bonds of friendship, shared interests and aims, and a common history all Soviet people take pride in the achievements of the Kazakh working people. They feel this pride because they are class brothers sharing a single fate and devoting their lives to the common cause of building communism. This is the pride of people who have actively interfered in the fate of their comrades and who, in turn, have been spiritually enriched by their friendship.

As the Kazakh saying goes, 'The strength of a bird is in its wings, a man's strength lies in friendship.' These words have acquired great significance in the Soviet Union of today.

The major and revolutionary transformation of the republic's agriculture began with the Leninist Decrees on Land and on the allocation of funds for the irrigation works in Turkestan, and the Obukhovskaya commune organised on the lands of Eastern Kazakhstan by the representatives of the working people of Peter [Petrograd, now Leningrad — Ed.], who brought to the Kazakh steppes their Bolshevist energy, will-power and proletarian discipline.

Thus Kazakhstan's very first efforts to build up its own industry were made with the help of the working people of the whole country. Russians, Kazakhs, Ukrainians, Byelorussians, and, indeed, representatives of all the Soviet peoples took part in the building of the Turksib [Turkestan–Siberian railway — Ed.] and the mines of Karaganda, the Emba oilfields and industrial enterprises in the regions of Rudny Altai, Chimkent and

Balkhash. Workers, engineers and technicians from Moscow, the Urals, Leningrad, the Donbass and other industrial centres volunteered assistance to the workers at the construction sites in Kazakhstan, gave them the benefit of their experience and helped to train local personnel.

The working people of Kazakhstan are well aware that the tremendous industrial progress of their own republic as well as that of the other Soviet republics is the result of the combined effort of all the peoples of the Soviet Union and is a vivid testimony to the advantages of a planned socialist economy encompassing the whole of our multinational country.

As Vladimir Lenin said, 'We do not rule by dividing, as ancient Rome's harsh maxim required, but by uniting all the working people with the unbreakable bonds of living interests and a sense of class. Thus our union, our new state is sounder than power based on violence which keeps artificial state entities hammered together with lies and bayonets in the way the imperialists want them' (*Collected Works*, Vol. 26, p. 480).

The reclamation of virgin and fallow lands is a major labour achievement of the Soviet people. It has gone down in our history as a heroic feat of the entire nation, and as an embodiment of the unity of action of all the Soviet peoples from all republics. The whole multinational working class of the Soviet Union took an active part in supplying the state farms on virgin land with modern machinery. In these unforgettable years an endless flow of new equipment was delivered to Kazakhstan; tractors from Volgograd, Chelyabinsk, Kharkov and Minsk, trucks from Gorky and Yaroslavl, agricultural machinery and spare parts from Uzbekistan and the Baltic and other republics.

Answering the call of the Party, hundreds of thousands of patriotic-minded people from the Russian Federation, Ukraine, Byelorussia and other fraternal republics voluntarily went to Kazakhstan. Combining their efforts, these representatives of all the nations of our country reclaimed the virgin lands. It is not by chance that many of these state farms now bear the glorious names of the cities and regions of fraternal Soviet republics.

Our people will never forget the great work of our fine young people, the Komsomol members of the 1950s, who won over the virgin lands, brought life to the vast expanses of Kazakhstan and harnessed Nature which had lain dormant for centuries, to serve man and communism.

Together with you, our comrades from Kazakhstan, we take pride in the fact that your manufactures are now exported to more than seventy different countries, which in itself is not a bad recommendation of the quality of your products. Maintain the good name of your produce from Kazakhstan, comrades, and do not slacken your efforts to improve standards still more . . .

. . . Kazakhstan today is a comprehensively developed socialist republic. There can be few auls or villages without a school, a library or a cultural centre. In tsarist days only two out of every hundred Kazakhs could read and write, whereas the Republic has now outstripped many advanced countries of the world in the rate and scale of training specialists. This is not surprising, since the republic now boasts over 10,000 general education schools with 3 million pupils. Over 200 higher and specialised secondary schools in Kazakhstan are training skilled personnel for work in the national economy and culture.

A land where a literate man was formerly as rare as a tree in a waterless desert has educated thousands upon thousands of teachers, doctors, engineers, agronomists, writers, artists and composers.

A land where, in the past, the term 'scientist' was not commonly known, for there were, in fact, no scientists, now has over 200 scientific institutions which are working successfully.

The Republic's Academy of Sciences is making a great contribution to the advance of science. There are over 25,000 research workers in the Republic.

The culture of socialist Kazakhstan is today diverse and flourishing and its best achievements are held in high regard by all Soviet people.

Bourgeois falsifiers sometimes make allegations to the effect that the cultural revolution in our country was accompanied by 'a loss of national traditions'. The Soviet Union of today, however, graphically demonstrates the complete groundlessness of these allegations. It is quite true that the grandchildren and great-grandchildren of the outstanding Kazakh scholars Chokan Valikhanov, Ibrai Altynsarin and Abai Kunanbayev are actively contributing in their native language to the treasurehouse of Marxism–Leninism and are studying and adding to the cultural wealth of other peoples, and of mankind as a whole from its very beginnings. But it is equally true that, under socialism, the distinctive culture of the Kazakh people, as well as that of all the nations and nationalities of the Soviet Union, have reached unprecedented heights.

Their contribution to the common cultural heritage of our socialist motherland has grown immeasurably.

All this, comrades, is one of the most vivid manifestations of the transforming force of socialism. This is the true, Leninist cultural revolution in practice!

> *Speech at a celebration meeting of the*
> *Central Committee of the*
> *Communist Party of Kazakhstan and*
> *the Supreme Soviet of the Kazakh*
> *SSR to mark their fiftieth*
> *anniversary. 28 August 1970*

Though the Azerbaijan people have traversed a long path in their development, their true history really began only five decades ago, when with the fraternal help of the Russian proletariat and the Red Army units, the workers and peasants of Azerbaijan overthrew the oppressive bourgeois-landlord Mussavatist government. The road to national freedom and social justice then opened up for the Azerbaijan people . . .

Once master of their own fate, the working people of Azerbaijan, under the guidance of the Communist Party and with the active participation of all the fraternal republics of our country, rapidly restored the republic's ruined economy, built up powerful socialist industry, realised Lenin's plan for a co-operative system of agriculture, made the cultural heritage of the past accessible to the whole people and created a new socialist culture.

Before the revolution, the overwhelming majority of the population of Azerbaijan was illiterate, whereas today the republic enjoys complete literacy and a high level of education and culture . . .

We are all aware of the great attention Lenin gave to the building of socialism in Transcaucasia, for he held that the example of a well-organised socialist way of life in the Transcaucasian republics would be the most effective propaganda for our cause among the many millions of people in the East.

Today, when we are marking the fiftieth anniversary of Soviet Azerbaijan, we have the right to declare with pride that, headed by the Leninist Party and with the fraternal assistance of all the peoples of our country, the working people of the republic are faithfully carrying out Lenin's behest. Soviet Azerbaijan, which has been transformed from a former colony on the borders of the Russian Empire into a flourishing republic in a country building communism, is convincing proof of the powerful creative force of socialism and an inspiring example for young national states, and for peoples fighting for social and national independence.

Azerbaijan today is a republic with extensive and diversified industry, highly developed agriculture and its own distinctive socialist culture.

From the Caspian shores of this republic, 300 types of industrial goods are exported to almost sixty countries of the world. This is a graphic testimony to the high industrial level reached by Azerbaijan during the years of Soviet power . . .

The standard of living and the way of life of the Azerbaijan people have changed beyond recognition. Alexei Maximovich Gorky knew pre-revolutionary Baku well and described the city thus: 'Among the chaos of oil rigs, the long and low workers' barracks, hastily put together from rust-coloured and grey rough-hewn stones and closely resembling primeval shelters, pressed themselves to the ground. Never before have I seen so much dirt and garbage around a human dwelling, so many broken window-panes and such wretched poverty in the small cave-like rooms.'*

Such was the Baku of tsarist Russia, a Baku recalled by only a few, very old people.

It happened to be my first visit to Azerbaijan and it is for the first time that I saw its capital city, and probably for this reason my impressions are so very vivid. I must state outright: Baku is a beautiful city! One can see that it was built and is being built by people who love their land deeply and who care for their national traditions, while at the same time skilfully making use of modern planning and construction techniques. It is very pleasant to live and work in such a city.

Here, in Baku, I happened to see a very interesting sculpture, a symbol

*M. Gorky, *Collected Works in 30 Volumes*, Goslitizdat, Moscow, 1952, Vol. 17, pp. 115–16.

of the emancipation of Azerbaijan women, showing a woman furiously tearing off her yashmak.

We are all aware of the unhappy associations of the yashmak for women, since it symbolised their lack of rights and servile position. In fact, the yashmak differed little from prison bars, the only difference being that the woman actually had to wear this fence which separated her from the world.

The liberation and emancipation of women was one of the Soviet government's major tasks. Soviet power has made women fully fledged members of socialist society and they have now noticeably 'ousted men from the health service and education'. There are many women engineers, agronomists and research workers. Today the women of Azerbaijan constitute 40 per cent of the republic's total work force, and quite a number of working women have been elected deputies to the Supreme Soviets of the Republic and of the USSR.

Just consider, for instance, how many women there are in this hall. And this is perfectly natural, for the daughters of the Azerbaijan people now occupy many top posts in the Republic's economic and cultural life and hold responsible executive, state and Party jobs. And they work well! Just look how many Gold Stars, orders and medals the women participants in our anniversary meeting have brought with them to this hall! These awards of the motherland are the best jewellery ever worn by women on earth!

The CPSU Central Committee is confident that the republic's Party organisation will continue to devote its full attention to the most important matter in hand — concern for the daily life of working women, their intellectual development, and their increasing participation in socialist production, social life and state administration . . .

We are convinced that in the course of the future joint work in all the spheres of building communism, fraternal co-operation between the Union Republics will become more extensive and comprehensive, and the mutual exchange of the achievements of material and spiritual culture will intensify, thereby leading to the further *rapprochement* of socialist nations and nationalities. In this the Party sees the guarantee that the creative forces of the whole Union will flourish as never before as the Soviet people confidently march towards a communist tomorrow.

*Speech delivered at a celebration
meeting of the Central Committee of
the Communist Party of Azerbaijan
and the Supreme Soviet of the Azerbaijan SSR to mark their fiftieth
anniversary. 2 October 1970*

. . . The USSR is more than a state, it is a voluntary, indissoluble socialist union of all Soviet peoples, being part of their very existence and forming the essence of their civic consciousness. Soviet people are deeply aware that their strength lies in their firm unity, on their readiness to help one another and together advance towards the great aim of communism under the leadership of the Communist Party. The fraternal peoples of our country have always stood together; in time of severe trial and in time of jubilation they share the joy of victory and the bitterness of failure, they are united by common goals and are pursuing the same course . . .

For the Armenian people the road to social and national independence was far from easy or simple, and the working people of Armenia suffered many hardships. With its rich and ancient culture, this nation was compelled for centuries to fight and defend the fruits of its labour and to uphold its rights to existence. After each wave of foreign invasion, the Armenian people restored from ruined cities and villages their unique cultural relics and monuments, and continued to march forward with full confidence in their future.

While fighting both internal and external oppressors, the working people of Armenia were increasingly drawn towards the democratic and revolutionary forces in Russia, regarding them as a powerful and loyal ally. The struggle of the Russian proletariat against tsarist autocracy showed the working people of Armenia that the only correct way to freedom and social progress was through revolutionary struggle and socialist transformation. They came to realise that there could be no justice and happiness in a world where one man exploited another and where a handful of the rich had everything while the working people had nothing.

The best sons of the Armenian people took a most active part in the proletarian movement in Russia from the very beginning. An outstanding group of revolutionary internationalists appeared who realised that the interests of the working people of Armenia were inseparably linked to those of their comrades in Russia. Having linked the destiny of their own people to the historic mission of the entire Russian proletariat and the victory of the socialist revolution in Russia, they unhesitatingly took the road pointed out by Lenin and became his disciples, friends and comrades-in-arms.

There is no doubt that Armenian communists justified the trust and hopes which their people placed in them. They made a worthy contribution to the development of the all-Russia revolutionary movement, to the foundation of the Marxist Party, a party of a new kind, and, together with communists of the whole country, took an active part in assailing the old world and in building a new, socialist one.

The great Lenin valued highly the role played by the Bolsheviks of the Caucasus in the struggle to build our Party and to cement its ranks, and in the education of the working people in keeping with the principles of proletarian internationalism. In 1913, Vladimir Ilyich wrote in a letter to Maxim Gorky: 'In Russia and in the Caucasus the Georgian + Armenian + Tatar + Russian Social-Democrats have worked *together*, in a *single* Social Democratic organisation *for more than ten years*. This is not a phrase, but the proletarian solution of the problem of nationalities. The only solution . . .'*

Soviet power in Armenia, as elsewhere in our country, was strengthened and tempered in fierce class battles, overcoming incredible difficulties. Many of the comrades who are present here remember well the grave problems the Armenian people inherited. As a result of the anti-popular, adventurist policy of the bourgeois nationalists, the Dashnaks, the economy was in a state of ruin. Dislocation, hunger and disease, which caused many thousands of deaths, reigned supreme. However, once masters of their own destiny, the Armenian people were able to heal these wounds quickly. Under the leadership of the Communist Party and with selfless support from other Soviet peoples, they have built on their ancient land a new, young and just society, which knows neither

*Lenin, *Collected Works*, Vol. 35, pp. 84–85.

exploitation, nor oppression, nor class or national animosity. They have built socialism . . .

Soviet Armenia has arrived at the threshold of its fiftieth anniversary with outstanding achievements in all spheres of economic, social and cultural life . . .

Many products developed and manufactured by Armenian scientists, engineers and workers have won high praise both in our country and abroad . . .

The Armenian countryside has changed completely. Gone are the small farms with tiny plots of land on which people could barely make a living. A system of large-scale production based on collective- and state-farms, with up-to-date machinery, has been set up and is successfully developing. Farmers can now enjoy a flourishing social and cultural life and they have become the enthusiastic builders of a new, socialist world . . .

Comrades, Soviet Armenia today is a republic of advanced science and comprehensively developed socialist culture.

The national culture of Armenia has a long history behind it and the Armenian people have made a notable contribution to world civilisation.

Centuries pass, but the powerful impact of such masterpieces of national poetry as the heroic epic *David of Sassun* does not diminish. Neither have the verses of the great bard Sayat-Nova who lived more than 200 years ago lost any of their freshness or novelty. As before, those who visit your wonderful country admire the great craftsmanship of Armenian architects and the unique beauty of ancient monuments.

Residents of Yerevan are justifiably proud of the famous Matenadaran, a magnificent collection of ancient Armenian manuscripts. Those who visit it seem to come into direct contact with the millennia-old history of the Armenian people. And the more one ponders over the lessons of this history, the more reason one has to affirm with a feeling of pride that it is the victory of Soviet power that saved the ancient culture of the Armenian nation, and that it is the victory of socialism that rejuvenated the spiritual life of this talented people and created the best conditions for their harmonious development.

Indeed, comrades, it seems incredible today that the people of an ancient culture that had a written language as far back as the fourth century were 90 per cent illiterate before the revolution. And yet this

27

people, the simple working people of Armenia, shepherds, farmers, bricklayers and artisans, handed down from generation to generation pages of ancient books and manuscripts. They preserved these pages as a precious relic of the past even though they could not read them.

Only Soviet government made this possible. It delivered the Armenian working people from the eternal darkness of illiteracy, giving them not only these manuscripts but also the whole rich culture of Armenia.

Immediately after the victory of Soviet power in Armenia, the Republic's first educational establishment — the Yerevan State University — was established.

Whereas before only a few Armenians had managed to receive a higher education, and even then only outside Armenia, today, young people from many countries come to Armenia to study. The Armenian Soviet Socialist Republic now outstrips many advanced capitalist countries in the number of students per thousand of population.

Thanks to the new social conditions created by socialism and the help of other Soviet peoples, the Armenian people have achieved notable progress in the field of science. In the Republic today there are about 100 research institutes successfully working on urgent problems of theoretical mechanics, chemistry and geology, and in such advanced areas as biophysics and cybernetics.

Soviet Armenia and indeed our whole country are rightly proud of some of the Republic's scientific achievements and, above all, of the Byurakan astrophysical observatory. This splendid scientific centre is headed by Comrade Ambartsumyan, an outstanding scientist, Hero of Socialist Labour and President of the Academy of Sciences of the Armenian SSR. Incidentally, he has been recently re-elected President of the International Council of Scientific Unions. Using the terminology of his own field of research, I could safely say that the name of Academician Ambartsumyan is shining on the horizon of Soviet and world science as a star of the first magnitude.

Many famous names among the republic's artists, writers and actors speak eloquently of the high level of Armenian culture.

It would be sufficient to mention here the great master of contemporary painting, Martiros Saryan. Those who have seen exhibitions of this marvellous artist's work will always remember their joyous meeting with true art, an art glorifying the proud, austere and yet tender land of

Soviet Armenia.

It would probably be difficult today to find a corner of our vast country where Aram Khachaturian's exciting works, which are profoundly national works and which at the same time have assimilated the best achievements of Soviet and world musical culture, are not known.

Our Party has always had great respect for artists and intellectuals. It has high regard for artists and writers, who clearly understand their role in and responsibility to society, who are worthy representatives of our progressive socialist art and who assert communist ideals in their work. Their best works are always national in form and are characterised by a clear class vision of the world, Party spirit, and socialist content.

It is such works, comrades, that are genuinely popular and find a way to the hearts of all Soviet people, who cherish them as works of lasting value and as the common heritage of all Soviet people. It is such works that truly enrich the culture of the fraternal peoples of the Soviet Union.

The history of Soviet Armenia repeatedly shows that a nation's prosperity is achieved not through isolation, but as a result of harmonious and mutually enriching development within the fraternal family of socialist nations and peoples.

The establishment of the Armenian socialist state and the comprehensive and successful development of Soviet Armenia's economic and cultural life are striking evidence of the constructive power of socialism and of the Leninist nationalities policy of the Communist Party.

People say that when fellow-countrymen living abroad who still remember pre-revolutionary Armenia visit the republic today, they cannot hide their amazement and admiration at the changes in the life of the Armenian people. Incidentally, such feelings are expressed even by those who do not find Soviet power to their liking. If even they have to acknowledge the outstanding achievements of Soviet Armenia, then, comrades, we can be pleased with our progress.

*Speech at a joint meeting of the
Central Committee of the
Communist Party of Armenia and
the Supreme Soviet of the Armenian
SSR to mark their fiftieth
anniversary. 29 November 1970*

Five years have passed since the 23rd Congress of the Communist Party of the Soviet Union.

These have been years of our people's intense labour. In implementing the plans outlined by the Party, the Soviet people have scored great successes along all the main lines of communist construction . . .

These have been years of successful development of socialist social relations and Soviet democracy, years of the further flourishing of the fraternal friendship of the peoples of the USSR and of considerable strengthening of the political and defence might of our great country — the Union of Soviet Socialist Republics . . .

The past 5-year period has been an important one in the fulfilment of social tasks. Real incomes per head of population have increased by 33 per cent, as compared with the 30 per cent provided for by the Directives of the Party's 23rd Congress, and the 19 per cent in the preceding 5-year period . . .

Social consumption funds have increased by 50 per cent . . .

More than 500 million square metres of housing have been put up in the past 5 years. This means that an equivalent of more than fifty large cities with one million population each were built in the country. Most of the family house-warmings were celebrated in separate apartments with modern amenities.

The systems of public education and health have made good headway. The Soviet people's health and longevity are an object of the Party's and the state's constant concern. In 1966–70 we trained 151,000 doctors, or 22,000 more than in the preceding 5 years. The network of medical institutions was expanded considerably.

For some years, most Soviet workers and office employees have had a 5-day work week with 2 days off. Paid annual leaves have been lengthened for a considerable part of the working people . . .

The Ninth Five-Year Plan is sure to be an important stage in Soviet society's further advance to communism, in building its material and technical basis, in augmenting the country's economic and defensive might. *The main task of the Five-Year Plan is to secure a considerable rise in the living standard and cultural level of the people on the basis of high rates of growth of socialist production, increase in its effectiveness, scientific and technical progress and accelerated growth of the productivity of labour* . . .

Setting a substantial rise in the standard of living of the working people as the main task of the Ninth Five-Year Plan, the Central Committee believes that this will determine not only our activity for the coming 5 years, but also the general orientation of the country's economic development over the long term. In setting this course the Party proceeds primarily from the postulate that under socialism the fullest possible satisfaction of the people's material and cultural requirements is the supreme aim of social production.

From the first days of Soviet power our Party and state have been doing their utmost in this respect. But for well-known historical reasons our possibilities were limited for a long time. Now they are substantially greater, which enables the Party to raise the question of centring economic development still more fully on improving the life of the people.

The Party also proceeds from the fact that a higher standard of living is becoming an ever more imperative requirement of our economic development, one of the most important preconditions for the rapid growth of production.

This approach follows not only from our policy of further accentuating the role of material and moral labour incentives. The question is posed much more broadly: to create conditions favourable for the all-round development of the ability and creative activity of the Soviet people, of all working people, that is, to develop the main productive force of society . . .

Apart from the increase of incomes in payment for labour, *the social consumption funds*, too, are to be raised considerably. It is planned to increase them by 40 per cent, so that in 1975 they will amount to 90,000 million roubles. These sums will be used for the further improvement of the medical services and the development of education and the upbringing of the rising generation.

The social funds will also be used to finance a number of other important social measures, including improvement of the living conditions of large families and needy families, women working in production, pensioners, and students . . .

To carry out the new measures relating to wages and salaries and greater allowances out of the social consumption funds, aimed at raising the standard of living, 22,000 million roubles are allocated in the current

31

5-year plan as against 10,000 million in the Eighth Five-Year Plan.

House-building will continue on a still larger scale. In the next 5 years we are planning to build housing totalling 565–75 million square metres which will enable us to improve the living conditions of approximately 60 million people. Considerable funds are also being allocated for the public utilities and for town and village improvement . . .

One of the Party's central tasks is to draw the working masses into the management of production on an ever larger scale. What we must achieve is, as Lenin emphasised, that every working person, every politically-conscious worker should feel 'he is not only the master in his own factory but that he is also a representative of the country' (*Collected Works*, Vol. 27, p. 403).

We have immense possibilities for this. The people's participation in economic management is not confined to resolving economic tasks in individual production collectives. A broader approach has to be adopted to this, in view of the role which our Party and the Soviet state play in economic management. Their policy, including their economic policy, is dictated by the basic interests of the working people. It is charted by representatives of the working people in the elective organs, with the masses participating broadly in the discussion of major plans and decisions. The working people also actively take part in the control of the fulfilment of these decisions. The Party will continue to promote all these forms of socialist democracy.

A big role is played in economic management by the primary Party organisations, which unite millions of workers, collective farmers and office employees. Utilising their right to control the economic activity of enterprises, they effectively influence matters concerning production. A big role is played by the trade unions in resolving economic problems, promoting socialist emulation and mass technical innovation and strengthening labour discipline.

In the period under review there has been a marked upswing of activity by production conferences, workers' meetings and general meetings of collective farmers. Concern must be shown to secure a further enhancement of their authority and bring the key questions of the life of the enterprises up for their discussion. It is necessary to encourage the practice of the heads of amalgamations and enterprises and also of top-level officials of ministries regularly accounting for their work directly to the workers.

Alongside questions of production, questions of labour protection and the improvement of everyday conditions must, naturally, receive the closest attention of the collectives. The practice of drawing up plans for the social development of collectives deserves encouragement. The procedure of concluding and checking collective agreements should be improved.

It is our duty to translate Lenin's behests still more fully into life and get all the workers, collective farmers and intellectuals to become conscious fighters for the implementation of the Party's economic policy, to act like statesmen and fully display their abilities, initiative and economic acumen . . .

Comrades, in its policy our Party has taken and will go on taking into consideration the interests of such large social groups as young people, women and pensioners . . .

On the Party's initiative a series of important measures has been put into effect during the past 5 years to improve the working conditions for women and, at the same time, lighten their household chores. Let me remind you at least of the fact that maternity leave procedures have been extended to collective-farm women and more crèches, kindergartens and everyday service establishments have been opened. You all know, comrades, that further steps in this direction have been planned for the next 5-year period.

The aim of the Party's policy is that Soviet women should have further possibilities for bringing up their children, for taking a larger part in social life, and for recreation and education, and that they should have greater access to the blessings of culture. All these are important tasks, and the new 5-year plan will be a noteworthy stage in their implementation.

A large group of our society consists of pensioners, of labour and war veterans. The delegates to this Congress know that in recent years citizens going on pension have been given wider opportunities to take part in labour activity. Many Party organisations are evolving useful forms of work with pensioners. But we shall act correctly if we take steps to employ the experience and energy of our veterans more extensively in social and labour activity.

Comrades, one of the greatest achievements of socialism is the practical implementation by the Party of the *Leninist national policy*, a policy promoting equality and friendship among peoples.

Many of the fraternal republics recently marked their fiftieth anniversaries. This was an imposing demonstration of the florescence of socialist nations, of the monolithic unity of all the peoples of our country. Next year we shall mark the fiftieth anniversary of the Union of Soviet Socialist Republics. For its political significance and socio-economic consequences the formation of the USSR occupies a prominent place in the history of our state.

All the nations and nationalities of our country, above all, the great Russian people, played their role in the formation, consolidation and development of this mighty union of equal nations that have taken the road to socialism. The revolutionary energy, dedication, diligence and profound internationalism of the Russian people have quite legitimately won them the sincere respect of all the other peoples of our socialist motherland.

Further progress along the road of the all-round development of each of the fraternal Soviet republics, along the road of the further gradual drawing together of the nations and nationalities of our country, has been made during the past few years under the Party's leadership. This drawing together is taking place under conditions in which the closest attention is given to national features and the development of socialist national cultures. Constant consideration for the general interests of our entire Union and for the interests of each of its constituent republics forms the substance of the Party's policy on this question.

The Party will continue to strengthen the Union of Soviet Socialist Republics, consistently pursuing the Leninist line of promoting the florescence of the socialist nations and securing their gradual drawing together. The Party will continue to educate all the working people in the spirit of socialist internationalism, intolerance of nationalism, chauvinism, national narrowness and conceit in any form, in a spirit of profound respect for all nations and nationalities.

A new historical community of people, the Soviet people, took shape in our country during the years of socialist construction. New, harmonious relations, relations of friendship and co-operation, were formed between the classes and social groups, nations and nationalities in joint labour, in the struggle for socialism and in the battles fought in defence of socialism. Our people are welded together by a common Marxist–Leninist ideology and the lofty aims of building communism. The multinational Soviet people demonstrate this monolithic unity by their labour and by their unanimous approval of the Communist Party's policy.

The past 5-year period has witnessed a further advance towards the consolidation of our society's unity. We shall go on doing everything to strengthen the community of interests of all the classes and social groups of our country in order to promote the process of drawing them together . . . Comrades, during the period under review the Party has accomplished considerable and extremely diverse work aimed at further strengthening the Soviet state and perfecting the entire political organisation of our society. The principal orientation of this work — in accordance with the tasks of communist construction — has been and remains the further development of socialist democracy.

In our country, as everybody knows, the organs of people's power — *the Soviets of Working People's Deputies* — are the foundation of the socialist state and the fullest embodiment of its democratic nature. This, comrades, is a mighty force. Today they comprise over 2 million deputies, who administer the affairs of our state of the entire people at all its levels. With them at the Soviets there is an army of 25 million activists, dedicated voluntary assistants.

Permit me to remind you that the need to enhance the role of the Soviets was underscored in the decisions adopted by the 23rd Congress of the CPSU. To achieve this a lot has been done over the past years. To this end the powers of the district, town, rural and settlement Soviets have been extended also in such an important field as coordinating, within the limits of their competence, the work of factories and economic organisations situated in their territories. Their material and financial resources have been enlarged and they are getting more trained personnel.

The work of the Soviets has, on the whole, become more active and many-sided. The deputies now meet more regularly with their electorate and give an account of their work to them. Also important is the fact that the press, radio and television are gradually making a practice of reporting the work of the Soviets more fully.

Greater control is exercised by the USSR Supreme Soviet and the Supreme Soviets of the Union republics over the work of ministries and departments and over the state of affairs in the key sectors of economic and cultural development. The larger number of standing commissions and the more efficient organisation of their activities are enabling the deputies to display more initiative, delve deeper into the work of the executive bodies and participate more actively in drafting laws.

The Party attaches great importance to *perfecting Soviet legislation*. During the period under review attention was concentrated on the legislative regulation of questions such as improving the public health services, strengthening family relations, further bettering labour relations and ensuring nature conservation and the rational utilisation of natural wealth. On all these questions the USSR Supreme Soviet and the Supreme Soviets of the Union republics have passed the appropriate laws after broad discussions with the participation of millions of citizens.

Another point, comrades. There is now a pressing need for a special law defining the status, powers and rights of deputies — from the Supreme to the settlement Soviets — and also the duties of officials with regard to deputies. It seems to me that the passage of such a law would enhance the authority and activity of deputies.

The successful realisation of the tasks facing us presupposes the precise and efficient work of the *state apparatus*. Hence the increased demands made on the administrative apparatus. The introduction of modern means and methods of administration, begun in recent years, creates the condition for a more rational organisation of the administrative apparatus, for cutting its operational costs and reducing its personnel. Steps have already been taken in this direction, and they will be continued.

Most of the employees of the state apparatus are highly trained, conscientious and considerate people. Their work merits the highest appreciation and respect. But it must be admitted that there still are callous officials, bureaucrats and boors. Their conduct evokes the just indignation of Soviet citizens. Relying on public support, the Party is and will go on making resolute efforts to achieve more efficiency in the work of the administrative apparatus.

The way we see it, efficiency in administration organically combines an attentive, solicitous attitude to the needs and cares of the working people with a prompt consideration of their applications and requests. An atmosphere of goodwill and of respect for man must reign in every institution.

In the system of Soviet socialist democracy an important place is occupied by the organs of *people's control*, in whose work millions of factory and office workers and collective farmers now take part. The Party will continue doing everything to secure the steadfast implementation of Lenin's precepts on constant and effective control by the broad masses.

Comrades, an important feature of the socialist system is that in our country the working people participate in the administration of society not only through state organs but also through a ramified network of mass organisations such as, above all, the trade unions and the Komsomol.

Today our trade unions have more than 93 million members. This is practically the entire working class, the whole of the working intelligentsia and numerous sections of rural workers.

The trade unions are one of the key links in the general system of socialist democracy, in drawing the working people into the administration of the affairs of the state and society. They participate in solving many problems of economic development — from the drawing up of state plans to the management of each enterprise. They play an important role in the production and social work of the personnel of factories, building projects and offices. They help to inculcate a communist attitude to labour and social property, and work to satisfy the cultural and everyday requirements of the people and protect their health.

The safeguarding of the legitimate interests of the working people remains one of the basic tasks of the trade unions. It is no secret, for example, that we still have enterprises where overtime is systematically practised, where people are unnecessarily deprived of days off and where, here and there, labour safety is poorly organised. The trade unions can do much to eliminate these abnormal phenomena.

The Party's line is to continue enhancing the role and efficiency of the trade unions. Without assuming petty tutelage over the trade unions, the Party organisations must do everything to promote their activity and initiative, strengthen them with cadres and make more exacting demands on Communists working in trade unions.

The Party will continue giving constant support to the trade unions as the largest organisations of the working people and seeing to it that they are able to fulfil their roles as school of administration, school of economic management and school of communism more fully and successfully.

In the country's social and political life an important place belongs to the *Lenin Komsomol*, which unites over 28 million young men and women. It would be hard to name a sector of economic and cultural development where the energy, creative initiative and ardour of Komsomol members have not been displayed. Komsomol shock building projects, team contests of skill by young workers, student building detachments, youth production brigades and summer work and recreation camps are among the concrete and vital tasks being accomplished by the Komsomol, which is the leader of Soviet young people.

The Komsomol's central task has been and remains to bring up young people in the spirit of communist ideals and devotion to our Soviet motherland, in the spirit of internationalism, and actively to propagate the norms and cultural values of our society.

The different groups of our young people — young workers, collective farmers, specialists, students and schoolchildren — have their own special features. The Komsomol must be able to work with each of these groups. On it largely depends the correct and timely vocational orientation of young men and women, and the education of the rising generation in a spirit of profound respect for work at factories, farms and in the fields.

In recent years there has been a considerable extension of the Komsomol's range of tasks in questions of the labour, education, recreation and everyday life of young people. Party organisations have begun to show more determination in assigning responsible sectors of work to Komsomol members. The Komsomol is now more active sociopolitically. An indication of this is that over half a million young people have been elected to organs of state power — the Soviets of Working People's Deputies. Nearly 20 per cent of the deputies to the USSR Supreme Soviet are young people.

The Party constantly draws new forces from the Komsomol. In the period after the 23rd Congress 45 per cent — or 1,350,000 — of new members came from the Komsomol. In the same period the number of Communists working in the Komsomol has doubled. This conforms to the 23rd Congress directives on strengthening the Party nucleus in Komsomol organisations. It is worth making it a rule that Komsomol members admitted to the Party should continue working actively in the Komsomol until they are given other assignments by their Party organisation.

The Party is justly proud of the young builders of communism. Our duty is to pass on to the rising generation our political experience and our experience of resolving problems of economic and cultural development, to direct the ideological upbringing of young people and to do everything to enable them to be worthy continuers of the cause of their fathers, of the cause of the great Lenin.

In the development of socialist democracy an important task is to enhance the role of our *work collectives*, which are the basic units of socialist society. This is a major field of struggle for stepping up the labour and social activity of Soviet people. The new, socialist qualities of the working people and the relations of friendship and comradely mutual assistance take shape in these collectives. The responsibility of each to the collective and of the collective for each of its members is an inalienable feature of our way of life.

During the period under review the Central Committee and the Soviet Government have continued taking steps *to strengthen legality and law and order*, to educate citizens to observe the laws and rules of socialist community relations. The work of the militia, the procurator's offices and the courts has been improved.

It is not only the task of the state apparatus to strengthen legality. Party organisations, the trade unions and the Komsomol are in duty bound to do everything to ensure the strictest observance of laws and promote the legal education of the working people. Respect for legality and for the law must become part and parcel of the make-up of every person. This is particularly true of persons in office. No attempt to deviate from or to go round the law is to be tolerated, no matter what the motives. Nor can we tolerate any violation of the rights of individuals and infringement of the dignity of citizens. For us Communists, champions of the most humane ideals, this is a matter of principle.

The fight against crime remains a serious task. Stricter punishment has lately been established for some kinds of crime. Alongside punishment, as provided by the law, a great measure of concern is displayed in our country to find ways and means of discouraging and preventing crime . . .

Comrades, as you know, questions of democracy are now at the centre of the ideological and political struggle between the world of socialism and the world of capitalism. Bourgeois ideologists and revisionists raise a hypocritical hue and cry, alleging that we have no democracy. They offer us all sorts of 'advice' on how to 'improve' and 'democratise' socialism. But their concern is not for socialism, of course. They would like to return us to bourgeois practices and, therefore, try to force bourgeois democracy on us, a democracy for exploiters, alien to the interests of the people.

A vain, useless venture. Soviet people have their own democracy, a socialist democracy, with their own principles and traditions for developing it. There is no freedom in general, just as there is no democracy in general. This is a class concept. That is how Lenin put the question, and that is how our Party puts it today. We see the meaning and content of socialist democracy in the increasingly broader participation of the masses in the administration of state and social affairs. In our country the entire political system of society and the steadily growing initiative of the people serve the building of communism. This sort of democracy is vital to us and it is an indispensable condition for the development and consolidation of socialist social relations.

The Party's constant concern is that our socialist democracy should steadily develop and that every person should feel he is a citizen in the full sense of the word, a citizen interested in the cause of the entire nation and bearing his share of the responsibility. The party will go on consistently implementing this very line . . .

Comrades, the new make-up of the Soviet man, his communist morals and outlook are consolidated in constant and uncompromising struggle with survivals of the past. Communist morals cannot triumph without a determined struggle against such of their antipodes as money-grubbing, bribe-taking, parasitism, slander, anonymous letters, drunkenness and the like. The struggle with what we call survivals of the past in the minds and actions of people is a matter that requires constant attention by the Party and all the conscious, advanced forces of our society.

During the period under review the Party CC has taken steps to create in our society a moral atmosphere that would help to establish a respectful and solicitous attitude to people, honesty, exactingness to oneself and others, and trust combined with strict responsibility and a spirit of true comradeship in all fields of social life, in work and everyday relations. In short, our aim has been that in our country everybody should live and work better . . .

In the Directives of the 23rd Congress of the CPSU the task was set of completing the transition to *universal secondary education of the young people* in the main by the end of 1970. To this end the network of general education (day and evening) and special secondary schools (vocational schools, and so on) was additionally enlarged and the number of other vocational schools giving their pupils a complete secondary education was increased. As a result, although we were unable to reach the set target we have drawn much closer to it: today about 80 per cent of the pupils finishing an 8-year school go on to receive a complete secondary education. We feel that one of the most promising ways of implementing universal secondary education (while preserving the leading role of the general education school) is to build more vocational schools offering a secondary education.

The number of institutions of higher learning has continued to grow. More than sixty new institutions of higher learning, including nine universities, were opened during the past 5 years. Today not only every Union republic but also many Autonomous republics have their own universities . . .

The development of all links of public education has resulted in the complete fulfilment of another important directive of the 23rd Party Congress: over 7 million specialists with a higher or secondary special education have been trained in the country during the past 5 years. This is a good and extremely needed addition to the army of builders of communism.

The public education system has to ensure the training of large contingents of specialists, including many new professions. Today progress is so swift in all fields that the education received by young people is only a foundation that requires the constant acquisition of knowledge. This makes the systematic improvement of the qualification of cadres extremely important.

> *Report of the Central Committee to*
> *the 24th Congress of the CPSU.*
> *30 March 1971*

There are events in the history of every people which sharply change its destiny and open up a new epoch. For the Georgian people such an event was the declaration of Soviet power in Georgia in 1921. Fifty years is not a very great age even in the life of an individual. It is a short period in the case of nations and states. This day, the day of the fiftieth anniversary of socialist Georgia and its Communist party, may be considered the triumph of youth and the blossoming of your beautiful Republic . . .

The roads traversed by Georgia through the centuries and millennia were rough and winding. Transcaucasia attracted hordes of invaders. There were few who did not attempt to conquer this land. However, the misfortunes which befell the Georgian people did not break them or diminish their creative power. This power time and again revived Georgia from ruins and ashes. The constructive genius of the Georgian people, however, unfolded in full measure, in full strength, only when the shackles of the exploiting system had been thrown off.

Never before had the Caucasian mountains, their caps white with eternal snow, seen such an upsurge of universal social creativity, such a thirst for light, freedom and progress stemming from the very soul of the people! In an historically brief period, this former semi-feudal province of the Russian Empire has turned into a socialist state with a modern industry and well-developed agriculture, a Republic of total literacy, advanced science and culture . . . The path which Georgia has followed is the path of our entire great community of peoples.

The very nature of the socialist social system and the consistent implementation of the Leninist policy on the national question by the Party have united the peoples of our country and transformed their friendship into a motive force for progress of Soviet society, into an inexhaustible source of energy and creative activity of all nations and nationalities of the Soviet Union. There is probably no person who does not feel everlasting love for and devotion to the land of his grandfathers and great-grandfathers, to his own culture, his own mother tongue, traditions and customs. In a socialist society, however, these sentiments — the sentiments of patriotism — transgress the bounds of one's nationality and are filled with a new content.

All of us, in whatever republic we live, are Soviet patriots, children of the socialist motherland. Our own land, our motherland, comprises the infinite expanses stretching from the Pacific to the Baltic Sea, from the

Arctic Ocean to the Pamirs and the Caucasus. And whatever has been created in this land by the effort of the people — beautiful towns, gigantic industrial complexes and blossoming fields, cascades of electric stations, values of spiritual culture — all this is the product of our common efforts, our common property, the property of the Soviet people.

The unbreakable friendship of the peoples is the product of socialism. It is the offspring of our social system and the nationalities policy of the Leninist Party. Its roots, however, extend deep into the period in history when the peoples of tsarist Russia rose to join the common ranks of fighters against the monarchy, against exploitation and oppression. The sons of the Georgian people have a worthy place in these ranks.

The history of the revolutionary struggle in Georgia is inseparably linked with the history of the revolutionary movement of the Russian people, of all the peoples of the Caucasus, with the activities and teaching of Lenin . . .

Lenin personally rendered constant assistance to Georgian Communists in their struggle for a new socialist Georgia. You, of course, know of Lenin's numerous speeches, letters and telegrams which show that he found time to go into the concrete problems of Georgia's economic and cultural development.

Guided by Lenin's instructions, leaning on the fraternal assistance of the Russian Federation and of the other Union Republics, the working people of Soviet Georgia had successfully laid the foundations of socialism. In the years of the first 5-year plans a network of plants and factories, collective and state farms, schools, colleges and libraries was built in the Republic. Far-reaching socio-economic reforms were implemented and a cultural revolution carried out. The victory of socialism in Georgia became a fact . . .

Tremendous changes have taken place in your Republic, too. These changes can be seen in everything — in the new appearance of towns and villages, in the new factories, electric power stations and institutes, and in the new tracts of fertile land. They can also be seen in the new outlook of the working people — the working class, the peasantry and the intelligentsia.

The Georgian working class today is practically a million-strong army of skilled people, more than half of whom have a secondary education. They are working at modern enterprises, producing complex machines, valuable equipment and other high-quality commodities . . .

The collective-farm peasantry of the Republic are not lagging behind the workers. They, too, are people of the new Soviet formation. The industriousness of the Georgian peasants has long been known. Today this industriousness is augmented by the strength of the collective, by the arsenal of agricultural machinery and implements, some of which are unique. They are skilled in the use of modern agricultural methods. It is thanks to their effort that Georgia has been turned into a blossoming orchard.

The new, people's intelligentsia of Georgia is playing a tremendous constructive role. It is no longer a narrow group of a chosen few. Now it comprises tens of thousands of teachers and doctors, engineers and agronomists, scientists and production managers, cultural workers and instructors at higher schools. Together with the workers and the peasants, the Georgian intelligentsia is giving all its knowledge, intellect and talent for the benefit of the people . . .

Thanks to the tireless labour of the Georgian workers, peasants and Georgian intelligentsia, the economy and culture of Georgia occupy an important place in the economic and cultural development of the whole of the Soviet Union.

Diverse industrial goods bearing the trademarks of enterprises of Tbilisi, Kutaisi, Sukhumi, Batumi, Rustavi, Chiatura, Tskhinvali, and many other towns of the Republic are reaching all corners of our country. Georgia holds a leading place in the production of grapes and citrus fruit, tobacco, tea, tung oil and vintage wines in the country.

Georgian scientists play an important part in the development of Soviet science. The schools of mathematics, physiology and other sciences established here are the pride of our science. Today Georgia has not only well-equipped institutes, but distinguished and world-famous scientists who with the scientists of other Republics are making a tremendous contribution to the country's scientific and technological progress.

Georgian art — one of the powerful and fruitful streams in Soviet culture — is highly appreciated and loved in the Soviet Union. Georgian music, poetry, drama and cinema are enriching the inner world of the Soviet people, inspiring them with kindness and radiant ideals, and with the desire to struggle against everything which hinders a happy and joyous life . . .

In pointing out the achievements of the Communist Party and the working people of Georgia, we also point out the achievements of all Soviet Communists, of all the working people of the country. One cannot imagine present-day Georgia without its specialists who have been trained at higher schools not only in Georgia, but in Moscow, Leningrad, Kiev, Gorky, Baku, Yerevan and many other cities. One cannot imagine present-day Georgia without its intellectual wealth which it draws from the treasure house of culture and art of all the peoples of the Soviet Union. Modern Georgia grew out of the unbreakable economic, scientific, technological and cultural bonds which link Georgia organically with other fraternal Republics and peoples of our motherland.

Such is our socialist reality: all are working for one and one works for all. Such is the real, tangible result of the triumph of the friendship of the peoples of the USSR, of the Leninist nationalities policy of our Party. That is why, comrades, the anniversary of every Republic is a festive occasion for all Soviet people. This is why numerous guests from all the Republics of the Union are present in this hall. There is no force in the world capable of shaking the friendship of the Soviet peoples — one of the greatest gains of socialism.

> *Speech at a meeting of the Central Committee of the Communist Party of Georgia and the Supreme Soviet of the Georgian SSR to mark their fiftieth anniversary. 14 May 1971*

This Congress is a major event in the life of our country. It owes its significance to the important role which the trade unions, uniting in their ranks 98 million Soviet working people, play in the building of communism . . .

Our trade unions operate in a society of triumphant socialism, and that is what determines their basic characteristics. In their struggle for the interests of the working people they have gone beyond the confines of the 'protective function', since the exploiting classes have been long done away with in our country. To be sure, trade unions are called upon today to protect the working people from 'departmental overzeal', as Lenin put it, and from bureaucratic excesses which unfortunately we still come across, but their functions are by no means limited to this. One of the basic distinctions of Soviet trade unions is that they take a direct and active part in the development of society, in raising production and increasing its efficiency, and in economic management . . .

Trade unions which have been invested by law with extensive rights in matters of wages, rate setting and payment scales may help considerably, in particular, to increase the role of payment according to work done, which is a major form of material incentive. New possibilities in this direction have opened up now that the production collectives have at their disposal considerable funds derived from the incomes of their enterprises.

I have mentioned this because of the many instances where there has been an indiscriminate approach in the matter of payment for work and the apportioning of the material incentive funds. To be concerned for the welfare of the working people does not mean to be a good uncle for all workers regardless of their contribution to social production. Everywhere wages should be *earned*, and everyone should be aware that the size of these wages directly depends on his contribution to the production achievements of one's collective . . .

While improving material incentives we must also considerably raise the role of moral incentives.

In our country these incentives are widely used, including such high marks of recognition of one's work as the awarding of orders and honorary titles. Such forms of encouraging the best workers and foremost collectives will certainly retain their full significance.

However, moral incentives should not be limited to awards. Also very important is the ability to create at each enterprise and in each collective such an atmosphere and public opinion that all know who are the workers, and how they work, and each is given his due. Every worker must be able to feel sure that his good work and praiseworthy conduct in the collective will be always acknowledged and appreciated and earn him the respect and gratitude of his workmates. By the same token, everyone should know that no tolerance or leniency will be shown to shirkers, loafers, footloose workers and bunglers and nothing will shield them from the anger of their workmates . . .

Vladimir Ilyich Lenin directly linked achievements in socialist construction with 'iron discipline while at work' (*Collected Works*, Vol. 27, p. 271). He included in the essential rules of behaviour for the Soviet man such injunctions as: '. . . do not be lazy . . .', and 'observe the strictest labour discipline . . .' (*Ibid.*, p. 243). Lenin regarded any breach of discipline either by workers or by economic executives as intolerable.

It is precisely because trade unions protect the interests of the working people that they should not — must not — shield those who fail to observe socialist discipline. This calls for an exacting proletarian approach. You should make the fullest possible use of your extensive rights and possibilities in this matter.

It is appropriate to recall, comrades, that Lenin's definition of the role of trade unions as a 'school of communism' implies above all the fostering of communist consciousness which is to be inseparably linked with the production activity of people, their work for the benefit of society. The keystone of the trade unions' educational work is the inculcation in the mass of the working people of a truly socialist, communist attitude to work and to public property . . .

Comrades, mention has already been made of the contribution made by trade unions towards raising the living standards of the working people, through participation in the effort to boost production. The significance of this activity of trade unions can hardly be overestimated. But trade unions also fulfil important functions which are directly linked with concern for the living and working conditions of Soviet people, for their welfare.

The competence of trade unions covers many questions concerning wages, material incentives and social insurance; the unions have considerable material facilities for organising health-building holidays and cultural opportunities for the working people, sanatorium and health-resort treatment, tourism, physical culture and sports activities. Trade unions also have great possibilities in such important matters as improving the everyday living conditions of working people, for example, public catering and services. All this affects the interests of millions of people.

This aspect of the activity of trade unions has a direct bearing on such an important issue as the use of free time. Marx observed that free time is the measure of public wealth. Yet free time can truly be considered as a public asset only when it is used in the interests of man's all-round advancement, of developing his abilities and, through this, for still further multiplying the material and cultural potentialities of the entire society. Socialism has furnished all necessary conditions for this; it has given the Soviet man enough free time to rest, to raise his educational and cultural level, to build up his health and promote his physical development, to bring up his children and to meet a variety of other interests. But can we say that free time is always used rationally, to one's benefit and to the benefit of society as a whole? Unfortunately we cannot say so.

Not infrequently this time is senselessly wasted, and sometimes it is used to the detriment of the person concerned and of those around him and, in the final count, to the detriment of the common good. Involved here are instances of anti-social behaviour which are still present. We have been taking and will continue to take stern measures along state and administrative lines to eradicate anti-social manifestations. However, a great role in fighting anti-social behaviour belongs to the public, to workers' collectives and hence to trade unions . . .

The Communist Party, which guides the work of the trade unions, shows great concern for the improvement of their activities and creates conditions necessary for their successful work. Over the past several years, the Central Committee of the Communist Party initiated laws which considerably extended the rights of trade unions, and especially those of them which immediately concern the interests of the working people. Of particular importance are the 'Fundamental Labour Legislation in the USSR and the Union Republics' and 'The Rights of Factory and Office Trade Union Committees' adopted by the Supreme Soviet of the USSR.

The Communist Party favours a more active participation of industrial and office workers through trade unions in the management of industrial enterprises. Production conferences and workers' meetings, at which working plans for factories, plants and state farms, social development schemes and other questions are discussed, are an important form of socialist democracy, public control, a form of drawing the working people into the sphere of industrial management.

Speech at the 15th Congress of the Trade Unions of the USSR. 20 March 1972

In his report at a celebration meeting Leonid Brezhnev summarised the results of the half-century socio-economic development of the state. He paid special attention to the advancement of democracy under socialism, the questions of the Leninist national policy and its consistent implementation, and the problems of peace and international co-operation. He also touched upon current and long-term economic tasks facing the country.

The formation of the USSR was a direct continuation of the cause of the Great October Revolution, which opened up a new era in mankind's development; it was a practical embodiment of the great Lenin's idea of a voluntary union of free nations.

The 50-year history of the USSR is that of the emergence of the indissoluble unity and friendship of all the nations joined in the framework of the Soviet socialist state. It is the history of the unprecedented growth and all-round development of the state born of the socialist revolution, which is now one of the mightiest powers in the world. It is the history of the growth to manhood and the attainment of true prosperity — economic, political and cultural — of all the Republics that have united under the banner of the Soviet state, of all the nations, big and small, which inhabit the country . . .

I. THE FORMATION OF THE USSR
— A TRIUMPH OF LENINIST NATIONAL POLICY

Comrades, in these anniversary holidays one's mind, quite naturally, goes back to that distant time in December 1922 when the First All-Union Congress of Soviets adopted its Declaration and Treaty on the Formation of the USSR. The more one ponders historical facts, the greater the clarity with which one sees the wisdom of the Leninist Party, which consolidated the success of the October Revolution and the subsequent radical social changes by establishing the indissoluble union of equal Soviet Republics.

The struggle against the enemies of the Revolution and for the victory of socialism in our country required the closest unity of the peoples that had flung off the yoke of tsarism, the bourgeoisie and the landowners. The collapse of the old world, the break-up of the exploiting system, the establishment of the dictatorship of the proletariat and the consolidation of social property in the means of production went hand in hand with fierce class struggle, which developed into a civil war. The young Soviet country was savagely attacked by the forces of internal counter-revolution and world imperialism.

The working class confronted the unified counter-revolution with the great power of proletarian solidarity born of the Revolution. The sons of all the peoples of our country fought the enemy shoulder to shoulder under the revolutionary banners of the Red Army in the central areas of the country, in the steppes of the Ukraine and the Volga area, on the Don and the Kuban, by the White Sea and in the mountains of the Caucasus, in the sands of Central Asia and in the distant Amur territory. Together they went into battle for peace, bread and land, for the power of the Soviets. During the years of the Civil War, as in the unforgettable days of the Great October Revolution, the internationalist solidarity of the working class and of all the working people was one of the vital sources of our victory. In those early years after the October Revolution all the Soviet Republics then in existence had already formed a close political, military, economic and diplomatic alliance formalised in a number of treaties.

The Civil War and the defeat of the enemies of the Revolution were followed by a period of peaceful construction. Each Soviet Republic naturally faced these questions: What was now to be done? What forms of statehood were to be chosen? How were relations with the fraternal Republics to be built?

For the mass of working people the experience of the three revolutions in Russia, the Bolshevik Party's internationalist slogans, the Decrees on Peace and on Land, the policy of the Communists and Lenin's very name became a symbol of joint struggle for a new life. The working class and the working people of all nationalities wished to strengthen their unity, which had already borne such important fruit in the earlier period.

To advance along the path of socialist construction, all the Soviet Republics had first to cope with the dislocation, to rehabilitate the productive forces undermined by the wars, to overcome the backwardness and to improve the working people's living standards. These tasks could best and soonest be fulfilled by developing the economies under a common plan, making rational use of the potentialities for division of labour among the various parts of the country.

Finally, there was the continued threat of fresh imperialist intervention. It would have been hard to safeguard Soviet power and the country's independence, surrounded as it was by militarily strong capitalist powers, without the closest union, without uniting to the fullest extent the fraternal Republics' military, political and diplomatic efforts.

Thus, the vital interests of all the Soviet peoples, the very logic of the struggle for socialism in this country demanded the formation of a united multinational socialist state. But the establishment of such a state required the Party's organising role, correct policy and purposeful activity.

Indeed, the Communist Party did have the necessary theoretical basis for such a policy: the Marxist–Leninist doctrine on the national question. This doctrine constituted an important component part of the theory of socialist revolution.

The Communists have always viewed the national question through the prism of the class struggle, believing that its solution had to be subordinated to the interests of the Revolution, to the interests of socialism. That is why the Communists and all fighters for socialism believe that the main aspect of the national question is unification of the working people, regardless of their national origin, in the common battle against every type of oppression, and for a new social system ruling out exploitation of the working people.

Lenin spoke of this with the utmost clarity: 'We are consistent internationalists and are striving for the voluntary alliance of the workers and peasants of all nations' (V. I. Lenin, *Collected Works*, Vol. 29, p. 195).

But what was the basis for establishing such an alliance? Lenin was deeply convinced that it could be established only on the basis of complete equality and mutual respect of all its participants. Lenin stressed: 'We want a *voluntary* union of nations — a union which precludes any coercion of one nation by another — a union founded on complete confidence, on a clear awareness of brotherly unity, on absolutely voluntary consent' (*Collected Works*, Vol. 30, p. 293).

Thus, the unity of the working people of all nations is one of the basic prerequisites of the triumph of the Revolution. On the other hand, only the triumph of the socialist revolution can ensure the full triumph of the cause of national liberation. This was quite clearly stated by Karl Marx and Friedrich Engels in the Communist Manifesto: 'In proportion as the antagonism between classes within the nation vanishes, the hostility of one nation to another will come to an end.'

Such is the dialectics of the Marxist–Leninist approach to the national question: the way to cohesion, unity and the all-round integration of nations lies through their complete liberation from social and national oppression, through the creation of the most favourable conditions for the development of each nation.

The national question was an especially acute one in Russia because of its specific conditions. The exploiting classes of tsarist Russia deliberately spread national strife and hostility, acting on the 'divide and rule' principle, which oppressors have practised in every epoch. Although tsarist Russia was one of the major powers at the time, she herself was subjected to imperialist plunder. Accordingly, the Land of Soviets was faced, on the one hand, with the problem of creating fundamentally new relations between the nations and nationalities within the country — relations of trust, friendship, and fraternal co-operation — and on the other, the problem of defending and ensuring the national independence of the young Soviet state in international relations.

It was up to our Party to do what even the most advanced capitalist states boasting of their democracy have been unable and are still unable to do. It is, after all, a fact that even today the national question remains highly acute in the USA, Canada, and Belgium, to say nothing of Great Britain, where English imperialism has for many years been carrying on a savage war against the people of Northern Ireland, who have risen to struggle for their rights.

Literally within a week after the birth of the Soviet state its famous Declaration of the Rights of the Peoples of Russia put on record these principles of the national policy of the Soviet Government: the equality and sovereignty of the peoples of Russia; the right of nations to free self-determination, including secession and the establishment of an independent state; the abolition of all manner of national and national-religious privileges and restrictions; the free development of the national minorities; the need for a voluntary and honest alliance of the peoples of Russia and their complete mutual trust.

In the early years after the October Revolution, the Party, headed by Lenin, put in a great effort in explaining to the working masses its policy in the sphere of national-state construction. Among those who took an active part in this work were the prominent Party leaders — M. I. Kalinin and F. E. Dzerzhinsky, Y. M. Sverdlov and J. V. Stalin, S. M. Kirov and G. K. Ordzhonikidze, M. V. Frunze and S. G. Shaumyan, G. I. Petrovsky and A. G. Chervyakov, N. Narimanov and A. T. Dzhangildin, P. I. Stucka and M. G. Tskhakaya, and many other comrades.

The Party put its revolutionary energy, its great labour effort and will into the historic endeavour of creating a socialist multinational state. The Tenth Congress of the RCP(B) noted that the establishment of the Soviet system and the measures carried out by the Party '. . . transformed relations between the toiling masses of the nationalities of Russia, under-mined the old national hostility, cut the ground from under national oppression and won for Russian workers the trust of their brother workers of other nationalities not only in Russia but also in Europe and Asia, and raised this trust to enthusiasm and a readiness to fight for a common cause . . .'

The Party's work among the masses, the experience of national con-struction already gained by the RSFSR, the Ukraine, Byelorussia, the Transcaucasian Federation and the Autonomous Republics, and the powerful movement for unification which started in all the Republics — all of this paved the way for the establishment of a united socialist state.

There was need, however, to find forms of a union state, and to balance the powers of the all-Union organs and of the Republics in a way that would best ensure unity.

Different tendencies surfaced on these questions in the discussion which began in the autumn of 1922. Some believed that it was possible to consider only something like a confederation of the Republics, without setting up common federative organs vested with extensive powers.

53

Other proposed 'autonomisation', that is, the entry of all the fraternal Republics into the RSFSR on the basis of autonomy. It took Lenin's genius to overcome these erroneous tendencies and to find the only right way.

Lenin put forward the plan to establish one federal state in the form of a voluntary union of equal Republics. The power of the Soviets, which had sprung from the Revolution and which had already proved its viability in practice, was the natural basis for such a federal state. On 6 October 1922 a plenary meeting of the RCP(B) Central Committee supported Lenin's initiative and deemed it necessary 'to conclude a treaty between the Ukraine, Byelorussia, the Federation of the Transcaucasian Republics, and the RSFSR on their unification into a Union of Socialist Soviet Republics'.

The First All-Union Congress of Soviets opened in Moscow on 30 December and, in response to the proposals put forward by congresses of Soviets in the Ukraine, Byelorussia, Transcaucasia and the RSFSR, adopted its historic decision setting up the world's first multinational socialist state — the Union of Soviet Socialist Republics.

This event was a fitting outcome of the first 5 years of Soviet government, the workers' and peasants' power. The power born of the Revolution not only withstood all the storms, calamities and dangers but also united the working people of our multinational country into the mighty and solid Soviet Union!

That same day, 30 December 1922, the fine city of Moscow was named the capital of the Soviet Union . . .

Comrades, the formation of the Soviet Union and the subsequent formation and entry into it of new Union Republics have multiplied the forces and potentialities of the peoples of our country in socialist construction. The Union of Soviet Socialist Republics, a great socialist power, has come to occupy a fitting place in the world arena with great benefit for the cause of peace, freedom and independence of all the nations of the globe.

When closing the Tenth All-Russia Congress of Soviets, Kalinin said: '. . . Do we not cherish the name of the RSFSR? We do. It is a name we have won in the flames of military battles . . . I see flying above us the Red Banner with the five sacred letters: RSFSR. We, delegates to the Tenth Congress of Soviets, plenipotentiary representatives of the whole

Soviet Russian Federation, dip this cherished banner, battle-scarred and covered with glory, strengthened by the sacrifices of the workers and peasants, before the Union of Soviet Republics. We already visualise the raising of the new Red Banner of the Union of Soviet Republics. Comrades, in my mind's eye I see Comrade Lenin holding this banner. And so, comrades, let us go forward, raising higher this banner for all the working and oppressed people of the world to see.'

It is a half-century now that the victorious Red Banner of the Union of Soviet Socialist Republics has been proudly flown, epitomising the greatness of communist ideals, the ideals of social justice, peace, friendship, and the fraternal co-operation of nations. This banner has inspired us in labour and in battle, in days of great jubilation and in the hour of grave ordeal. Our present jubilee is, in a manner of speaking, a solemn vow given by the whole Soviet people, a vow of loyalty to our glorious banner, of loyalty to our great Union, a vow of loyalty to the sacred ideals of communism!

II. THE UNBREAKABLE UNITY AND FRATERNAL FRIENDSHIP OF THE PEOPLES OF THE USSR — A GREAT GAIN OF SOCIALISM

Comrades, the joining of all the peoples of the country into a solid union, the formation of one multinational socialist state has opened up unprecedented opportunities for our country's social, economic and cultural progress. It was as if history had itself quickened its march.

Comrades, consider this point. Since the establishment of the Soviet Union its industrial output has gone up 320-fold. Some may say, of course, that any comparison with 1922 is not indicative, because it had been a year of post-war ruin and famine. Indeed, that is so. In that case, let us compare 1972 with the pre-war year of 1940, the year by which our country had already well surpassed the pre-revolutionary level. In that period alone, the Soviet Union's industrial output increased 14-fold. Soviet industry now turns out in one month more than it did in the whole of 1940.

The Soviet Union's rapid economic growth has created a reliable basis for the steady rise in the well-being and culture of all the peoples of this country. Compared with 1940, the real incomes of the population have increased by more than 300 per cent, while retail sales have increased by over 600 per cent. The number of doctors in the country has increased by 370 per cent, and the number of citizens with a higher, and a complete or incomplete secondary education by 550 per cent.

Behind these figures lie deep-going changes in the economy, in socio-political relations, ideology and culture, which have changed the face of the whole of our society. And an important place among them is held by the new, socialist relations that prevail among all the peoples of our country.

Our Party was well aware that if all the consequences of national oppression and inequality were to be overcome there would be no need for more than the adoption of even the best and the most equitable laws. There was also need to overcome the economic and cultural backward-ness of the once oppressed nations and nationalities. In other words, it was not enough to abolish the legal inequality of nations; there was need to put an end to the actual inequality between them. Fulfilment of this task became one of the Party's main political goals.

Summing up the heroic accomplishments of the past half-century, we have every reason to say that the national question, as it came down to us from the past, has been settled completely, finally and for good. This is an accomplishment which can by right be ranked on a par with the victories in building the new society in the USSR, such as industrialisation, collect-ivisation and the cultural revolution.

A great brotherhood of men of labour, united, irrespective of their national origins, by a community of class interests and aims, has emerged and has been consolidated in this country; the relations between them have no equal in history and we have every right to call these relations the Leninist friendship of peoples. This friendship, comrades, is one of our invaluable gains, one of the most important gains of socialism which is most dear to the heart of every Soviet citizen. We Soviet people will always safeguard this friendship as our most cherished possession!

At present, on this fiftieth anniversary of the Union, the solution of the national question and the overcoming of the backwardness of the once oppressed nations are regarded by the Soviet people as an ordinary thing, something to be taken for granted. However, one must recall the scale and the complexity of the work that has been done in order to appreciate not only the wisdom but also the courage and the consistency of the

Bolshevik Party, which set itself this goal and achieved it.

Let us recall for a moment the state of the outlying national areas of the country at the time of the Revolution. In economic development Central Asia and Kazakhstan were on a level quite usual for colonial countries. Poverty, disease and ignorance were the lot of the bulk of the population. Suffice it to say that even in the early 1920s from 90 to 96 per cent of the people in the Central Asian Republics and 82 per cent in Kazakhstan could neither read nor write. The social structure of society was essentially a feudal one.

The mark of economic backwardness also lay on many areas of Transcaucasia and even on Byelorussia, which was close to the centre. All these areas, with the exception of a few large cities, still remained in the remote ages in economic terms, social make-up, the cultural level and living conditions of the working people.

Indeed, comrades, such was the picture no more than half a century ago, a time witnessed by millions of men and women who are still with us. That is the point at which we had to start, and, besides, to be the first to do so, because the proletariat of Russia and its Party had no one's experience to fall back on in tackling these most complicated tasks. The plain fact is that such experience simply was not there.

Those are the conditions in which the Party took, on Lenin's initiative, the line of accelerated economic, cultural and socio-political development of the outlying national areas.

The Party was aware that this line could be implemented in practice only through great and all-round assistance to the once oppressed nations and nationalities by the more advanced parts of the country, above all, the Russian people and its working class.

Such assistance and readiness to put in a great effort and even, let us plainly say, to make sacrifices so as to overcome the backwardness of the national outskirts and help them to develop at an accelerated pace was bequeathed by Lenin to the proletariat of Russia as a prime internationalist duty. The Russian working class, the Russian working people have fulfilled this duty with honour. This was in effect a great achievement by a whole class, a whole people, performed in the name of internationalism. This heroic exploit will never be forgotten by the peoples of our country.

The history of this exploit began literally from the earliest days of the Revolution. As early as 1918, Soviet Russia, herself starving and in ruins, allocated tens of millions of roubles for irrigation works in Turkestan. While the Civil War was still on, decisions were taken to extend financial, food and technical aid to Azerbaijan; sizeable funds were remitted to the railwaymen of Kharkov and the miners of the Donets Basin, and important support was rendered to the economy of Byelorussia, Armenia and Soviet Lithuania and Latvia.

The Tenth Congress of our Party, which concentrated on the tasks of peaceful construction, noted in its resolution: 'Now that the landowners and the bourgeoisie have been overthrown . . ., the Party's task is to help the working people of the non-Russian nations to catch up with the more advanced Central Russia.' One of the directives issued by the Congress in this context was 'the planned implantation of industry on the outskirts through a transfer of factories to the sources of raw materials'. In accordance with this many factories and plants were transferred, without charge, to the Republics of Transcaucasia, Central Asia and to Kazakhstan, and engineers, technicians, skilled workers, specialists, scientists, teachers and cultural workers were sent to these Republics.

The formation of the USSR marked a new stage in the development of the outlying national areas. Consistent and all-round assistance was rendered to them within the framework of an all-Union economic policy. Suffice it to say that for many years the budget expenditures of a number of Union Republics were covered mainly by subsidies from the all-Union budget. For instance, in 1924 and 1925 the share of revenues in the budget of the Turkmen Republic covered by that Republic itself came to just over 10 per cent. Even a large Republic such as the Ukraine at that time covered under 40 per cent of its budget expenditures with its own resources.

For many years the population in the Republics and regions facing the gravest material hardships was fully or partially exempted from agricultural and civic taxes. At the same time, the purchasing prices of farm produce were set at a level designed to promote the economic development of the once backward regions.

Vast assistance was rendered to the fraternal Union Republics in cultural construction, the development of education and the training of personnel. Large contingents of young men and women from the national Republics, regions and districts were enrolled at institutions of higher learning in the country's major centres. Dozens of universities and institutes were opened in the Republics. By the will of the Party the socialist cultural revolution rapidly spread to the remotest areas.

The efforts of the Party and the state over a period of many years yielded remarkable fruit. Look at Central Asia and Kazakhstan today! You will find not only first-class cotton fields in Uzbekistan and Turkmenia, the once fallow lands of the Kazakhs under crop, flowering orchards and new cattle-breeding farms in Kirghizia and Tajikistan. Today, these Republics are famed for a host of big, modern, beautiful cities, like Tashkent, Alma-Ata, Dushanbe, Frunze and Ashkhabad. There you will find large centres of metallurgy, mining and heavy industry, like Jezkazgan and Karaganda, Pavlodar and Navoi, first-rate power and water installations like the Nurek hydroelectric power plant and the Karakum canal. Central Asia and Kazakhstan have become major producers of oil and gas, chemicals and modern machines.

Since the formation of the Union, Kazakhstan's industrial output has increased 600-fold, Tajikistan's over 500-fold, Kirghizia's over 400-fold, Uzbekistan's about 240-fold and Turkmenia's over 130-fold. The gross cotton crop in Uzbekistan has gone up 120-fold and in Turkmenia 90-fold. Kazakhstan now produces almost 30 times more grain than it did in 1922.

The results of cultural development in Kazakhstan and the Central Asian Republics are equally striking. They have achieved virtually 100 per cent literacy. Almost one-half the population in each Republic are men and women with a higher or secondary (complete or incomplete) education. In Uzbekistan alone there are now more specialists with a higher or secondary special education than the Soviet Union had working in its economy in the late 1920s. Modern science has been firmly established in these Republics: in their national academies there are thousands of scientists engaged in fruitful research.

In the capitalist world achievements which are much more modest are frequently labelled 'miracles'. But we Communists do not consider what has happened in Soviet Central Asia and Soviet Kazakhstan as being in any way supernatural. You might say that it is a natural miracle, because it is natural under Soviet power, under socialism, in conditions of relations of friendship and brotherhood of nations that have been established in this country.

Evidence of this comes not only from Central Asia and Kazakhstan. In

59

the Soviet period the Transcauscasian Republics — Georgia, Azerbaijan and Armenia — have also made giant strides in advancing their economy. Each of them now has the most modern industries, and their subtropical agriculture has scored great successes. The ancient culture and art of the Transcaucasian peoples have flourished and have been enriched. They have large scientific centres, which are known all over the country.

Byelorussia, which went through an especially trying ordeal during the Great Patriotic War, has flourished in the fraternal family of the Soviet peoples. Fine cities and villages have been rebuilt and major industrial construction projects have been completed in Byelorussia, where the invaders trod a scorched earth during the war. Today, Byelorussia's industry makes excellent electronic computers, heavy-duty lorries, modern radio appliances, mineral fertilisers and synthetic fibre. The Republic has a large contingent of scientists and workers in culture.

Not long ago Moldavia was also a backward outlying area. If we do not count the war years and the early post-war years spent in rehabilitation, we find that this Republic has been developing in the family of Soviet nations for not more than a quarter-century. But in that short span it has gone a long way! The Republic has become one of the country's granaries, and one of its major centres of horticulture and wine-making. Its industrial output has increased 31-fold.

In short, on the basis of the Leninist national policy, at the cost of intense effort by the whole Soviet people we have achieved a state in which the term 'backward national outlying area', a usual one for old Russia, has disappeared. Comrades, this is a splendid achievement for our Party, an achievement of socialism, of the socialist friendship of nations!

It has benefited the once oppressed and backward nations in this country. It has benefited our great Soviet motherland, because it has made the USSR even mightier and more solidly united, because it has made the unity of the fraternal Republics truly indissoluble.

The socialist system, the relations of friendship and brotherhood between the nations have also opened up the broadest possibilities for accelerated development in the Republics and regions which at the time of the Revolution were at a relatively high level of economic development.

Among them is the Ukraine. It used to be one of the developed industrial and agricultural areas of the country. Ukrainian culture had long and rich traditions. But the Soviet Union has gone such a long way since then!

Take our famous working-class Donets Basin. Let us recall the old coal-mining town of Yuzovka with its huts, dirt and squalor. Compare it with the Yuzovka of today, the large modern city of Donetsk, with its broad avenues and green parks, blocks of modern flats, fine stadiums and Palaces of Culture. Let us recall the life of the Donets Basin miner before the Revolution and the horrible conditions in which he lived and worked. Compare this with the life of the Donets Basin or Krivoy Rog miner today, a man who takes pride in his trade, commanding the respect of the whole country, duly remunerated for his fine labour and enjoying all the benefits of modern culture. Similar comparisons are suggested everywhere: in Zaporozhye, Kharkov and Dnepropetrovsk, in the Kherson and the Transcarpathian areas.

Since the formation of the USSR, industrial output in the Ukraine has increased 176-fold. The present-day Ukraine has a powerful metallurgical industry, diversified engineering, large-scale ship-building, and well-developed chemical, light and food industries. The Soviet Ukraine also has large-scale and highly mechanised agriculture. All this and also splendid scientific centres and magnificent achievements in culture and the arts.

All this is the result of the great effort of the Ukrainian working people and also the result of their fraternal co-operation with the working people of all the other Republics of the Soviet Union. It is no exaggeration to say that the people of the Ukraine were able truly to rise to their full stature and to give full scope to their labour energy and talents only in the community of the Soviet Republics, the union which has enabled them to multiply their own strength!

Another graphic example is offered by the Baltic Republics: Lithuania, Latvia and Estonia. It may be recalled that when they joined the Union they could not be ranked among the backward outlying national areas. But on taking the socialist path they showed the highest rate of development in the Soviet Union. Compared with 1940, industrial output has gone up 31-fold in Latvia, 32-fold in Estonia and 37-fold in Lithuania. Their agriculture made good headway, and their culture flourished after it shook off the fetters of provincialism and stagnation in the backwoods of capitalist Europe. This remarkable growth proved possible only when these Republics united with the other Republics of the Union.

I should like to deal specifically with the results of the development of the Russian Federation, our biggest Republic, the first among equals, as it is by right called by all the peoples of our multinational country.

This Republic has had to play a special historical role. On the one hand, as the largest and most developed Republic, it became the mainstay in the development of the other Republics and gave them invaluable fraternal assistance. On the other hand, the Russian Federation is not just Moscow, Leningrad, Gorky and Central Russia's other old industrial towns. It is also a Republic which inherited from the past its own backward national areas. Its sixteen Autonomous Republics, five autonomous regions and ten national areas gained their statehood for the first time under Soviet power. On the territory of the Russian Federation there are dozens of peoples, including those who were threatened with extinction under tsarism.

Moreover, together with the large industrial and cultural centres, many fundamentally Russian areas inherited from tsarist Russia old, backward, out-of-the-way places, the countless provincial townlets and stagnant hamlets described with bitterness and pain by the Russian classical writers.

That is why the development of the Russian Federation required efforts in various directions. There was the need for rapid progress in the most advanced centres and regions which have played and continue to play the role of the main base, ensuring the advance of the whole of Soviet society. At the same time there was the need to overcome the backwardness over a large area of the Republic, to solve the national question, or, to be more precise, a multiplicity of national questions inherited from the past in the Federation itself. Finally, there were the vast territories in Siberia, the Far East and the North to be opened up.

The working people of the RSFSR fulfilled these great tasks with honour. Hundreds of new modern cities and industrial centres have arisen across the Republic on either side of the Urals. The Republic's old major cities, beginning with Moscow, our capital, and Leningrad, the cradle of the Revolution, have been rejuvenated. Rich natural stores of oil, gas, coal, metallic ores, gold and diamonds have been discovered and placed at the service of society.

The Federation's industry has made giant strides: in the 50 years its output has increased over 300-fold, going up over 11-fold during the post-war years alone. Just imagine what this means, considering the vast scale of the Republic's economy. The output of staple farm produce has been doubled and trebled. Soviet Russia's achievements in science, culture and education are also well known.

Comrades, our half-century of experience is graphic confirmation of Lenin's ideas about the advantages offered by a large-scale, centralised national economy as compared with a fragmented economy. The pooling of the economic potentials and resources of all the Republics accelerates the development of each, the smallest and the largest alike. Management and planning of the economy on the scale of the Union have made it possible to effect a rational location of the productive forces; they afford scope for economic manoeuvre, and have helped to enhance co-operation and specialisation, which yield an overall benefit well in excess of a mere arithmetical addition of the component efforts of each Republic, region and district.

This path has been tested, it is reliable, and we shall advance along it towards fresh achievements, towards fresh gains in communist construction.

On the basis of the deep-going and all-round socio-political changes over the past half-century our society has risen to a qualitatively new level, thereby realising the vision of the great Lenin, who emphasised that socialism 'creates new and superior forms of human society' (*Collected Works*, Vol. 21, pp. 38–39). Indeed, as the 24th Congress of the CPSU noted, *a new historical entity of men — the Soviet people —* has been established and become reality in this country.

This entity is based on the deeply rooted objective material and spiritual changes in the country's life, on the emergence and development in our country of socialist nations between whom relations of a new type have taken shape.

The economy of the Soviet Union is not a sum total of the economies of the individual Republics and regions. It has long since become one economic organism, formed on the basis of the common economic aims and interests of all our nations and nationalities.

The economic condition of, say, Uzbekistan depends not only on the cotton crop in the Republic itself, but also on the work of the machine-builders of the Urals and Leningrad, the miners of the Kuznetsk Basin, the grain-growing state farms of Kazakhstan and the makers of electronic computers in Byelorussia. Similarly, the prosperity of the Ukraine depends not only on the successful work of her working people but also on the results of the work of the oil-industry workers of Tataria and Bashkiria, of the timber industry in the Komi Autonomous Republic, and the engineering industry in Moscow, Gorky and Kuibyshev. There are hundreds and thousands of similar examples. The scale of our work tends to outgrow the boundaries not only of economic regions but also of the Union Republics.

In the past 50 years radical changes have also taken place in the sphere of social relations. In the Soviet Union, the exploitation of man by man has long since been eliminated. The whole Soviet people now consists of socialist classes and social groups. It is welded together by common purpose and outlook. Communism is its goal, and Marxism–Leninism the basis of its world outlook.

The working class, the chief productive force of society and the most progressive class of the present epoch, the collective-farm peasantry, which has shed the private-property mentality, and the Soviet intelligentsia, whose whole creative effort is dedicated to the cause of communist construction, have changed.

Large contingents of the working class have been formed in all the Republics, Union and Autonomous, and in all the national regions and areas. It is the working class, by nature the most internationalist class of all, that plays the decisive role in the process of bringing closer together all the nations and nationalities of our country. It is the workers of all nationalities, united in close-knit production collectives, that are erecting industrial installations, wherever they may be located, building the railways, and laying the canals, the oil pipelines and the electric-power transmission lines linking the various parts of the country, the Union and the Autonomous Republics, and the territories and regions into a coherent economic whole.

In each of the Soviet Republics, in each region and in each major city you will find men and women of many nationalities living as neighbours and working together. Throughout the country there is a growing number of mixed marriages, which now run to millions.

The more intensive the economic and social development of each national Republic, the more pronounced the internationalisation of every aspect of our life in these Republics. Take Soviet Kazakhstan, which has been growing so rapidly. Living there with the Kazakhs are now millions of Russians, hundreds of thousands of Ukrainians, Uzbeks, Byelorussians and people of other nationalities. Kazakh culture is developing and becoming richer as it absorbs the best elements of Russian, Ukrainian and other national cultures. Is this good or bad? We Communists confidently say: it is good, it is very good, indeed!

In the half-century of the USSR, a Soviet socialist culture has emerged and flourished in this country, a culture uniform in spirit and basic content, which comprises the more valuable features and traditions of the culture and life of each Soviet nation. At the same time, any one of the Soviet national cultures does not merely feed on its own sources, but also draws on the spiritual riches of the other fraternal nations and, for its part, adds to the latter and has a beneficial effect on them.

Common, internationalist features are becoming ever more pronounced in the varied national forms of Soviet socialist culture. In a progressive process, the national culture is increasingly enriched by the achievements of other fraternal nations. This process is in the spirit of socialism and in the interest of all the nations of our country, laying the groundwork for a new, communist, culture that is free of any national barriers and equally serves all men of labour.

We already have good reason to say that Soviet culture is socialist in content and in main tendency of development, is varied in national form, and is internationalist in spirit and character. It is thus an organic compound of the spiritual riches being created by all the Soviet nations.

Comrades, there are no abstract formulas: this is life itself. In Turkmenia or Moldavia, for instance, people read and appreciate Pushkin, Shevchenko, Gorky, Mayakovsky, Sholokhov, Tvardovsky, Fedin and Stelmakh as they do their own national writers, while the Russian or the Ukrainian has adopted, as part of his own cultural heritage, the ancient but never-ageing epics of Shota Rustaveli, the fine works of Villis Lacis, Abai Kunanbayev and Chinghiz Aitmatov and the splendid poetry of Yanka Kupala, Samed Vurgun, Rasul Gamzatov, Eduardas Mezelaitis, Mustai Karim and many, many others.

The rapid growth of bonds and co-operation between the Soviet nations and nationalities serves to enhance the importance of the Russian language, which has now become the linguistic medium of mutual communication for all of them. And, of course, comrades, we are all glad to see that Russian has become one of the universally accepted world languages.

Thus, both in the material and the spiritual spheres, a break-down of national barriers is taking place — a process which Lenin more than once described as important — with prerequisites being formed for a further drawing together of the Soviet nations. The powerful source of their unity lies in the common history of the whole Soviet people and all its constituent nations and national groups, and the common traditions, attitudes and experience stemming from the half-century of their joint struggle and joint labour.

The heroic exploits in defence of the socialist motherland were the most convincing expression of the Soviet people's unity. The union and friendship of all its nations and nationalities have stood the severe trials of the Great Patriotic War, in the course of which the sons and daughters of the same Soviet motherland not only succeeded in safeguarding with honour their socialist gains, but also saved world civilisation from the barbarity of fascism, thereby lending powerful support to the peoples' liberation struggle. The glory of this country's heroes, its valiant defenders, will not dim through the ages.

Today, our Armed Forces are a reliable shield for the socialist motherland and a guarantee for its people's peaceful labour in building communism. The Soviet people deeply respect and love their army, because they know that they need a well-equipped army so long as forces of aggression still exist in the world. The Soviet Army is also a special kind of army in that it is a school of internationalism, a school that fosters feelings of brotherhood, solidarity and mutual respect among all Soviet nations and nationalities. Our Armed Forces are one friendly family, a real embodiment of socialist internationalism.

Apart from their glorious military record, Soviet people of every nationality are also brought together by the legendary feats of the shock workers in the early 5-year-plan periods, the heroic labour of post-war rehabilitation, the exploits of the men and women who developed the virgin lands, the unprecedented scale of the great construction projects of our day, and the opening up of the northern and eastern areas. Joint labour and struggle have forged the Soviet people's common traditions, which are a source of pride and are cherished by every Soviet citizen.

The emergence in our country of a new historical entity of men, the Soviet people, is, comrades, our great accomplishment. We are justified in regarding it as a summary of the economic and socio-political changes that have taken place in this country in the past 50 years.

Lenin's Party, its collective reason and unbending will, its organising and guiding role, was the force that paved the way for the formation of the great Union of Soviet Socialist Republics, a force that has guided its development over the half-century, and that is now confidently leading it forward.

The CPSU is a Party of Leninist internationalists both in ideology and policy, and in structure and composition.

The Bolshevik Party was the first political party based on the principle of uniting proletarian organisations in which workers of different nationalities formed a single fighting force. Lenin wrote back in 1905 'To dispel any idea of its being national in character, the Party called itself "Rossiiskaya" and not "Russkaya" ' [The adjective *Russkaya* (Russian) pertains to nationality, *Rossiiskaya* (Russian) pertains to Russia as a country — Ed.] (*Collected Works,* Vol. 8, p. 496). Upon the formation of the Soviet Union, the Party emphasised this special feature by changing its name first to 'All-Union Communist Party (Bolsheviks)' and then to 'Communist Party of the Soviet Union'.

The Party unites the foremost representatives of all the country's nations and nationalities. It is the most vivid embodiment of the USSR working people's militant fellowship and friendship, the inviolable unity of the whole Soviet people. All Communists in this country, whatever their nationality, are members of the single Leninist Party. All of them enjoy equal rights and have equal duties, bearing equal responsibility for the country's future.

It stands to the Party's credit that millions upon millions of Soviet men of every nation and nationality have adopted internationalism — once the ideal of a handful of Communists — as their deep conviction and standard of behaviour. This was a true revolution in social thinking, and one which it is hard to over-estimate. The Party's success is largely due to its implacable attitude to any departures from the Leninist national policy within its own ranks, its resolute struggle against all manner of deviations, its firm stand for and creative development of the great Marxist–Leninist theory.

Lenin is known to have repeatedly emphasised the complexity of tackling the national problems, the need to show tact and tolerance with respect to national feelings, those of the smaller nations in particular, and the need gradually to foster in the latter a spirit of internationalism. But Lenin always demanded that the *Communists* of any nationality should take a clear and principled stand on the national question, and never allowed for any indulgence in this matter. He always waged a relentless struggle against any manifestations of nationalism or great-power chauvinism among Communists.

Is it right, some may ask, to talk of such problems now that our multinational socialist state has been in existence for 50 years and has been developing successfully, and now that the Soviet people have started to build communist society? Yes, comrades, it is right.

As I have already mentioned, we have successfully dealt with those aspects of the national problem that we inherited from the pre-revolutionary past. But in a mature socialist society, national relations continue to be a constantly developing reality, which keeps putting forward fresh tasks and problems. The Party never loses sight of these questions, tackling them in due time in the interest of the country as a whole and of every Republic in particular, in the interests of communist construction.

It should be remembered that nationalistic prejudices, exaggerated or distorted national feelings, are extremely tenacious and deeply embedded in the psychology of politically immature people. These prejudices survive even when the objective premises for any antagonisms in relations between nations have long since ceased to exist. It should also be borne in mind that nationalistic tendencies are often intertwined with parochial attitudes, which are akin to nationalism.

Neither can we afford to overlook the fact that nationalistic survivals are being encouraged from outside in every way by politicians and propagandists of the bourgeois world. Our class adversaries zestfully seize on all cases of this kind, inflating and encouraging them in the hope of impairing — if only a little — the unity of the peoples of our country.

Lastly, comrades, there are also objective problems in our federal state, such as finding the most correct way of developing the individual nations and nationalities and the most correct balance between the interests of each nation and nationality and the common interests of the Soviet people as a whole. In dealing with these problems, our Party closely follows Lenin's injunction that the maximum concern has to be shown for the development and interests of each nation.

The further drawing together of the nations and nationalities of our country is an objective process. The Party is against pushing the process; there is no need for that, for it is determined by the entire course of our Soviet life. At the same time, the Party considers as impermissible any attempt to hold it up, to impede it on some pretext, or to give undue emphasis to national distinctiveness, because this would go against the general line of development of our society, the internationalist ideals and the ideology of Communists, the interests of communist construction.

Lenin could not have spoken more clearly on this score: 'The proletariat cannot support any consecration of nationalism; on the contrary, it supports everything that helps to obliterate national distinctions and remove national barriers; it supports everything that makes the ties between nationalities closer and closer' (*Collected Works*, Vol. 20, p. 35).

As the Party resolves the problems of the country's further development along the way mapped out by Lenin, it attaches great importance to the continuous, systematic and deep-going education of all Soviet citizens in the spirit of internationalism and Soviet patriotism. For us these two concepts comprise an unbreakable whole. Needless to say that they are cultivated in the people by the Soviet way of life, by all our reality. But conscious efforts of the Party, of all the workers of the politico-ideological front, are also required. Our work in this area is an extremely important part of the general effort of building communism.

Comrades, the accomplishments of the past 50 years are a source of pride for all Soviet people and impart in them unshakable confidence in the future of our great motherland.

The path travelled in this half-century instils in us faith in the strength of our Party, our state, our fine people. If the obstacles that faced us in the past failed to stem our victorious march to socialism, then no one and nothing can block our path now that the Soviet Union has reached such heights. All the aims set by the Party of Lenin are certain to be attained.

The mighty winds of the times, the winds of history, are filling the sails of the ship of socialism. And, irrepressibly, our ship is sailing farther and farther ahead to the radiant horizons of communism! . . .

III. THE SOVIET UNION FOLLOWS THE PATH CHARTED
BY THE 24th CPSU CONGRESS

Dear comrades, for almost 2 years the Soviet people have been working to carry out the decisions of the 24th Congress of the CPSU, which charted a wide-ranging programme for our country's economic and social progress. The tasks that were set by the Congress are immense in scale and extremely complex. The thing is that we Communists are restless people. We want to do as much as we can to improve the life of the people, for their happiness, and to do it as quickly as possible . . .

We are confronted with extensive work, comrades, in state development and in the further promotion and improvement of socialist democracy. The basic directions of this work were outlined in the Resolution of the 24th Congress of the CPSU. This includes a still more active participation of the masses in management, a fuller implementation by the Soviets of their multi-form functions in the administration of social life; a more consistent application of the principle of the accountability of executive organs to representative organs; the further strengthening of socialist legality; an improvement in the work of the people's control bodies.

One of the major questions of the further development of the Soviet Union that we shall have to resolve in the immediate future is that of the Constitution of the USSR.

Each of our Constitutions has been an ascendant stage in the development of the socialist Soviet state, a new phase in the unfolding of socialist democracy. The 1918 Constitution of the RSFSR legislatively recorded the birth of the state of the dictatorship of the proletariat created by the October Revolution. The 1924 Constitution of the USSR was the first Constitution of the multinational Soviet state and it formalised the voluntary union of the fraternal Republics in a single state. The present 1936 Constitution reflected the abolition of the exploiting classes and consolidated the victory of socialism in our country.

But life moves on. During the three and a half decades that have passed since the adoption of that Constitution fundamental changes have taken place in the development of Soviet society, in world development and in the alignment of the class forces on the international scene. What is the main substance of these changes? Briefly speaking it lies in the following.

Instead of the foundations of a socialist economy we now have a mature and technically well-equipped economic system in both town and countryside. This system has taken shape under conditions of victorious socialism, i.e. since the adoption of the 1936 Constitution.

With the working class retaining its leading role, there has been in our country a marked convergence of all classes and social groups, and the social homogeneity of socialist society has increasingly grown. The essential distinctions between labour by hand and by brain and between the working and living conditions in town and countryside are being rapidly erased.

Since the war, our society has accomplished a tremendous leap forward in cultural development. Today there is total literacy in the Soviet Union, with two-thirds of the working population having a secondary or higher education.

There has been considerable headway in the promotion of socialist democracy: law and order has been strengthened, legislation has been developed, and the role and activity of the Soviets have been enhanced.

All these fundamental changes have enabled our Party to draw the important theoretical and political conclusion that a developed socialist society has been built in the Soviet Union by the selfless labour of Soviet people under the leadership of Lenin's Party. Having completed its great, historic mission the state of the dictatorship of the proletariat has gradually grown into a socialist state of the entire working people, with the working class remaining the leading force. The world's first country of victorious socialism has been the first to start the practical work of building communism. Far-reaching changes have also taken place in the Soviet Union's international position.

There are grounds for considering that all these changes in the life of our motherland and the tasks confronting our society under the new conditions must be reflected in the Constitution of the USSR. We have spoken of this before, and the appropriate preparatory work is being conducted. Today it is the opinion of the Party Central Committee, the Presidium of the Supreme Soviet and the Council of Ministers of the USSR that it is time to complete this work. We expect to submit the appropriate proposals for the new text of the Constitution for nation-wide discussion before the next Party Congress.

This will doubtlessly be a great, historic event in the life of the Soviet Union. It will not only help Soviet people and the whole world to get a better understanding of what we have achieved and sum up the results of what we have accomplished, but also shed new light on the further progress of our Soviet socialist society, advancing to communism.

*   *   *

Dear comrades, a remarkable, historic road has been traversed during the past half-century by the USSR, founded by Lenin, the home of almost a quarter of a thousand million free and equal people of over 100 nationalities. Soviet people have every reason to love their great motherland and to be proud of her. This feeling of love for the Soviet motherland has permeated the speeches of representatives of all the nationalities of our country at the anniversary meetings that have been held during these days throughout the Soviet Union and hundreds of thousands of letters from the working people dedicated to the glorious anniversary.

During the imperialist world war 58 years ago Lenin counterposed to the unbridled chauvinism fanned by the exploiting ruling classes a proletarian, communist understanding of national pride. He wrote of the national pride of the Great Russians, in other words, of the Russians, who can justifiably be proud of the glorious revolutionary traditions of their people, of the deeds of heroes of the liberation struggle, of heroes who came from their midst. That is how Lenin, true son of the Russian people and a great internationalist revolutionary, understood the feeling of national pride. He called upon class-conscious Russian proletarians to be faithful 'to the proletarian brotherhood of all the nations of Russia, i.e. to the cause of socialism' (*Collected Works*, Vol. 21, p. 106).

Today, half a century after the formation of the Union of Soviet Socialist Republics, we can speak with full grounds of a broader understanding, of the great sense of patriotism of our whole people, *of the national pride of the Soviet man*.

The arrogant sense of superiority of one nation over another, let alone the mad idea of national or racial exclusiveness, is alien and odious to Soviet people. Soviet people are internationalists. That is how they have been educated by the Party and by our entire reality. But regardless of

72

nationality or language, all Soviet people are proud of their great motherland, the herald of a new era in mankind's history. They are proud of the inspired labour of millions, who have, under the leadership of the Communists, built a new, truly just and free society and created an unbreakable fraternal union of many peoples. They are proud of the feat accomplished by millions of heroes — sons and daughters of these peoples, who laid down their lives in the joint struggle for these gains. They are proud of the great achievements of emancipated labour, of the achievements of science and the flourishing of culture which assumes diverse national forms, of the entire way of life of the Soviet people, who have shown mankind new horizons and new moral values and ideals.

The national pride of the Soviet man is a feeling that is vast, all-embracing and immensely rich in content. It is broader and more profound than the natural national feelings of each of the peoples forming our country. It has absorbed all the finest accomplishments of the labour, courage and creative genius of millions of Soviet people.

The whole country takes pride in the labour achievements of workers and collective farmers, in the outstanding discoveries of the scientists of all our Republics, in the skill of the craftsmen, in the immortal creations of the folk art of each of the fraternal nations. The fine original works of literature, painting and music of each of the peoples of the Soviet Union have long ago become our common property, comrades. All this and very much else that is simply impossible to list comprises the integral and common incalculable national wealth of Soviet people. Justifiable pride is taken in all this by every Soviet citizen, by all the sons and daughters of our great multinational country, by all the peoples living in it.

The farther we advance in the building of communism, the more multi-form and stronger become the economic, cultural and other relations linking all the peoples of the USSR, the stronger and deeper will be the lofty sense of that great community we call the national pride of the Soviet man.

Comrades, it would be impossible to over-estimate the contribution that the Union of Soviet Socialist Republics, created on Lenin's initiative, has made in the course of half a century to the history of mankind under the leadership of the Communist Party. The fact that the USSR was the first to build a socialist society and was the first to show in practice what really equal fraternal relations between peoples are will undoubtedly be remembered and valued by all peoples for all time to come.

Today the Soviet Union is forging ahead.

The Soviet Union is moving towards communism.

We know that the road to it will not be an easy one. Utmost exertion of the efforts of each of the peoples of our country and of all of them together will be needed. We know that great and inspired labour, organisation and a high level of political consciousness will be required. We also know that the Soviet people possess all these qualities and will be able to display them and achieve the great objectives that have been set. The earnest of this is our common firm determination to complete the work started under Lenin's leadership in the legendary days of the October Revolution. The earnest of this is the united will of the Soviet people, which has found its expression in the policy of our Leninist Communist Party.

*Report at a joint meeting of the
Central Committee, the USSR
Supreme Soviet and the RSFSR
Supreme Soviet to mark the fiftieth
anniversary of the USSR.
21 December 1972*

1973 – 6

Comrades, next year our country will solemnly celebrate the fiftieth anniversary of Soviet Uzbekistan and of the other Union Republics of Central Asia. Looking back over the path traversed, we speak, with good reason, about the historic leap which the peoples of Central Asia have made in their social development as a result of the Great October Socialist Revolution and the victory of socialism.

The present reality of Uzbekistan, and of the neighbouring fraternal Republics, which is in striking contrast to the past, compels many foreign figures who visit you to call a miracle what has taken place in Central Asia over the years of Soviet power.

Miracles do not exist, of course, but we understand the emotional character of this definition which vividly reflects the scope of our common accomplishments.

The flourishing of Soviet Central Asia and its impetuous progress are the immediate result of the Leninist nationalities policy pursued by our glorious Communist Party. This policy is based on the principles of internationalism, it is a vivid example of embodying in concrete deeds the historic mission of the working class which, by emancipating itself, emancipates all the oppressed popular masses. It has invariably proceeded, and continues to proceed, from the realisation of the tremendous potentialities of the independent historic creativeness of the revolutionary masses of the East and is doing all possible to enable these potentialities to be used to the full.

Since the early days after the October Revolution, the Bolsheviks' nationalities policy has been an organic combination of ardent solidarity and moral support with real and variegated fraternal aid. All parts of our country, including the central regions, hit by economic dislocation in the years of intervention and Civil War, needed big capital investments, educated and skilled personnel, but Soviet power took pains to ensure accelerated progress of the so-called national provinces, and a tremendous contribution to this was made by the Russian people who selflessly shared with their Central Asian brothers everything they had.

In the years of socialist construction, the all-round progress of Central Asia became the common concern of the entire Soviet state. The first all-Union projects — Turksib, the great Ferghana Canal, the Tashkent Textile Mills and many others — were built there. Big financial allocations, machines and equipment in short supply, and whole enterprises were shipped to Central Asia from the centre.

The Party invested in the cause of socialist construction in Central Asia its most valuable capital — the labour, talent and enthusiasm of its best workers. Our Party found in its ranks, in the midst of the working masses and promoted thousands upon thousands of able organisers, people with a sense of the new. The popular masses awakened from medieval slumber, grew aware of the need of change, and became masters of their destinies.

Today we recall with gratitude and respect the first fighters for Soviet power, the initiators of the socialist transformations on your land, people reared by the Leninist Party, such as Comrades N. Turakulov, K. Atabayev, A. Ikramov, F. Khodzhayev, Y. Akhunbabayev and many others. Comrades M. V. Frunze, G. K. Ordzhonikidze, V. V. Kuibyshev, J. E. Rudzutak, I. M. Vareikis, whose names are carefully and gratefully preserved in the memories of the people, worked in Central Asia in the same ranks with them. They led the great endeavours of the popular masses in creating new social relations and establishing socialism in their land.

The Communists set up schools on Uzbek land, started publication of books, magazines and newspapers in their native language, opened first-aid points and hospitals, armed the dehkans, farmhands and all working people with a new world outlook, inspired them to struggle for socialist ideals. It was extremely complicated, I would even say fine, delicate work, when it was necessary to overcome quite a few prejudices and preconceived notions left from the past. It called for persistence, courage and firmness, particularly necessary for breaking the resistance offered by alien class forces. In the past decades, the Party carried out a cultural revolution in the Leninist sense of the word on Uzbek land.

In the blossoming Uzbekistan of today we proudly see the results of the Party's titanic work, of the selfless work done by millions of workers and collective farmers, by scientists and intellectuals. It is a joy to see your splendid cities, your modern factories and plants, your thoroughly cultivated fields and your blossoming orchards.

More than a hundred industries, including machine building, mining, metallurgy, the production of gas, oil and coal, chemistry, radio engineering, electronics, the production of cotton and silk fabrics and, to add to this, gold — such is industrial Uzbekistan today. Your agriculture — a multibranch economic complex meeting your Republic's requirements and the interests of the Soviet Union as a whole — is developing intensively and dynamically.

The regeneration of Uzbekistan under socialism is of tremendous social and political importance. An army of skilled industrial workers, 1,500,000-strong, has taken shape in the Republic. The working class is the backbone of socialist Uzbekistan, an active conductor of the Party's policy in communist construction, a reliable ally and support of the collective-farm peasantry. The successes achieved by Uzbekistan's foremost workers, who include representatives of various nationalities, are known all over the country. The names of metallurgist Said Nuritdinov, scraper operator Mirzaraim Dzhumabayev, excavator operators' team leader Khadzhi Alikulov, boring-machine operator Boris Yefremov, excavator operator Mikhail Narushev, weavers Aishi Abdurakhmanova, Lidiya Kazantseva, Yevgenia Gubina, Bella Stadnichenko and many, many others are widely known. Their achievements are a model for thousands upon thousands of the Republic's working people. The heights they have attained mark the standards which the entire Uzbek working class has to — and certainly will — achieve.

Each Soviet Republic has its own special place in the development of the Soviet economy. Cotton production is Uzbekistan's main contribution to the common cause. I am not in the least belittling the significance of other branches of the economy, but Uzbek cotton plays the key role on the Republican and all-Union scale.

In assessing the labour of Uzbekistan, the Soviet people always speak highly of its thorough and skilful cotton-growers. We know how much effort and love for his job the cotton-grower gives to raise and gather in a high crop.

The Party and economic *aktiv* has gathered in session today. And when cotton was referred to as 'white gold' there, I added that this 'white gold' had been made by hands of gold!

The great work of master cotton-growers — Khafiz Palvanov,

Mamadjan Dadadjanov, Tursunoi Akhunova, Shaimardan Kudratov, Svetlana Prodan, Maria Kovalyova, Enver Aliyev, Djavat Kuchiyev and many others — enjoys well-earned esteem in our country.

Uzbekistan's culture has blossomed out to an unprecedented extent in the years of Soviet power. The glorious humanistic traditions of ancient Uzbek culture have received a new lease of life as they became enriched with socialist ideals and aspirations.

Today it would be appropriate to remind you of an episode of a rather distant past. In 1920, when the Civil War was still on, a 'science train' was dispatched from Moscow to Tashkent on Lenin's initiative. A big group of Russian scientists brought with them a library, instruments and reagents for laboratories. Here in Tashkent they helped establish Central Asia's first university which today bears the name, dear to all of us, of Vladimir Ilyich Lenin.

What a glorious road Soviet Uzbekistan's culture and science have traversed since! On this festive day I should like to pay a tribute of respect to your scientists — Academicians Vladimir Petrovich Shcheglov, Vladimir Ivanovich Popov, Abid Sadykov, Sabir Yunusov, writer Kamil Yashen, poetess Zulfiya, composer Mukhtar Ashrafi, film director Kamil Yarmatove, People's Artists of the USSR Sara Ishanturayeva, Galina Zagurskaya, Shukur Burkhanov and many, many others. The work of these prominent representatives of our socialist science and culture has won national distinction.

While assessing the profound and many-sided social achievements of Uzbekistan, we cannot but make a special note of the emancipation of women.

Charles Fourier, one of the early ideologists of the socialist trend, rightly noted that the extent of the development of civilisation is determined by the position which the woman occupies in society. It is common knowledge that here, in the East, the woman was especially oppressed and without rights. That is why we all note with pride, as a great achievement, the fact that today Uzbek women are taking an active part in the construction of communism, that dozens and hundreds of labour heroes, schoolteachers, doctors, prominent scientists and cultural figures have emerged from their midst . . .

Socialism is the most humane and democratic social system of all systems that history has known. It has generously placed all the material

78

and cultural values at man's service, to help his development and promote his weal. Solicitude displayed by society and the state for man — this great social achievement of which we Soviet people are rightly proud, steady improvement of living and cultural standards of the Soviet people — these are the main goals of the policy pursued by our Party, as laid down by the 24th CPSU Congress.

Work, work and work again, inspired, skilful and well-organised work of Soviet people who are building a happy life with their own hands is a sure way to the achievement of these goals. Man gives to society and society gives to man. Such is the relationship between the individual and society under socialism. Work is a duty and this is the basic law of our life, the cardinal condition for the well-being of each Soviet family and each Soviet citizen.

In society based on exploitation it is people who have inherited their pompous titles of princes and barons, the greedy landlords — bailiffs and squires, money-bags who grow rich from the labour of others — the bankers and manufacturers that enjoy prestige. In our country prestige is enjoyed by advanced workers, innovators of production and masters of the trade regardless of where they work. Honour and respect are accorded to heroes of labour, and others trying to keep up with their achievements. These features are the norm in Soviet life.

Comrades,

Back in the very early stage of socialist construction in our country, Vladimir Ilyich Lenin formulated the central task of our Party's internal policy in the preliminary thesis of his report at a trade union congress as follows: 'Work discipline, higher labour productivity, work organisation, increased output, relentless fight against slipshod work and red tape.'* This, Lenin stressed, was the guarantee of victory.

These words by Lenin have definitely lost none of their importance to this day, comrades.

We cannot fail to see that we have not yet done everything possible and necessary to ensure the organisation of work and the required standard of labour discipline. We have no right to tolerate poor labour discipline at some of the factories, on some collective farms and state farms and at establishments or to put up with situations where people are negligent towards their responsibilities at work. It is necessary to resolutely combat

*Lenin, *Collected Works*, Vol. 42, p. 308.

such conduct. We must hold high our labour prestige and make those who disregard it answerable for such behaviour. It is the duty of the Party organisations, government bodies, trade unions and the Komsomol to see that this is observed.

Comrades, we must unremittingly keep within our field of vision all the problems connected with boosting labour discipline and must not permit even a shade of formal attitude to this most important problem. In modern production, fitted out with up-to-date equipment, the importance of labour discipline has grown especially high.

The cost of wasted time, negligence and mistakes is now totally different. A man with a spade wasting half an hour in idleness is one thing, but an operator of a powerful excavator, combine harvester or tower crane wasting the same half-hour is quite another matter. These are totally different things.

It is a fact that capitalist labour discipline is based on the fear of unemployment and on lack of social rights. We put an end to this long ago. Our ideal is conscientious discipline which implies a thrifty attitude, creative resourcefulness and broad possibilities for working people's initiative.

At the same time we should see to it that the very working conditions contribute to the strengthening of discipline. This calls for steady improvement of planning, management and labour organisation. It is necessary to develop and improve the system of material and moral incentives which would help raise the standards of discipline and labour productivity; it is important to conduct systematic ideological and political work to instil a conscientious and creative attitude to labour. In cases when measures of persuasion fail to produce the desired results, it is necessary to take decisive measures against persistent loafers, bad workmen, drunkards and violators of labour discipline. This line is justified, it proceeds from the interests of our society and of the whole of our people. It will meet with the approval of all honest workers.

Here, comrades, we cannot but mention the role which a working collective is called upon to play in accomplishing these tasks. The opinion and influence of the collective in which a man works every day can, not infrequently, do much more than any official measures.

Comrades, together with our entire country, the working people of Uzbekistan share the pride for the great accomplishments of the Soviet people in implementing the decisions of the 24th Congress of the Party. Our union is developing, economically, culturally and socially, as a single and integrated entity, and the friendship, co-operation and mutual assistance of the Soviet peoples have become a mighty factor in the general progress of our splendid country . . .

The Communist Party of Uzbekistan is a large and militant detachment of the CPSU, like all the Parties of the Central Asian Republics and of other Union Republics. All the successes, the present and the future of your Republic, are inseparably linked with its ideological, political and organisational activities. The Republic's army of Communists, almost half a million strong, has always been and will remain a faithful assistant of the Leninist Central Committee of our Party. The strength of our Central Committee and that of our entire Party lies in that the Central Committee reposes boundless trust in the Communists of your and other Party organisations and, for their part, all our Communists are boundlessly devoted to their Leninist Central Committee. That is where our strength lies, comrades! We are profoundly convinced that the Communist Party of Uzbekistan, its Central Committee and its Bureau will continue to fulfil with honour the tasks facing it and to preserve unbreakable loyalty to the great cause of Lenin.

> *Speech at the joint celebration*
> *meeting of the Central Committee of*
> *the Communist Party of Uzbekistan*
> *and the Supreme Soviet of the Uzbek*
> *SSR, on presentation of the Order of*
> *Friendship Among Peoples.*
> *24 September 1973*

By promoting the principles of peaceful co-existence, we are working for something which billions of people all over the world cherish most of all: the right to life itself, and deliverance from the danger of its destruction in the flames of war. At the same time, we are thereby also working to ensure favourable international conditions for the social progress of all countries and peoples. This means recognition of each people's right to choose the social system it wants. This means simple and clear rules of intercourse between states. Breaches of these rules tend not only to undermine equality in relations between countries, but also to produce armed conflicts, for nowadays the peoples of the world refuse to tolerate any *diktat*. And they are perfectly within their rights in rebuffing aggression. With the world split into two systems, the only basis for international security is full and scrupulous observance of the principles of peaceful co-existence, and in particular non-interference in the internal affairs of states.

In this connection one cannot help noting that in the recent period some Western circles have been in effect trying to circumvent these principles by proposing something like a new edition of the 'cold' or, if you prefer, 'psychological' war. I am referring to the campaign conducted under the hypocritical slogan of 'defending human rights' in the socialist countries.

Some of those who have initiated this campaign claim that *détente is impossible unless some changes are effected in the internal order of the socialist countries. Others leave the impression of not actually opposing détente*, but declare with amazing frankness their intention to use the process of *détente* to weaken the socialist system, and, ultimately, to secure its destruction. For the public at large this tactic is presented as concern for human rights or for a so-called 'liberalisation' of our system.

Let us call a spade a spade, dear friends. With all the talk of freedom and democracy and human rights this whole strident campaign serves only one purpose: to cover up attempts to interfere in the internal affairs of the socialist countries, to cover up the imperialist aims of this policy. They talk of 'liberalisation', but what they mean is elimination of socialism's real gains and erosion of the socio-political rights of the peoples of the socialist countries.

We have no reason to shun any serious discussion of human rights. Our revolution, the victory of socialism in this country have not only proclaimed but have secured in reality the rights of the working man whatever his nationality, the rights of millions of working people, in a way capitalism has been unable to do in any country of the world.

From the bourgeois standpoint such human rights as the right to work, education, social security, free medical aid, rest and leisure, and the like, may be something secondary or even unacceptable. Just one figure:

nearly 100 million people are at present unemployed in the non-socialist countries. Many capitalist states violate the rights of national minorities and foreign workers, and the right of women to equal pay for equal work. This is probably why many Western powers have not yet subscribed to international covenants establishing the social and political rights of man.

The staggering socio-economic changes that have taken place in our country are the result of the far-reaching and conscious political creativity of the masses, and also of their will to safeguard the system they themselves have created from every possible incursion. For this reason, Soviet people will not tolerate any encroachment on the sovereignty of our state, the protector of their socio-political gains. This sovereignty is not an obstacle to contact and exchange; it is a reliable guarantee of the rights and freedoms hard-won by our people.

Soviet laws afford our citizens broad political freedoms. At the same time, they protect our system and the interests of the Soviet people from any attempts to abuse these freedoms. And this is in full conformity with the International Covenants on Human Rights ratified by the Soviet Union, which say that the rights they enumerate 'shall not be subject to any restrictions except those which are provided by law, are necessary to protect national security, public order, public health or morals or the rights and freedoms of others . . .' We subscribed to this.

And what kind of freedoms are those who are attacking us talking about?

For example, we have a law banning the propaganda of war in any form. There is legislation prohibiting the dissemination of the ideas of racial or national strife and hatred, and of those which degrade the national dignity of any people. There are laws combating immoral behaviour, laws against the moral corruption of society. Are we expected, perhaps, to repudiate these laws in the name of free exchange of ideas and information? Or are we to be prevailed upon that this would serve the cause of *détente* and closer international ties?

We are being told: 'Either change your way of life or be prepared for cold war.' But what if we should reciprocate? What if we should demand modification of bourgeois laws and usages that go against our ideas of justice and democracy as a condition for normal interstate relations? Such a demand, I expect, would not improve the outlook for sound development in interstate relations.

It is impossible to fight for peace while impinging on the sovereign rights of other peoples. It is impossible to champion human rights, while torpedoing the principles of peaceful coexistence.

To put it in plain language, no one is any longer able to subvert the socialist world, but regrettably it is still possible to subvert peace. For peace depends on multilateral efforts, and not least of all on mutual — and I stress — mutual respect for the principles of sovereignty and non-interference in internal affairs. As concerns the Soviet Union, our ship of state cutting through the ripple of propaganda campaigns directed against socialism will continue on its course, seeking constructive solutions to the problems of international life that are facing the world today.

> *Speech in the Kremlin at the World Congress of Peace Forces.*
> *26 October 1973*

The Komsomol has always been and remains the Party's militant reserve and reliable assistant. This is no abstract formula, but real life, real practical activity. Remarkable is the fact that today two-thirds of the Party's replenishment, more than it was ever before, is supplied by the Komsomol. In the 3 years following the 24th CPSU Congress about 1,000,000 Komsomols were admitted to the Party ranks. Young Communists continue to work in the Komsomol, constituting the Party nucleus of Komsomol organisations.

The vital connection between the Party and the Komsomol is also expressed in the fact that tens of thousands of youth leaders have been elected to Party steering organs — from the bureaux and committees of the primary organisations to the CPSU Central Committee.

And take a look at the composition of the Soviets, the organs of our state power. Young people under 30 constitute one-fifth of the deputies to the USSR Supreme Soviet, and the share of young people in local Soviets is even greater — nearly one-third. Young people work actively in the trade unions and other mass organisations of working people. The best Komsomols are promoted to responsible sections of Party, economic and cultural construction.

Without exaggerating, we can say that no major problem — whether concerning the affairs of the Soviet Union, a region, district, or labour collective — is handled without the participation of youth. In our country the Komsomol, all young men and women, enjoy unlimited possibilities to express their creative forces and initiative.

It has always been a tradition with Communists to put trust in young people, to take support from their inherent enthusiasm and noble aspiration to work for the common good, and at the same time to help young people find a correct orientation in life and to arm them with the knowledge and experience of older generations. In future the Party will continue to reinforce these traditions, develop youth activity and draw them into participation in managing the affairs of socialist society on an even broader scale.

Speech at the 17th Congress of
Komsomols. 23 April 1974

The election campaign is drawing to a close. Millions of voters have met with their candidates and discussed what heartens the people and what causes them concern. These meetings became an impressive demonstration of the monolithic unity of the Party and the people, the unity of all classes and social groups of our society, of all the nations and nationalities that inhabit our great country. This inspires us, comrades, instils confidence in new victories on the road to planned milestones of communist construction.

Allow me wholeheartedly to thank you, all the working people of the Baumansky and Sokolnichesky districts of the capital, for nominating me as a candidate to the Supreme Soviet of the Soviet Union.

For nearly a quarter of a century I have had the honour of representing the interests of the working people in the highest organ of state power of the country. It is the seventh time that I address an election meeting of this kind.

85

I must say frankly that it is impossible not to feel excited on the eve of a speech. This stems from a feeling of responsibility, from profound, sincere gratitude for the trust, for the honour bestowed on me.

Many kind words have been said about me here. These words should apply, above all, to the Communist Party that reared and educated me and which I joined 45 years ago, to its Central Committee which leads the country to communism along the Leninist course.

In keeping with a good, long-standing tradition our election meetings are of a businesslike nature. These meetings always mean a serious discussion of the way the voters' instructions are fulfilled, of the content of the Party's political election platform.

On the eve of the previous elections, the CPSU Central Committee, addressing the Soviet people, emphasised that the Party would be striving to strengthen the might of our motherland for the sake of further victories of communism, for the sake of peace on earth, for the sake of improving the life of every Soviet family, for the benefit of all Soviet people.

Yes, comrades, everything is done for the benefit of man, for the benefit of the people. These simple words sum up the most profound meaning and purpose of the activity of the Communist Party.

It is for this great goal that Karl Marx and Friedrich Engels laid the foundations of scientific communism and the mighty political movement called upon to liberate man from all forms of oppression. It is for this goal that Vladimir Ilyich Lenin built the Party of Bolsheviks under whose guidance the proletariat of Russia carried out the victorious socialist revolution.

From the first years of Soviet power, the Party, the state have been striving to use all possibilities to improve the position of the working people. But it was difficult to establish socialism in our country. For a long time, we were waging a struggle to hold out, to survive. We had to overcome age-old backwardness, to create large-scale industry, to make millions of people literate, to form specialist cadres. We had to live through the grimmest war and to raise from ruins thousands of cities and villages, factories and plants.

The labour and endurance, selflessness and enthusiasm of the communists and non-Party people, of workers and peasants, of those who advanced in the front ranks and who sacrificed much in order to preserve and consolidate the main thing, socialism, merit the greatest respect.

Those years have long since become legendary. But it is important to remember them so as to grasp more fully and more vividly the scope of the changes.

A different situation exists now. An advanced socialist society has been created in our country by the persistent, heroic labour of the millions. And now, too, we certainly have to allocate vast funds for the accelerated development of the country's economic potential, and to ensure its defence might. But our resources are now immeasurably greater and this makes it possible to do what we have always been striving for: to place the emphasis of the Party's practical work on increasing the prosperity of the Soviet people.

The previous elections were held in our country at a time when the Eighth Five-Year Plan period was nearing completion and the Ninth Five-Year Plan period was to be started, in an atmosphere of preparation by the Party and the entire Soviet people for the 24th CPSU Congress. And the Congress summed up the main task of the 5-year plan as follows: to raise considerably the material and cultural levels of the life of the people on the basis of high rates of development of socialist production.

Reporting on the work that has been done since June 1970, we, at the same time, report on how the decisions of the Congress are being implemented. You know the specific data about the state of the national economy. They were given in the address of the CPSU Central Committee to the voters. Many problems of our development were covered in the election speeches of Party and state leaders who spoke before me.

Sharing the views and judgements of my comrades in the Politburo and the Central Committee, I would like to emphasise the main, principled aspect of the state of affairs: the course proclaimed by the Congress for raising the prosperity of the working people is being translated into specific, tangible deeds.

Within 4 years of the 5-year plan, the state will spend 50 per cent more than in the previous 5-year plan period just on new measures to raise the living standards of the people.

This will have a noticeable effect on the standard of living of teachers and doctors, railway workers and farm machine operators, students, pensioners and other population groups. During this period, the wages of 47 million factory and office workers will be increased. The increase in pensions, allowances, grants and other payments will boost the incomes of 30 million people. Much has been done to improve living conditions. In 4 years more than 45 million people will have moved into new flats. Such is our scope.

Vast changes are taking place in the development of agriculture whose lagging behind in the past seriously limited the possibilities for improving the life of the people.

The Party succeeded in finding and applying such levers which, taken as a whole, ensure steady progress in this important branch of the economy. Economic conditions stimulating its development have been created. Comprehensive mechanisation, electrification and chemicalisation are being implemented; land improvement schemes are being implemented on a large scale. Large-scale work for specialisation and concentration of agricultural production is being conducted. All this will enable the working people of the rural areas to use effectively the achievements of contemporary science and technology.

I wish to confirm again that the Party will firmly and consistently continue to implement the course for further raising the level of agriculture to meet fully the country's growing needs.

The 24th Congress pointed to a certain gap between the output of consumer goods and consumer demand. In recent years, this gap has been narrowed. Industry has considerably increased the output and improved the quality of many consumer goods, including household appliances, furniture, cars and other durable goods.

Comrades, mapping out the roads of development of society, the Party proceeds both from current needs and from long-term goals, from what we wish our country to be like by the end of this century.

Every 5-year-plan period is an important step in the development of our society. But the Tenth, so to say jubilee, Five-Year-Plan period will hold a special place, and not only as regards the scale of planned targets which is, naturally, growing. The point is that in accordance with the directives of the 24th Party Congress, the new 5-year plan is being drawn up in line with the general perspective for national economic development for 1976–90 and will be an integral part of this overall perspective.

This means that the next, 25th CPSU Congress and the USSR Supreme Soviet of the new convocation will be discussing and adopting not merely another 5-year plan but documents that truly have the significance of a programme that will become important milestones on the highroad of communist construction.

At this time when these plans are being drawn up it is still too early to give specific figures for the growth of national income, of output of this or that product. But since these plans are drawn up on the sound basis of Party policy, Party decisions, their direction is obvious and it is possible to speak about it in quite a definite way.

The 24th Party Congress stressed that the long-term orientation of the country's economic development would be determined by the course for attaining a further marked increase in the well-being of the working people. On behalf of the Central Committee of the Party, I can assure you, comrades, and through you all the Soviet people that this principled stand of the Party will be strictly maintained . . .

The rapid development of the national economy will create new opportunities for carrying out highly important social and economic tasks.

During the three coming 5-year-plan periods we must provide an abundance of quality food products, consumer goods, to ensure the wide development of services and the adequate growth of the real incomes of the population.

In our long-range plans we shall be able to provide for reconstruction of most cities and villages in our vast country. At the same time such a complex task as providing a well-appointed apartment for every family will be solved. Not a single country in the world has been able to carry out such a task so far, whereas we are tackling it and shall cope with it.

Certainly, all these are not easy problems. The rates of advance will depend directly on how we work, on the successes of industry, agriculture, science and technology. The labour, brain and hands of those who make steel, who extract oil, who design machinery, who build plants and power stations, who sow and harvest grain, have been and remain the only source of our prosperity. And it is you alone, comrades, the working people, who can bring into being all we plan and all we hope for, looking into the future.

High labour productivity, economic effectiveness — this is what determines in the most direct way the extent of the share of the national wealth which society can allocate for improving the life of the people. This is precisely why the Party has come to the conclusion regarding the great importance of passing over to intensive methods of running the economy, placing the emphasis on qualitative factors of growth. The first estimates in connection with the preparation of the long-term plans have confirmed that all this becomes a requisite for successful economic development.

Already the present-day national economy which is developing at a far greater rate than the growth of manpower resources requires the utmost economy of living labour. This requirement will become even more pronounced in future, since economic development will acquire still greater scope, and more and more people will be engaged in science, education, medical care and services. This means that the rapid growth of the national economy must be achieved without greatly increasing the number of people engaged in material production, by raising labour productivity. Hence, in order to fulfil our plans, the workers and collective farmers must be equipped with more efficient machines, new transfer lines, powerful tractors, harvesters, other agricultural machines, the latest technology.

The Party regards scientific and technical progress as the core of its entire economic policy. It must penetrate all fields of production, encompassing daring scientific discoveries, hundreds and thousands of improvements in technology, new mechanisms and instruments — all that saves and facilitates work, that makes it more productive and interesting.

In the final analysis, labour productivity is the most important, the most essential thing for the victory of the new social system, Lenin said. This Leninist injunction has assumed particular importance in the present epoch, an epoch of scientific and technical revolution. And our Party never forgets about this.

The turn to intensive methods of economic development is accompanied by quite a few important and complex tasks in economic management. It requires improved planning, more efficient use of economic levers and strict economic accounting. The Party has worked and will continue working on all these problems.

In a word, we are faced with huge tasks with regard to the economy and to improving the people's well-being. What is necessary to solve them is to pay daily heed to tying in improvement of the activity of all the echelons of economic management with a widespread movement of millions upon millions of the working people, with enhancing their activity, with their attitude of taking a thrifty and responsible approach to their work. In this lies the essence of the Party approach to economic management. Its correctness has been confirmed by the entire history of socialist construction. We are confident that the key to our future economic successes lies in this, too.

Comrades, besides the economic aspect, our long-range planning encompasses other aspects of development of society. Socialism's goal is to satisfy also the social, spiritual, moral needs of the people.

It is important for each person to realise that he enjoys equal rights with the other members of society, can always reckon on a just, respectful attitude to himself, can count on the solicitude of the state, on help and support of the collective. Each person is interested in taking an active part in the affairs of his enterprise or institution, in the affairs of his state. Each person wants to be confident of tomorrow, of a settled future for his children. We have created all the conditions for satisfying these social requirements. This is a great gain of socialism. We must cherish it and multiply it like all the other social wealth.

It is more complex to sum up the results of social development than of economic development and, what is more, for a short period of time: the dynamics of social processes cannot always be expressed in figures. As for tendencies, they can be traced clearly enough.

The main tendency is that Soviet society becomes more and more united and consolidated. Our country for the first time in history copes with problems of unprecedented scope and significance regarding deep-going changes in the pattern of social relations. Classes and social groups that make up Soviet society continue to draw closer together. And this, comrades, is very good: we advance further and further towards communism.

A new historical entity of people, the Soviet people, has developed in our country. This means that common features of behaviour, character, world outlook of Soviet people, features irrespective of social or national differences, become increasingly marked.

This means that the alliance of the working class and the peasantry, which has always been the basis of the socialist system, has found its development in the indestructible political and ideological unity of these classes with the intelligentsia which has long since firmly taken socialist positions. And today we can rightfully speak of the strong alliance of all working people, workers by hand and brain, the alliance of the working class, the collective-farm peasantry, and the people's intelligentsia as a fact of our reality. This alliance in which the working class plays the leading role, is strong and inviolable.

The furthering of the social homogeneity of society is a sound basis for the further development of social democracy, of the political system of advanced socialism.

Fully confident that we are right we maintain that it is socialism and only socialism that ensures in practice the exercise of democratic freedoms. Genuine democratism permeates all spheres of our society, effectively ensures both the interests and rights of the entire people and the interests and rights of each citizen. Our Leninist Party is the chief vehicle of the principles of socialist democracy, the guarantor of its progressive development.

Four years ago we spoke of a need for new specific measures for enhancing the activity of the Soviets at all levels. Since then, laws which extended the rights and material resources of the Soviets have been adopted. The law on the status of deputies substantially extended the scope of their activities. The Soviets have become more active. The deputies are becoming more exacting and displaying greater statesmanship. And this is very important for it indicates that the Party's work is yielding results.

Democracy is just an empty word if it does not cover the surroundings in which the person does his daily work, applies his creative energy. Therefore it is of fundamental importance to strengthen democratic principles in production.

And in this we are quite consistent. The Party demands that any law, any decision concerning the principles and methods of the operation of enterprises should provide without fail for the participation of the working people in economic management. Recently, for instance, a statute regarding production associations was passed. Throughout the entire document the idea is to enhance the role of public organisations and collectives of the working people in drafting and implementing plans, for improving working and living conditions, for improving the entire activities of the association. There is no doubt that Party organisations, the trade unions, the Komsomol will succeed in exercising their extensive rights in the interests of each collective and the whole of society.

The broadening of the working people's participation in the activities of the Soviets, in economic management, the growth of the activity of trade unions, the Komsomol and other public organisations make it imperative to raise the political level of the working people, to give more publicity to the work of the Party, Soviet and economic bodies. Much has already been done in this respect. And we shall continue to proceed along these lines.

The fundamentals of labour legislation, of legislation on education and on public health, on environmental protection, adopted by the Supreme Soviet in recent years continue our principled line: to steadily extend and enhance the rights of the individual, of the working person. On the whole it can be said that our legislation has been greatly renewed in recent years, has become more stable and democratic.

Speaking of the strengthening of socialist legality we mean two aspects of the matter. Firstly, the strictest protection of the rights of the citizen, prevention of any arbitrary acts whatsoever including those committed by officials. Secondly, we mean the strictest observance of Soviet laws, of the code of public order by all citizens. Crime, any forms of anti-social behaviour are a social evil and we must fight against it every day, firmly and resolutely. I am confident that the Soviet people share and support the way the question is formulated.

I should like to say a few words about the legal regulation of economic activity. Unfortunately, for a long time, these questions have not been given due attention and as a result many unresolved problems have piled up. In each branch of the national economy, thousands of various directions and instructions are in effect. Just try to figure all these out! Especially since many of those instructions have become obsolete, contain unjustified restrictions, petty regulation. This hampers initiative, runs counter to new demands made of the economy nowadays.

I believe that the newly elected Supreme Soviet, the government, the ministries and departments will tackle this matter in earnest.

The development of socialist democracy presupposes the steady improvement of the state apparatus. It is important that responsibility of officials be enhanced everywhere, and the organisational pattern be improved wherever necessary.

We shall continue to resolutely and consistently assert the Leninist, Party style in the work of state bodies. This was the subject of serious discussion at the last plenary session of the CPSU Central Committee. It was said that in affirming the Party style of work, we must intensify the struggle against all manifestations of red tape.

It is already difficult for an overtly rude person or bureaucrat to show himself for what he is. But the more difficult it is for the bureaucrat to get along in our society the more skilfully he adapts himself and assumes new aspects.

But the essence remains the same: to sacrifice substance for form, to neglect the interests of the state, society, people for the sake of departmental and parochial interests. Some workers try to evade decisions, the reasonable risk entailed in each matter, personal responsibility. From the very outset they are not as concerned with how to set up work in the best way as they are with how to securely protect themselves with papers to justify themselves if things go wrong. There are not so many people like that in our apparatus, of course. But even though they are few in number they can nevertheless do great harm.

Our country is vitally interested in having in all managerial positions — be it in state or economic bodies, cultural institutions, public organisations — competent and able people devoted to the cause of socialism, good organisers with a sense of the new, who are unassuming and approachable people, who can lead the collective and at the same time learn from it.

Lenin used to say that under socialism, for the first time in the history of civilised societies, the mass of the people would rise to independent participation in everyday administration. In our country this has been achieved. In practice, in life, our state is managed from top to bottom by means of the everyday participation of the masses. And this is an important source of the dynamism of our society, of the stability of the political system of socialism.

Comrades, the spiritual life of the Soviet people, their culture are becoming more interesting and varied with every passing year. This is natural.

Nowadays the rate of social progress, the rate of our advance to communism all the more markedly depend on the intellectual potential of society, on the development of culture, science and education. In all these spheres we have achieved much, implementing the historic decisions of the 24th Congress of the Party.

Owing to the strides in education the Soviet people can be regarded today as one of the world's most educated peoples. Completion of the transition to universal secondary education by the end of the current

5-year-plan period will expand the mass basis for new achievements in all spheres of social life. This is also the aim of the Party's line of developing institutions of higher learning into active centres of science and culture.

Soviet science accomplishes much on all fronts of communist construction. More and more it actively affects production, daily living, it changes the way of life of tens of millions of people. This year Soviet scientists and together with them the entire country and the people as a whole are proudly celebrating the 250th anniversary of the main headquarters of our science, the USSR Academy of Sciences, which has been headed for many years now by our outstanding scientist, Mstislav Vsevolodovich Keldysh. We are fully confident that Soviet scientists will continue to make a great contribution to the material and spiritual progress of our great motherland.

Scientific quest and direct concern for man's welfare in his everyday life are, one could say, most closely interrelated in medicine, in the public health system. The people highly appreciate the work of the 5-million-strong army of physicians, scientists, medical workers who guard the health of the Soviet people.

Socialist culture, drawing on all that is best and most progressive of what mankind has created or is creating, enriches the inner world of the people, makes their lives brighter and more interesting. It helps provide a better understanding of the meaning of our labour, our struggle, the grandeur of our goals.

Speaking of artistic creation, one cannot fail to note that in recent years many works in Soviet literature and cinema and theatre productions have profoundly, truthfully, and movingly depicted the immortal feat of the Soviet people in the Great Patriotic War. The Party highly appreciates such works. For ever new generations of the Soviet people, the heroism of the people who saved world civilisation will always be a patriotic example, an example of courage and nobleness.

Soviet spectators, readers and listeners become more and more exacting. The country is awaiting new highly artistic works that are fundamental in content about our contemporaries from the writers and all people in Soviet art.

The Party considers it its task to ensure the most favourable conditions for the development of socialist culture and science. We want to continue to strengthen the creative intelligentsia's bond with the life of the people, the working class and rural workers. We want intellectual values, so essential for the people who are building communism, to multiply in a democratic, exacting, and comradely atmosphere.

I am sure that people in Soviet science and culture will always be equal to their historical mission.

These are, comrades, some matters of the Party's domestic policy, of our social development, which I deemed necessary to touch upon. I believe we may draw the following conclusion: the Party's previous election platform is being successfully implemented.

This is further convincing proof that the words and deeds of the Leninist Party are never at variance. The Soviet people know this full well. They believe in their Party and by their everyday deeds support its policy. This is the basis of all our successes, the basis of our optimism, our unshakeable confidence in the triumph of communism . . .

Speech to the Baumansky District
electorate, Moscow. 14 June 1974

Today all of our great country is celebrating . . . the fiftieth anniversary of the birth of the Moldavian Soviet Socialist Republic and the Communist Party of Moldavia.

The Moldavian people's lot was not an easy one. All through the centuries of their history they had to wage a hard and persistent struggle to survive, assert their right to freedom and independence and a dignified life. In this struggle the Moldavians have always had the support of Russian progressives. Works by Pushkin and Tolstoy, Gorky and Korolenko are connected with the life and the destiny of this land and its unique culture.

The revolutionary movement in Moldavia matured under the marked influence of the Petersburg 'League of Struggle for the Emancipation of the Working Class'. Social-Democratic circles and groups organised in Moldavia at the turn of the century. Lenin's *Iskra* was once printed underground not far from this hall in Kishinev.

The glorious sons of the Moldavian people — Mikhail Frunze, a general of the Revolution, Grigory Kotovsky, the legendary army commander, and Sergei Lazo, the indomitable fighter for the freedom of the Soviet motherland — are the pride of all Soviet people.

The Great October Revolution brought a radical change in the destiny of the Moldavian people who, led by their Bolshevik Party, had established Soviet power in all of Bessarabia by the beginning of 1918. However, the forces of international imperialism which attacked the young state of workers and peasants managed, through the ruling classes of monarchic Romania, to wrest the land between the Prut and the Dniester away from the Soviet motherland for 22 years, forcibly dividing the Moldavian land and the Moldavian people. Those were hard times for the people of Bessarabia, as can be seen from the words of Henri Barbusse, the well-known French communist author:

'This once prospering land', he wrote, 'has been reduced to a miserable state. Eighty per cent of the fields lie abandoned. An end has been put to national education because, as an official newspaper put it, national schools are "sources of Bolshevism" . . . There is one secret agent from the political police department for every three people.'

The struggle of the working people for the restoration of Soviet power, led by the underground Communist organisation of Bessarabia, never abated for a single day. The restoration in 1940 of Soviet power in Bessarabia and its reunification with the Moldavian ASSR was an act of historical justice. The Moldavian Soviet Socialist Republic was formed and, in accordance with the will of all the people of Moldavia, joined the USSR as a Union republic. And when the grim time of war came, the Moldavians fought courageously, shoulder to shoulder with the other peoples of our great motherland, against the fascist invaders, and fought fearlessly in partisan units and patriotic underground organisations.

After 3 years of occupation which caused the people untold suffering, the fascists were cleared from the Republic. The brilliant encirclement and rout of the Jassy–Kishinev grouping of the enemy troops has gone down forever in the annals of glorious Soviet Army victories.

The victory of the Soviet people in the Great Patriotic War enabled the Moldavian people, who had joined the close-knit family of Soviet nations for all time, to begin to build a new, socialist life in conditions of lasting peace. Abroad, too, in the neighbouring Balkan Peninsula, events took a new turn: the peoples of Bulgaria, Romania and Yugoslavia put an end to the exploiter system and set out to establish socialism.

Comrades, many of those who themselves took part in the struggle for Soviet power in Moldavia, her defenders and liberators from the fascist invaders and veterans of socialist construction in the Republic, are present at our celebration meeting. Allow me to greet them cordially and wish them good health, long life and fruitful work!

All those who contributed to the development of the new Moldavia, who built factories and cities here, cultivated orchards, taught children or did any useful job honestly and efficiently, all of them can say today with true satisfaction: 'We have not worked in vain', and they may well feel proud of their prosperous socialist Republic . . .

Moldavia, which had practically nothing in the way of industry before the Revolution, now has modern mechanical-engineering, chemical, and power-engineering enterprises; a mighty building base has been developed and there are large-scale light industry and food industries.

But the main thing is that the working class — now half of the gainfully employed population of the Republic — has developed along with industry. The farmers and wine-growers of yesterday are today making tractors, precision instruments and electronic equipment.

The foremost representatives of the Moldavian working class are not only highly skilled, but also have a well-developed sense of civic duty, and a proprietory concern for the development of our people's economy.

Such people as Stepan Bogoslovich Myndryanu, a tool-maker at the Kishinev tractor factory, who, having fulfilled his personal 5-year-plan assignments in 3½ years, is now working on the assignments for 1976; Dmitry Vladimirovich Kretsula, a building team leader, Valentina Alexandrovna Firsova, a weaver at the Bendery Silk Mills, and Valentin Dmitriyevich Iovitsa, a turner, are well known in the Republic, and all over the country. Today we express our gratitude to them and to all front-rank workers of Moldavia for their dedicated labour and we wish them success in the future.

We all rejoice also at the great transformations in the Republic's agriculture. Moldavia, with her fertile land and excellent climate, was only able to realise her potential under Soviet government thanks to socialist forms of economic management — the collective and state farms — to the supply of powerful agricultural machinery, and to the people who, having become the masters of the land, are doing shock-work, working with enthusiasm, in a new way.

The Moldavian SSR figures prominently today in Soviet agriculture. Although rather small both in size and population, Moldavia produces nearly a third of all the grapes in the Soviet Union, more than a third of the tobacco and large quantities of vegetables, fruit, sugar-beet, sunflower seed, grain and animal products.

The Moldavian peasant has always understood the land and loved it — has always been known for his industriousness. The people working on the land in Moldavia today still possess these qualities. And, along with that, there are new factors today — they work for their own benefit, they have developed skills and a high level of culture, they are able to use agricultural science and technology, and they have the know-how to get as much as possible from the land. That is the secret of the bumper harvests for which the Republic is famous.

Foremost Moldavian agricultural workers have received due country-wide recognition and become the recipients of signal awards. They include Semyon Mefodiyevich Lungu, Grigory Semyonovich Tukhar and Nina Andreyevna Moskalu — machine operators in composite teams who grow 5–6 tons of grain crops per hectare: Yevgeniya Mefodiyevna Kuryshina, Pantelei Andreyevich Guryuk and Maria Alexeyevna Gimpu, wine-growers who raise 15 and more tons of grapes per hectare; Vladimir Grigoryevich Abakumov, who grows 30–40 tons of fruit per hectare; Afanasy Ivanovich Nikoara, who gets 50 and more tons of vegetables from each hectare; Valentina Grigoryevna Petrashku, Grigory Petrovich Palamar and Fyodor Yemelyanovich Popa, who are experts in mechanical milking. They are just a few of the many.

Dear friends, unfortunately, I cannot mention here all those whose skill and industry have earned them respect in Moldavia and, indeed, throughout the country.

Speaking today of the achievements in the Moldavian countryside, my mind goes back to the early 1950s, when collective and state farms on the western bank of the Dniester in the Republic were just starting out. It seems that just a short while ago we were discussing, at the conference hall of the Central Committee of the Communist Party of Moldavia in Kievskaya Street not far from here, questions connected with the organisational, political and economic strengthening of the young collective and state farms and choosing Party members to go to the countryside to rebuild life in the Moldavian villages along socialist lines. It was a tense and difficult period, but we should speak of it with kind words because it was then that we laid the basis for the successes of today.

Developing new industry, transforming agriculture — everything that has been done and is being done now to develop the economy is for one main purpose in our country, the greater well-being of our people. I shall only give one, but an extremely vivid, illustration of the changes in the lives of the Moldavian people. I am referring to the new image of towns and villages in Moldavia.

Yesterday and today I rode along Kishinev streets. I must say, comrades, to me it looked quite different from the city where I used to work. I remembered what it was like in the 1950s, when the debris was not yet cleared, and the first few multistorey buildings were going up; the first trees had just been planted for the park on the Buyukan hillside. In the hollow, people were digging with their spades what is now Lake Komsomolskoye. The park has grown, the lake is a feast for the eye and there are beautiful modern buildings everywhere around. Housing has multiplied 22-fold in the city since the war. Today Kishinev's population borders on the half-million.

That is how things are now and not only in the capital and the other towns. The Moldavian villages, where well-appointed collective and state farm communities with schools, hospitals, clubs and sports grounds have come into being, are also barely recognisable today.

And, perhaps, what is most important is that these reinvigorated towns and villages are coursing with new, vibrant life — a life enriched by the wealth of socialist culture.

This land, where only one person in ten could sign his name, now has a 300,000-strong force of research associates, engineers, agronomists, teachers, doctors and people in literature and the arts. One can well say that never before in the history of the Moldavian people has there been such an all-round and intensive upswing in national culture as today when it is developing on the basis of socialism, closely tied in with the cultural development of all the fraternal peoples of our country.

The contribution made by Yemilian Bukov, Ivan Cheban and Petrya Dariyenko, Tamara Cheban and Maria Biyeshu, Leonid Grigorashenko and Vasily Zagorsky, Academician Ya. Grosul and A. Zhuchenko,

D.Sc. (Biology), along with that of many other Moldavian writers, actors, artists, composers and scientists, has become a component part of the common cultural treasury of the Soviet people.

The progress made by Soviet Moldavia, regardless of whether we speak of the development of her socialist statehood or her economic or cultural development, is inseparably linked with the efforts of the Communists. They fought for the bright future of their people, for the triumph of socialism on Moldavian soil without sparing themselves or their lives.

On this festive occasion I would like to praise the contribution made by the big detachment of Communists whom the Central Committee of our Party sent to the Moldavian Republic in the early post-war years. Their tireless efforts to build a socialist Moldavia shall not be forgotten.

The Communist Party of Moldavia, one of the tried and tested detachments of our Leninist Party, is now successfully proceeding to carry out the 24th CPSU Congress decisions, doing much to develop the economy and further the communist education of the working people.

Sincerely congratulating the Communists of the Republic on the jubilee, I wish them every success in all their undertakings and initiatives!

Dear comrades, we have no doubt that the working people of Moldavia will succeed, under the guidance of their Party organisation, in making their Republic even richer and more beautiful and will make a worthy contribution to the common cause of our people — the building of communism.

We are certain that this cause will succeed for it is a common cause. The main source of our strength lies in the fraternal co-operation, mutual assistance and the unity of the Soviet peoples.

Moldavia is an eloquent example of this. From the standpoint of history only a little over a quarter of a century has gone into building socialism in your Republic. Even so, Moldavia has managed to catch up with the other Soviet Republics and to keep abreast. In the main this was possible because the Moldavian people were able to rely on support from all the fraternal peoples of our country, on the Soviet Union's industrial, scientific and engineering potential, and to make the most of the experience gained in building socialism in our country.

The Soviet Republics built socialism in close fraternal unity and by joint effort. And that is how we shall proceed towards communism . . .

*Speech at a joint celebration meeting
of the Central Committee of the
Communist Party of Moldavia and
the Supreme Soviet of the Moldavian
SSR to mark their fiftieth
anniversary. 11 October 1974*

The document which we are to sign, summing up the results of the past, is oriented, in its content, to the future. Understandings that have been reached cover a wide range of most topical problems, i.e. peace, security, co-operation in various fields.

Relations between participating states have been placed on the solid basis of the fundamental principles which are to determine rules of conduct in their relationships. These are the principles of peaceful co-existence for which the founder of the Soviet state Lenin fought with such conviction and consistency and for which our people are fighting to this very day.

The Conference has also determined directions and specific forms of co-operation in the fields of economy and trade, science and technology, environmental protection, culture, education and contacts between individuals, establishments and organisations.

Possibilities of co-operation now extend also to such areas where it was unthinkable in the years of the cold war, for instance, broader exchanges of information in the interests of peace and friendship among nations.

It is no secret that information media can serve the purposes of peace and confidence or they can spread all over the world the poison of discord between countries and peoples. We would like to hope that the results of the Conference will serve as a correct guideline for co-operation in these fields as well . . .

The experience of the work of the Conference provides important conclusions for the future, too. The main conclusion which is reflected in the Final Act is this: no one should try, on the basis of foreign-policy considerations of one kind or another, to dictate to other peoples how they should manage their internal affairs. It is only the people of each given state, and no one else, that have the sovereign right to decide their own internal affairs and establish their own internal laws. A different approach is a flimsy and perilous ground for the cause of international co-operation . . .

Speech at the Conference on Security and Co-operation in Europe at Helsinki. 31 July 1975

Comrade delegates,
Esteemed guests,
It is 5 years since the 24th Congress of the CPSU convened in this hall. A mere 5 years. But how eventful they were. For Communists, for our entire people, it has been a period of events and undertakings of truly immense significance.

The world is changing before our very eyes, and changing for the better. Our people, our Party have not been passive onlookers of these changes. No, we are active participants in them. The labour of the Soviet people, who are building communism, and the activity of the CPSU and the Soviet state on the international scene are contributing palpably to the cause of social progress. Are we not entitled to take pride in this and feel deep gratification over the impact of our ideas, the effectiveness of our policy and the constructive energy of our people?

The previous, 24th Congress set a number of major fundamental tasks. Today, knowing how these tasks were put into effect and what results were achieved, we can confidently say: the course we chose was correct.

In home policy, faithful to Lenin's behest of giving top priority to improving the condition of the masses, the Congress set the task of assuring a considerable rise in the people's living standard and cultural level. It also showed the way to achieve this by considerably raising the efficiency of social production on the basis of scientific and technical progress, and accelerating the growth of labour productivity.

Following this course, we have reached new frontiers in the building of the material and technical basis of communism. The might of our mother-land has grown. Soviet people are better off materially and richer spirit-ually. For us this is unquestionably the most important.

Soviet society's moral and political unity and the fraternal friendship of all the peoples of our country have grown still stronger. Our socialist democracy has made further strides, and all aspects of the life of our society have become fuller and brighter. Soviet people have become still more active in labour, in management, in public and state affairs. And what can be more pleasing than to see the people's energy unfold and their creative forces grow . . .

What must be mentioned first are the successes in fulfilling the task which the 24th Congress of the CPSU defined as being of paramount significance, the task of *raising the living standard of the people*. The history of our country knows of no comparable far-reaching social pro-gramme as the one that has been put into effect in the period under review.

Suffice it to recall that the funds allocated for the implementation of new social measures were equal to the total sum invested during two preceding 5-year periods. *Per capita* real incomes have increased by almost 25 per cent. In order to give an idea of the changes taking place I shall cite only one fact: compared with 1965, in 1975 the number of people with a monthly income of 100 roubles and more per member of the family has grown eight and a half times. This figure is evidence of a fundamental change in the living standard and way of life of tens of millions of people.

The housing of 56 million people has been improved during the 5-year period. The allowances and benefits paid out of the social consumption funds have grown by 40 per cent. Pensions and allowances for factory and office workers and for collective farmers, and scholarship grants for students have been increased. Major positive changes have taken place in the conditions of the working people's life in rural localities . . .

. . . The orientation and character of our economic development have thus been fully consistent with the fundamental guidelines and Directives of the 24th Congress of the CPSU. *Under the leadership of the Communist Party a further major advance has been made during the Ninth Five-Year Plan period in building the material and technical basis of communism, in raising the people's living standard and ensuring the country's security. Such is the political result of the Party's economic work during the period between the 24th and the 25th Congresses. Such is the cardinal result of the heroic labour of the Soviet people.*

Our Congress has every reason to express its sincere gratitude to everybody — Communists and non-Party people, men and women, labour veterans and young people — to everybody whose work has made our motherland more beautiful and more powerful than it has ever been.

It has long been noted that the continuous succession of days that resemble one another, that routine, day-to-day work — and all of us are engaged in this work — often prevents us from fully appreciating the significance and scale of what is taking place around us. Even space flights have become customary and commonplace, to say nothing of the commissioning of new factories or, say, the settlement of new residential districts. That is, probably, as it should be. Indeed, comrades, that is as it should be. For every morning tens of millions of people begin another and most ordinary working day: they take their places at machine tools, go down into mines, drive out to the fields, bend over microscopes, computations and charts. They most certainly do not think of the greatness of their work. But in carrying out the plans charted by the Party they, and nobody else, are raising the Soviet Union to new and ever higher summits of progress. And in calling ours a time of great accomplishments we pay tribute to those who have made it such — we pay tribute to the working people . . .

In terms of the principal objectives and the basic orientations of economic activity the Ninth and Tenth Five-year Plans [1971–5 and 1976–80 —Ed.] are what may be described as an integral whole. I mean the long-term orientation of the Party's economic policy, in which we see, to use Lenin's words, 'the general plan of our work, of our policy, of our tactics, of our strategy. . .' (*Collected Works*, Vol. 33, p. 501).

Just as any other strategy, the Party's economic strategy begins with the formulation of tasks, with the identification of fundamental, long-term aims. The most important of these has been and remains a steady rise of the people's living standard and cultural level. Economic strategy also covers a precise determination of the means, of the ways of attaining the set aims. These are the dynamic and balanced growth of social production, the enhancement of its efficiency, the speeding up of scientific and technical progress, the growth of labour productivity and the utmost improvement of the quality of work at all levels of the national economy.

From this ensues the principal tasks of the Tenth Five-Year Plan as it has been formulated in the document of the Party's Central Committee on the guidelines for national economic development.

In accordance with the decisions of the preceding Congress the work of drawing up the Tenth Five-Year Plan was conducted in parallel with the elaboration of the primary guidelines for the country's long-term economic development up to the year 1990. Needless to say, the orientations for 15 years cannot and should not be of the same mandatory nature and as detailed as the 5-year plans. They pursue a different purpose, namely, to determine well in advance the character and magnitude of the tasks facing us, to concentrate efforts on fulfilling them, see possible problems and difficulties more clearly and facilitate the preparation and implementation of programmes and projects extending beyond the 5-year period.

Much work remains to be done on concrete long-term targets and assignments. But from the estimates that have already been made it follows that in 1976–90 the country will roughly double the material and financial resources it had in the preceding fifteen years. New possibilities are thereby being created for the solution of the basic socio-economic problems set in the Party Programme and by the last few congresses. This concerns, notably, *a further rise in the Soviet people's well-being, an improvement in the conditions of their work and everyday life, and considerable progress in public health, education and culture, in fact everything that helps to mould the new man, the harmoniously developed individual, and improve the socialist way of life.*

During the past 15 years *per capita* real incomes have approximately doubled, while the total volume of material benefits and services has increased approximately 2.4 times. This gives an idea of the scale of the tasks that can be set for the next 15 years. More and more high-quality foods and consumer goods will be made available to Soviet people with each 5-year period. Much will also be done in resolving other major social problems, notably the housing problem.

An essential advance in these areas has been planned for the Tenth Five-Year-Plan period. Permit me to remind you of some concrete figures.

During the next 5 years it is planned to increase the wages of factory and office workers by 16–18 per cent, and the incomes of the collective

106

farmers from the socialised economy by 24–27 per cent. The benefits and allowances to be received by the population from the social consumption funds will grow by 28–30 per cent. Over 31,000 million roubles, or 6000 million roubles more than in the previous 5 years, are to be allocated for the development of the food, light and service industries.

It is planned to increase the volume of retail trade by 60,000 million roubles. It should be emphasised that with the creation of the necessary conditions and the accumulation of resources the Party will continue its policy of ensuring stable state retail prices of basic commodities and reduce the prices of certain types of goods.

In drafting the guidelines, the Central Committee gave special attention to housing construction. The target for the next 5 years is 550 million square metres of housing. We shall strictly require that designers and builders improve the layout of flats and build good, high-quality and handsome houses. At the same time, provision is made for a substantial increase in the production of furniture, household appliances and crockery. In a new flat everything must be pleasing to the eye. In precisely this way — comprehensively and all-sidedly — we strive to resolve the housing problem . . .

Regrettably, the work of some medical institutions still evokes justified criticism from the people. The Ministry of Public Health must draw the proper conclusions from this. Large allocations are being made for the promotion of the health services during the Tenth Five-Year-Plan period. They must be used properly and in full. It is the direct duty of the Central Committees of the Communist Parties of the Union Republics, the territorial and regional committees and the local Soviets to focus attention on these questions.

The party's concern for the working people is also manifested in the measures for the further promotion of education and culture . . .

In putting forward a broad social programme the Party acts in the belief that its fulfilment will help to enhance the labour activity of workers, collective farmers and intellectuals, and serve each person as a further incentive to work better. There is no need to explain how important this is. For the growth of production, an increase in output and an improvement of quality are the main and decisive conditions for raising the people's standard of living . . .

THE PARTY IN CONDITIONS OF DEVELOPED SOCIALISM

Comrades, the results of the past 5-year period provide convincing evidence that the CPSU has been following the Leninist line. It has lived up to its role of the political leader of the working class, of all the working people, of the whole people. The Party has once again demonstrated the power of its scientific vision and the realism of its policy, and its capability of directing the energy of the masses towards the fulfulment of the tasks of communist construction.

Our Party holds high the revolutionary banner of Marxism–Leninism and proletarian internationalism, fulfilling with honour its historical mission and tirelessly working for the triumph of communist ideals.

THE PARTY'S FURTHER DEVELOPMENT.
QUESTIONS OF CADRE POLICY

In the period under review, the Party continued to grow and gain in strength. On the basis of observance of the Leninist rules of Party life and the principles of Party leadership, the ideological and organisational unity of the Party ranks has been further consolidated.

Since the 24th Congress, nearly 2.6 million men and women have been admitted into the CPSU. At present the Party has 15,694,000 members. Of them 41.6 per cent are workers, 13.9 per cent collective farmers, nearly 20 per cent intellectuals in the technical fields, and over 24 per cent workers in science, literature, the arts, education, public health, management and the military spheres.

In characterising *the growth of the Party and the work to improve its qualitative composition*, I should like to consider the following fundamental points. Under developed socialism, when the Communist Party has become a party of the whole people, it has in no sense lost its class character. The CPSU has been and remains a party of the working class. We are deeply pleased with the fact that 58 per cent of those now joining the Party are workers. This is natural and is a reflection of the leading role of the working class in the life of society.

In the period under review, more than 11 per cent of those joining the Party were collective farmers. The steady admission of collective farmers into the ranks of the Party is in line with the interests of further consolidating the alliance of the working class and the peasantry.

Of those who are accepted as candidates for Party membership, roughly 9 per cent are foremen, shift engineers, section chiefs, agronomists, zootechnicians and others directly involved in the process of production. Thus, altogether almost 80 per cent of those joining the CPSU are men and women engaged in the sphere of material production, the decisive sphere of social life.

The percentage of Party members among specialists in the national economy, teachers, doctors and workers in science, literature and the arts has grown substantially. Today roughly one in four or five specialists is a Communist. That is good. After all, the Soviet intelligentsia has a very considerable role to play in implementing the scientific and technical revolution, in raising the people's cultural standards and in fulfilling all the tasks of communist construction.

The overwhelming majority, or more than two-thirds, of new Party members come from the Komsomol. The growing influx of young people into the CPSU shows that the Party's vital forces are inexhaustible, that our young generation is deeply committed to the ideals of communism.

In the past 30 years, membership of the CPSU has increased nearly 3-fold. The growth of its ranks will quite obviously continue. Such is the objective tendency stemming from the whole course of social development under socialism, and the growth of the Party's leading role and prestige. However, the CPSU does not press for numerical growth. It admits only those who have proved in practice that they are joining the Party, not for the sake of obtaining some advantages but to work selflessly for the benefit of communism, as Lenin put it.

And the further we advance and the bigger the tasks tackled by the Party, the more concern we should display about replenishing its ranks with fresh forces, drawing on those who have won the recognition of their primary Party branch, of their collective, on those who have shown themselves to be active in production and in social life. For this purpose, there is need to enhance the importance of the period of candidacy for Party membership. There is need to take a most scrupulous approach to the all-round testing of the political qualities and capabilities of candidates for Party membership, to their Marxist–Leninist education. We should not forget that every Communist must have a high ideological level, and be an active Party fighter and a front-ranker among the builders of communism.

The CPSU has been doing everything to enhance the prestige of Party membership, in accordance with Lenin's precepts. An important role in this was played by the exchange of Party cards carried out under a decision of the 24th Congress. There are good grounds for saying that the aims of the exchange have been attained. It has helped to invigorate the activity of Communists and Party organisations in the struggle to fulfil the tasks before them.

One important result of the exchange is that the Communists have become more exacting to each other, and that an atmosphere of intolerance of any breaches of the Rules has been created in the Party branches. The Party organisations acted on the premise that the exchange of cards was not a Party purge. At the same time, they took scrupulous care to see that no one unworthy of the lofty title of Communist should remain in the Party. Almost 347,000 persons did not receive new Party cards in the period of the exchange. They are those who allowed themselves departures from the rules of Party life, committed breaches of discipline and lost touch with their Party branches.

Comrades, our Party is now a great and mighty organism. It includes 14 Central Committees of the Communist Parties of the Union Republics, 154 territorial committees and regional committees, 10 area committees, 4,243 city and district committees and 390,000 primary branches, including 150,000 branches at enterprises in industry, construction, transport and communications, collective and state farms and other production units. You are very well aware of the importance of having all the units of the Party working smoothly, actively and purposefully. This can be achieved only through unfailing application of the Leninist rules of Party life and principles of Party leadership, and the principle of democratic centralism. The Party has always displayed a highly principled approach, standing up for these principles and combating any breaches of them. In this context, the decisions of the 20th Party Congress, whose twentieth anniversary now falls due, were highly important. A key role in strengthening and developing the Leninist rules and principles of Party life has been played by the decisions of the October 1964 Plenary Meeting of the Central Committee and the 23rd and the 24th Party Congresses. The consistent development of inner-Party democracy and the growing demands being made on every member of the Party — these Leninist principles are not a thing of the past. This is the basis for the development of the Party in our day as well.

The fulfilment of the directives set by the 23rd and the 24th Congresses on the questions of Party development has helped to give greater depth to inner-Party democracy and collective leadership, and to develop the forms of Party organisation and methods of activity. All of this has been most forcefully expressed in the report and election campaign held before the Congress.

Suffice it to say that the report and election meetings in the primary Party branches were attended by more than 94 per cent of the Communists, with one in four of those attending taking part in the debate. The meetings, conferences and congresses were keynoted by efficiency, a high level of activity and maturity of the Communists, and a high level of criticism and self-criticism. The Communists gave a principled appreciation of the work of the elective Party organs in implementing the decisions of the 24th Congress and determined the tasks for the future.

The course of the report and election campaign was extensively dealt with in the press and on the radio and television, thus, in effect, turning the Party committee reports to the Communists into reports to the working people. There is much profound meaning in this. The Party has no secrets from the people. It is vitally interested in having all the Soviet people know about its undertakings and plans, and in having them express their own views on these matters.

At the meetings, conferences and congresses, the Communists demonstrated the monolithic unity of the Party ranks, giving complete and unanimous approval to the Party's general line and the practical activity of the Central Committee and its Politburo.

Comrades, the dynamic development of Soviet society, the growing scale of communist construction, and our activity in the international arena insistently require a steady *raising of the level of Party guidance of economic and cultural development, the education of our men and women, and improvement of organisational and political work among the masses.*

In the period under review the Central Committee, the Politburo and the Secretariat of the Central Committee have worked with great intensity.

In this period the Central Committee held eleven plenary meetings to decide on the key questions in the life of the Party and of the whole country. The December Plenary Meetings in 1972, 1973, 1974 and 1975 were of special importance. They equipped the whole Party with a concrete analysis of important economic problems and brought to the fore the tasks which required the maximum concentration of effort . . .

The activity of the Politburo of the Central Committee was dynamic and efficient. Since the 24th Congress it has held 215 meetings. The Politburo regularly considered various questions relating to industry, agriculture and capital construction, and improvement of administration and management in every sector of the state and economic apparatus. Special attention was given to the fulfilment of the measures outlined by the 24th Congress for raising the people's living standards. There was regular discussion of the basic problems involved in improving inner-Party and ideological work. The Politburo gave much attention to various aspects of the country's external political activity and strengthening of its defences.

The Central Committee Secretariat, which has held 205 meetings in the intervening period, constantly dealt with the activity of the Party organisations and the selection and placement of cadres. Much more attention than before has been given to control and verification of the fulfilment of adopted decisions.

The Central Committee has made a careful study and summing-up of the experience of local Party organisations. It discussed the activity of a number of Central Committees of Communist Parties of Union Republics, territorial and regional committees, and city and district committees to establish how they exercised Party guidance of the economy and carried on organisational, political and ideological-educational work. The experience of labour activity by the masses has also been thoroughly analysed. Many valuable initiatives of Party organisations, collectives and individual working people in Moscow and Leningrad, the Ukraine and Kazakhstan, the Urals and Byelorussia, Central Asia and the Baltic area, the Transcaucasus and Moldavia were approved and recommended for extensive application across the country.

The decisions taken by the Central Committee, and its Politburo and Secretariat, adopted as a result of circumstantial and collective discussion, provided the Party organisations with a clear orientation and lucid directives, which helped to improve their work.

Comrades, letters from the working people are an important link between the Party and its Central Committee and the masses. Their number has been steadily growing as a reflection of the Soviet people's growing social involvement. They express support for the Party's policy and voice opinions on many basic questions concerning the life of the Party and the state.

The Central Committee is being regularly informed of everything that deserves notice in the letters of the working people. The most important proposals and opinions are considered by the Central Committee's Politburo and Secretariat, and are taken into account in the drafting of decisions and laws. Many of them have also been used in preparing the material for the present Congress.

In the Party's general undertakings, great importance attaches to the activity of the *republican, territorial, regional, area, city and district Party organisations*. The work of the Party's key units — the regional and territorial committees and the Central Committees of the Communist Parties of the Union Republics — has been growing ever more fruitful and meaningful from year to year. It is no exaggeration to say that they bear the main responsibility for implementing the Party's policy in the localities. We must give due credit to the persistence and purposefulness with which they have organised the implementation of the decisions of the 24th Congress of the CPSU, and worked to utilise our economic and political potentialities in order to bring about an upswing in every branch of social production and make it more efficient. They deserve much credit for their vigorous efforts to develop massive popular initiatives. It is indicative that in the past few years local Party organs have been putting forward many more major concrete proposals of all-Union importance than ever before.

The level of Party guidance directly depends on how much vigour and initiative is displayed by the *primary Party branches*, which make up the basis of our party.

The primary Party branches are in the forefront of economic and cultural construction, working in the very midst of the people. The whole of their active effort helps combine the Party's policy with the vital creativity of the masses, promoting the successful fulfilment of economic-political and ideological–educational tasks.

In the period under review, the CPSU Central Committee has

discussed reports on the work of a number of Party organisations at enterprises in industry, agriculture and construction, in scientific and educational institutions, and in ministries. Its decisions specifically emphasised that the primary Party branches must now exert an even more active influence on raising the effectiveness of production and accelerating scientific and technical progress, constantly seeking to create an atmosphere of concerted effort and creative quest in every collective, to educate our people and improve their working and living conditions.

The Party's guiding and mobilising role is not an abstract conception. It is life itself, it is our day-to-day practice. But the Party's role as organiser and inspirer of the masses is most evident at difficult moments. I have already mentioned how difficult 1972 was. At that time, we pitted our strength, our organisation and our will against the elements. The people were rallied and inspired by the Central Committee and the local Party organisations. A real battle for the grain harvest was started. Workers from the cities, men of the Soviet Army and students took an active part in this battle side by side with the collective and state farmers.

At that time I happened to visit the areas of the country that were crucial for success in the struggle for the harvest. The people were having a very hard time. But they were working with remarkable enthusiasm and energy. They did everything that was possible. Indeed, they did what many believed to be impossible. When one saw this one could not help feeling a sense of great pride for our Party and for our remarkable people.

Comrades, *the Leninist style of work* is an important condition for success in the Party's leadership. The Leninist style is a creative and scientific approach to all social processes, one which eschews subjectivism. It exacts a high standard of critical approach with respect to oneself and to others, rules out any self-complacency, and is opposed to any manifestations of red tape and formalism.

In this connection, I should like to consider the question of criticism and self-criticism. We have had serious and principled discussions on this subject at the plenary meetings of the Central Committee. This was done because with the growth in the scale and complexity of the task we have to tackle, an exacting, critical approach to all matters acquires especial importance.

In its resolution, 'On the State of Criticism and Self-criticism in the

Tambov Regional Party Organisation', the Central Committee raised a number of questions which are of importance for the whole Party. It drew attention above all to the very substance of the method of criticism and self-criticism. What is it? It is that every aspect of the activity of this or that organisation, of this or that individual should be given an objective evaluation. It is that the existing shortcomings should be subjected to all-round analysis in order to eliminate them. It is that there should be no liberalism towards shortcomings or to those who allow them. Trust and respect for people should go hand in hand with a demanding attitude towards those responsible for assignments. This is a law of Party work, and not only of Party work but of the whole of our work. Of course, comrades, every instance of incorrect response to criticism must evoke a sharp and swift response from the Party organs.

When we say 'sharp response' we do not, of course, mean any sharpness of expression, but the substance of the matter. The value of criticism lies in its authenticity, and in the social importance of the questions being raised. For its part, the value of self-criticism is determined by its sincerity, and a readiness instantly to start correction of mistakes and shortcomings.

Alongside the questions of criticism and self-criticism, the Central Committee also considered another problem, that of control and verification of adopted decisions. This has been repeatedly dealt with at meetings of the Central Committee's Politburo and Secretariat. This was dealt with in a special letter circulated by the Politburo to all Party organisations, and also in a number of decisions taken by the CPSU Central Committee.

There seems to be no need here for any special comments. It is obvious that adopted decisions must be fulfilled. After all, they are the decisions of the Party, they are its collective will and the concentrated experience of the masses. However, now and again some decisions are not fulfilled, or are fulfilled improperly or incompletely, because of lax control.

Now and again, when some decision is not fulfilled, a second and at times even a third decision is adopted on the same matter. In content they seem to be good. But the point is that they deal with something that should have already been done. So one cannot help asking: does not the new decision on an old subject turn out to be a kind of concession, an expression of liberalism? Does this not reduce the standard demanded? It is time to put an end to this practice!

Control and verification of fulfilment of adopted decisions are a key aspect of organisational work. They are the duty of every Party and government worker and manager, of every Party organ and of every primary Party branch. Here, it is necessary to enhance the role of the Secretariats of the Central Committees of the Communist Parties of the Union Republics, the territorial and regional Party committees, the Councils of Ministers of the republics, the Executive Committees of the Soviets of Working People's Deputies, and the collegiums of the Ministries and departments.

Much important work in this field is also being carried out by the Party Control Committee under the CPSU Central Committee, and the Party commissions of the local Party committees. In the period under review, they have raised a number of key questions of general importance concerning the struggle for strict observance of Party and state discipline.

In the verification of fulfilment, much importance attaches to the organs of the people's control. The Party organisations should make better use of their potentialities, and help them in every way to exercise their functions.

I say all this just now not because some sort of alarming situation has developed in our Party concerning the fulfilment of adopted decisions or the state of criticism and self-criticism. No, I want to make a different point. Undeviating practice of the Leninist style of work is a premise for the successful activity of all Party, Government and economic bodies, and for the realisation of all our plans.

Of course, neither the Party nor the nature of its activity is immune to change. At every stage, the Party's work is filled with new content. It is natural, therefore, that the new tasks which the 25th Congress is to set forth will still require scientifically based improvement in forms and methods of Party work.

Cadre policy is a powerful instrument by means of which the Party exerts an influence on the course of social development. In the past few years, many young and promising comrades who have shown themselves good and capable organisers in practical work have been promoted to leading posts. In the struggle to fulfil the Ninth Five-Year Plan and implement the tasks of domestic and foreign policy, our cadres have gone through an important school of political seasoning and have acquired a

116

wealth of experience.

The modern leader must organically combine within himself the Party approach and well-grounded competence, a sense of high discipline and initiative, and a creative approach to his work. At the same time, in every sector the leader must take account of the socio-political and educational aspects, be sensitive to the needs and requirements of people, and set an example in work and in everyday life.

Much significance attaches to the selection for Party work of politically mature, active specialists in the national economy who have experience in working with people. In the period under review, a number of measures have been taken in this direction. At present, 99.5 per cent of the secretaries of the Central Committees of the Communist Parties and the territorial and regional committees of the Party have a higher education, and more than 70 per cent of them have engineering, technical and agricultural training. It is a good thing that virtually all of them have worked as secretaries of primary Party branches and city and district Party committees. Among the secretaries of city and district committees 99.2 per cent have a higher education, with 60 per cent of them specialists in industry and agriculture. This line should be further pursued with even greater persistence.

A thoughtful and considerate attitude to our cadres has been firmly established in the Party. An end has been put to the unjustified re-shuffling and frequent replacements of cadres, a matter that was raised back at the 23rd Congress. Cadres are moved when this is made necessary by the interests of the matter at hand and the need to fortify this or that sector of work. That is not to say, however, that on the pretext of securing cadre stability it is possible to leave in leading posts those who fail to pull their weight, as the saying goes, and to cope with their duties. It is all the more impossible to leave in leading posts those who display irresponsibility and live on their old merits, believing that their post will of itself assure them of prestige and respect.

He who has lost his ability to make a critical assessment of his activity, he who has lost touch with the masses, who breeds toadies and boot-lickers, and who has lost the trust of the Communists cannot be a Party leader. I think that the Congress will support such an approach.

In its approach to the organisation of the training and retraining of cadres the Party takes into consideration the growing requirements, and

117

does everything that is necessary to help them raise their theoretical level, deepen their knowledge, and master the modern achievements in science, technology and organisation of production and management. In the period under review, 40,000 persons have been trained in the Party's educational institutions alone. Over 230,000 Party and government workers have taken retraining courses. Economic executives and specialists improve their qualifications in various institutes, departments, at the Institute of Management of the National Economy, and extension courses, where more than one million men and women are trained every year.

We must continue improving all this work. we should clearly give thought to the ways of raising to a new and higher level the training of leading Party cadres, especially those on the ideological front, to ways of steadily raising the ideological, theoretical and business standards of the comrades who are already engaged in leading Party work. The activity of the central Party educational institutions should be further improved. Here, we should both recall the experience of the past and also give thought to new and modern forms of training highly skilled cadres. The important thing is to provide the Party with an even more extensive reserve of experienced and theoretically mature comrades.

The Party puts a high value on its cadres, has trust in their creative potentialities, and displays concern in fostering and educating them. There is no doubt that our cadres, fully aware of their responsibility to the people, will continue to give all of their strength, knowledge and experience to the communist cause.

THE PARTY'S WORK IN THE FIELD OF IDEOLOGICAL EDUCATION

Comrades, the strength of our system derives from the consciousness of the masses. Accordingly, the Party believes it to be its constant concern to foster communist consciousness and readiness, determination and skill in building communism. In the period under review, *a major aspect of all our work has been the ideological education of our people, and the problems arising in the moulding of the new man, a worthy builder of communism.*

The CPSU has based its effort in communist education, like the whole of its revolutionary transforming activity, on the sound foundation of Marxist–Leninist theory. Marxism–Leninism is the only reliable basis for formulating the right strategy and tactics. It gives us an understanding of the historical perspective, helps us to determine the lines of our socio-economic and political development for years ahead, and correctly to find our orientation in international developments. Marxism–Leninism derives its power from its constant and creative development. That is what Marx taught. That is what Lenin taught. Our Party will always be loyal to their precepts!

Everyone knows that practice is the criterion of the validity of any theory. The revolutionary struggle of the working class and of all the other working people, and all the practical activity of the Communists have convincingly proved the validity of the theoretical tenets and principles expressing the essence of Marxism–Leninism . . .

In-depth research into questions relating to the development trends of our society and its productive forces is highly necessary. This applies, for instance, to the character and content of labour under developed socialism and to changes in the social structure. Improvement of distribution according to work, the combination of moral and material incentives, the socialist way of life and the development of our multi-faceted culture — consideration of all these problems requires a pooling of the efforts of scientists working in the various fields. There is also need for a further study of the problems relating to the development of our state system, and the forms and methods of our educational and ideo-logical work. In this context, much attention should be given to the study of public opinion.

Soviet scientists should not lose sight of the problems of environment and population growth which have recently assumed such a serious aspect. Improvement of the socialist use of natural resources and the formulation of an effective demographic policy are an important task facing a whole complex of natural and social sciences . . .

Speakers at the 24th Congress emphasised the importance of estab-lishing a creative atmosphere in scientific work. This task remains as important today as it was yesterday. It goes without saying that the creative comparison of views should proceed on the basis of our common Marxist–Leninist ideological platform. The important thing is that there should be consistent observance of the party principles in science, with

119

resolute rebuffs to the Right-opportunist and 'Leftist' views voiced by our ideological adversaries abroad . . .

In the sphere of ideological education, much importance attaches to political enlightenment. Here we have done a great deal. Consider the following fact by way of example. Within the Party education system alone, nearly 20 million persons, including over 7 million non-Party people, are studying. Our young people who are still at school — schoolchildren and students — are learning the fundamentals of political knowledge. The mass-scale study of Marxism–Leninism is a most important feature of the development of social consciousness at the present stage.

Today, as the Party is entering a new phase, it is important to display special concern for the content of Party education and the enhancement of its theoretical level, without relaxing our efforts to involve in Party studies ever greater masses of Communists and non-Party people . . .

In the intervening period, the Party organisations have made a great effort to promote the patriotic education of the working people and also to strengthen the internationalist consciousness of the masses. In this context, a tremendous role was played by the celebrations of the fiftieth anniversary of the USSR and the thirtieth anniversary of the Victory in the Great Patriotic War.

All of us, comrades, remember the enthusiasm and feeling with which our people marked those momentous anniversaries. The solid unity of all the classes and social groups, nations and nationalities of our country grew and was tempered in the labour exploits of the past half-century, and in the military exploits in the Great Patriotic War. This unity and cohesion of all the Soviet people, their loyalty to their great country, and the internationalist brotherhood of the peoples marked these anniversaries. Therein lay their vast political and educational importance.

One of the Party's most important tasks has been and remains the cultivation in the minds of the working people, the young generation in the first place, of the ideas of Soviet patriotism and socialist internationalism, of pride in the Land of Soviets, in our homeland, and readiness to stand up in defence of the gains of socialism.

In its resolutions on the work of the Party organisation in the Lvov Region and of the Tbilisi City Committee, the Central Committee drew the attention of Party organisations to the shortcomings in the matter of internationalist education. Today, we can note with satisfaction that the right conclusions from this have been drawn. The Party organisations have started to conduct the patriotic and internationalist education of the working people with more initiative and greater scope. Individual instances of nationalism and chauvinism, the non-class approach to the evaluation of historical events, departmental attitudes, and attempts to extol patriarchal ways are being successfully combated. These efforts have met with profound understanding and support among the working people, and have had a positive impact on the continued consolidation of the friendship and brotherhood of the peoples of our country . . .

It is concrete deeds, of course, that are the measure of success in the political education of the masses. The communist ideological spirit is an alloy of knowledge, convictions and practical action.

The current upswing in socialist emulation is a graphic result of the close *combination of political and labour education* . . .

We are all happy to see how deeply the Leninist ideas of socialist emulation have taken hold. We take pride in the fact that the Communists are in the forefront of the emulation, which exerts profound influence on economic practice, on the country's socio-political life and on the moral atmosphere. Our common militant slogan is to do our utmost to develop still further socialist emulation and the movement for a communist attitude to work.

Communist education implies constant perfection of the public education and occupational training system. This is especially important today, under the scientific and technical revolution which tends to change the nature of labour, and, consequently, also of men's training for work. We have been doing a great deal in this respect. But what has been and is being done still falls short of solving all the problems in this sphere.

It is obvious, for instance, that there is need for further and serious improvement of the whole system of general education, secondary schools in the first place. In modern conditions, when the volume of knowledge a man needs tends sharply and rapidly to increase, it is no longer possible to rely mainly on the assimilation of a definite sum of facts. It is important to develop in a young person the ability to augment his knowledge independently, and to find his bearings in the torrent of scientific and political information. Much remains to be done in this field. Of course, this work should be approached with great care and thought, without uncalled-for changes or hasty decisions. What does this require? Apparently, it requires an improvement in the training of teachers, an adjustment of the methods of instruction to the requirements of life, and provision of schools with modern study aids, including visual aids.

Here, at the Congress, it is fitting to recount the measures taken by the Party organs in the economic education of the working people. An extensive system of economic education was set up on the basis of the decisions of the 24th Congress. More than 42 million people have already taken advantage of it; 36 million are studying at the present time. This work should be continued. In advancing this economic education, we should see to it that it promotes to the utmost throughout the country the spread of advanced experience in labour organisation and the application of scientific and technological achievements in production.

Comrades, nothing adds so much to the stature of the individual as a constructive attitude to life and a conscious approach to one's duty to society, when matching words and deeds becomes a rule of daily behaviour.

Unfortunately, we still come across some who, though they have a knowledge of our policy and our principles, do not always apply them in practice, do not work to implement them, and take a conciliatory attitude to breaches of the rules of socialist community living. Any gap between the word and the deed, whatever its form, also does harm to economic construction, but especially to moral education.

We have achieved a great deal in improving the Soviet people's material welfare. We shall continue consistently to pursue this task in the future as well. But it is necessary that the growth of material opportunities should be constantly accompanied by a growth in our people's ideological, moral and cultural levels. Otherwise we may have relapses into the philistine, petty-bourgeois mentality. This should not be lost sight of.

The higher the level of our society in its development, the more intolerable are the still occurring departures from the socialist rules of morality. Acquisitiveness, proprietary tendencies, hooliganism, red tape and indifference to one's fellow humans run against the very grain of our system. In combating such phenomena, there is a need to make full use of the opinion of the working collective, criticism in the press, methods of persuasion and the force of the law — all the instruments at our disposal.

In the period under review, much attention in the activity of the Central Committee was given to various questions pertaining to the raising of ideological level, co-ordination and efficiency of the *mass media*. As a result, their information and propaganda impact on the development of the economy, science and culture and on the whole life of society has grown still more.

In the recent period, Soviet press printings and the number of publications have increased. More than 400 newspapers and 113 journals and magazines have been newly launched. According to the subscription figures, now every family gets an average of more than four periodicals — a high indicator. At the same time, it is well known that the supply of a number of publications falls short of the rapidly growing demand. Here, thought should be given, among other things, to increasing the production of newsprint and paper. There is hardly any need to argue that this is more than an economic question. There is also need to accelerate the renewal of the material and technical facilities of the newspapers, journals and radio and television.

The Party organisations must exercise day-to-day and practical guidance of the press and enhance its ideological level and efficacy. Unfortunately, some still tend to underestimate the social importance of the press. There are also some who gladly accept praise but pay no heed to criticism and are unable to draw the right conclusions. The Party committees will have to correct those who seek to brush off meaningful criticism and remain indifferent to the important problems raised in the press and to the working people's letters which it carries.

Comrades, everyone probably remembers that the 24th Congress gave serious attention to questions of *literature and art*. While commending all the vivid and talented works, the Congress noted some of the extremes which were likely to lead some writers and artists along a path lacking in creative prospects.

Today we can say that the approach of the 24th Congress to questions of literature and art has been fully justified. The intervening period has been characterised by a further intensification of the activity of all creative intellectuals, who have been making an ever more tangible contribution to the construction of communist society, which is the endeavour of the whole Party and of the whole people.

This positive and vivifying process has naturally been reflected in the new works of socialist realism which have been created in our country over the past few years. These works respond more frequently and, what is even more important, more deeply to the basic and essential ideas which animate the country, and which have become part and parcel of the personal histories of Soviet men and women.

Take the 'production topic', as it was once plainly designated. Today, it has acquired a truly aesthetic form. Together with the characters in fiction and drama, we care strongly about the success of the steelworkers or the director of a textile mill, the engineer or the Party worker. Indeed, even a seemingly particular issue like the award of a bonus to a team of builders becomes the subject of heated discussion as a matter of broad social significance.

The Soviet people's feat of arms in the Great Patriotic War is another important topic in the arts which in the recent period has been dealt with in truthful and impressive works. War veterans experience the emotion of joining the protagonists of novels, stories, films and plays in recrossing the front lines in the hot flames of battle and the bitter cold of the snows, and bow in veneration before the strength of the spirit displayed by their living and dead comrades-in-arms. Through the miraculous effect of art, the younger generation feels involved in the exploits of its fathers or of the young girls who died in the quiet dawn to gain immortality in the fight for the freedom of their homeland. Such is true art, which re-creates the past and helps to foster the Soviet patriot, the internationalist.

Another topic to which our literature and art have devoted much effort also deserves to be mentioned. It is the topic of morality, of moral quests. Though there have been some failures here, the achievements have been greater. It is to the credit of our writers and artists that they seek to bring out the best human qualities, like firmness of principle, honesty and depth of emotion, always in line with the sound and solid principles of our communist morality.

Another source of inspiration for our artists, writers, and poets has been the important and lofty topic of the struggle for peace, for the liberation of the peoples, and the internationalist solidarity of the working people in this struggle.

The intellectuals engaged in the arts have become more exacting with respect to their own and each other's works, and drab and mediocre stories and plays, to say nothing of ideological mistakes, are being duly assessed without regard for personalities. All of this largely goes to the credit of the writers' and artists' unions and their Party organisations.

The spreading movement in which our theatres and literary and art journals give encouragement and guidance in artistic matters to workers at factories and collective farms and on construction projects, such as the Baikal–Amur Railway and the Kama Motor Works, should be welcomed without any reservation. Amateur art groups, literary associations and people's theatre are directed by experienced masters. Thus an invigorating process is under way in which, on the one hand, art is being enriched with a knowledge of life, and, on the other, millions upon millions of working people are being introduced to cultural values.

The Party approach to questions of literature and art combines tact with respect for intellectuals working in the arts, assistance with their creative quest, and a principled stand. The main criterion in evaluating the social importance of any work of art has naturally been and still is its ideological direction. That is precisely the Leninist attitude taken by the Central Committee and other Party organs, which have been doing a great deal in this sphere of ideological activity. If some officials take an oversimplified approach and try to resolve matters relating to aesthetic creativity and diversity of form and individuality of style by issuing decrees, the Party does not ignore such cases and helps to rectify the situation.

Soviet writers, artists, composers and workers of the stage, screen and television, all those whose talents and professional skills serve the people and the cause of communism, deserve our deep gratitude. We are happy to see a young generation of creative intellectuals emerging on the scene with ever greater confidence. Real talent is rare. Talented works of literature and art are part of the national heritage. We know that the well-turned phrase, the play of colour, the expressiveness of stone and the harmony of sound which inspire our contemporaries will leave the hearts and souls of our descendants a memory of our generation, of our epoch, with its anxieties and accomplishments. Let us, therefore, wish our workers in culture, whether members of the Party or not, success in producing fresh works worthy of our history, of our present and our future, of our Party and people, and of our great homeland.

SOME QUESTIONS OF PARTY GUIDANCE OF STATE
AND SOCIAL ORGANISATIONS

Comrades, an important line of our whole work in communist construction is the all-round development of the political system of Soviet society. This means improvement of the socialist state system, further development of socialist democracy, consolidation of the legal basis of the life of the state and society, and invigoration of the activity of social organisations.

In carrying on this work, the Party and the Central Committee have always started from the premise that a developed socialist society has been built in our country and is gradually growing into a communist society, from the premise that our state is a state of the whole people, expressing the interests and the will of the whole people. We have always started from the premise that we now have a fully shaped new historical community, the Soviet people, which is based on the solid alliance of the working class, the peasantry and the intelligentsia, with the working class playing the leading role, and on the friendship of all the big and small nations of our country. We have sought to promote the all-round development of the activity of state agencies and social organisations, stimulating their initiative in every possible way.

In the sphere of state construction, the party devotes special attention to *the work of the Soviets*. In accordance with the proposals put forward at the 24th Congress, we have adopted a Law on the Status of the Deputy, clearly defining the rights and duties of deputies, and also the duties of state and social bodies with respect to deputies. This has yielded tangible results. On the initiative of deputies to the Soviets, many important matters are now raised and decided. Let me say that the proposals being put forward by the deputies on the basis of instructions from their electors reflect the requirements and needs of our people and of our life as a whole.

You will recall that some time ago laws were adopted on the initiative of the Politburo for extending the rights and material capabilities of rural, village, district and city Soviets. The experience gained in the period under review shows that this was done quite correctly. We might say that the work of the local Soviets has now acquired a new dimension. I think that the delegates will also support the proposal for the adoption of laws defining the competence of territorial, regional and area Soviets. Another matter we have constantly dealt with is *improvement of our legislation and consolidation of socialist law and order*. The framing by Party and Government organs and the adoption by the USSR Supreme Soviet and the Supreme Soviets of the Republics of laws on some of the key problems concerning our life are of major socio-political importance. A considerable role in this effort has also been played by the standing commissions of the USSR Supreme Soviet, whose activity has in general been markedly invigorated in recent years.

We have adjusted our legal regulations to the new level to which our society has risen. Legal provisions have been prepared for spheres of life which had earlier remained outside the framework of legal regulation, like protection of the environment, including bodies of water, the earth, the air, and so on. It is a very good thing that we now have well-grounded legislation making it possible to carry on purposeful work for the protection of nature.

The Politburo recently instructed the appropriate agencies to prepare proposals for further improving labour and administrative law and certain other laws in order to take account of the new phenomena in the life of our society.

Much also remains to be done to improve the legal regulation of economic activity. Our laws in this sphere should more effectively secure the fulfilment of the tasks of improving output quality and ensuring economy. They should be more effective in countering cases of defrauding the state, doctoring accounts, theft of socialist property, undue zeal in giving priority to local interests, etc.

The time has evidently come to issue a code of laws of the Soviet state. This will help to enhance the stability of our whole law and order. It will make our laws more accessible to all Soviet citizens.

It is quite natural, comrades, that we have been devoting and will continue to devote constant attention to improving the activity of the *militia, the procurator's office, the courts and the organs of justice*, which guard Soviet legality, the interests of Soviet society and the rights of Soviet citizens. The Party and the state have a high appreciation of the difficult and noble work done by the men and women in these institutions, and have shown concern to provide them with well-trained and worthy cadres.

The *state security organs* have reliably safeguarded Soviet society from the subversive activity of the intelligence services of the imperialist states, and all types of foreign anti-Soviet centres and other hostile elements. The activity of these organs is geared to the requirements stemming from the international situation and the development of Soviet society. Our CHEKA men cherish and carry on the traditions initiated by Felix Dzerzhinsky, that knight of the revolution.

The state security organs carry on all their work, which takes place under the Party's guidance and unflagging control, in the light of the interests of the people and the state, with the support of broad masses of working people, and with strict observance of constitutional rules and socialist legality. That is the main source of their strength, and the main earnest of the successful exercise of their functions . . .

Comrades, social organisations are an integral part of the Soviet political system. Altogether they involve nearly the whole of the country's adult population, and that is a significant fact. Our social organisations are one of the important channels through which citizens are enabled to participate in running the affairs of society.

Take the *trade unions*, the largest social organisation, with a membership of over 107 million. The work of the trade unions directly furthers the exercise of democracy in production, the basic sphere in which man's creative efforts are applied.

The trade unions have the task above all of protecting the rights and interests of the working people, and actively dealing with everyday, social questions. But they would be unable to do much in this sphere if production did not develop, and if labour discipline and labour productivity did not rise. It is precisely because our trade unions are dedicated to the working man's interests that their duty is to show concern for boosting production.

In the life of our society, the trade unions have an important role to play, and this puts many duties on them. The trade unions have to organise their work in such a way as to make it more fully conform with their rights and the degree of their responsibility. Take the following question. Everyone knows that a few years ago the sectoral management of industry was re-established and has been undergoing improvement. The concentration of production has been growing, and production associations are being set up. However, none of this has yet been duly reflected in the work of the trade unions. We have to settle the question of the structure of trade unions in production to make it accord more fully with the structure of management in industry, the question of the forms and methods of trade union activity in production associations, and the question of the powers of the governing bodies of sectoral trade unions.

In the recent period, the role of the trade unions on the collective farms has been growing. There is need to help make them more of a mass organisation which will be of considerable importance in tackling the tasks of boosting agriculture and improving the collective farmers' working and living conditions. All of these are very serious tasks. They need to be fulfilled.

Many kind words have been and are being said about our *Leninist Komsomol*. And this, comrades, is quite justified. The 35-million-strong army of Komsomol members is a reliable helper of the Party and its direct and militant reserve. Whatever the tasks the Party has set, the Komsomol has always tackled them with the enthusiasm of youth.

Let us recall the many good initiatives of the Komsomol over the past 5-year period, and its many fine achievements! The construction of the Baikal–Amur Railway, the high-priority Komsomol construction projects. In the 5-year period there were 670 of these, involving more than half a million young men and women. The Komsomol has taken charge of 1200 land-improvement and rural construction projects in the non-black earth zone of the Russian Federation. And we all know of the eagerness with which young people seek to join the student building teams! These teams have been doing very important work. In the Ninth Five-Year-Plan period they have done a volume of work worth roughly 5000 million roubles. Nor is it possible to overrate their importance as a school of labour education.

The labour glory won by the Komsomol is firmly established. But, comrades, we must understand that life itself keeps setting before the Komsomol growing demands. After all, it is in the Komsomol that young people are actively brought into conscious participation in communist construction. It is no easy task to foster such consciousness, especially considering the fact that one has to deal with young people whose character has yet to mature. They are prepared to respond sincerely and whole-heartedly to any good initiative. But encounters with formalism and a bureaucratic approach to educational work tend to extinguish their fervour. Our task is, however, not only to keep this fervour alive, but also to encourage it. We want our young people to retain their enthusiasm, their mental alertness and their youthful energy for the rest of their lives. This should be promoted by the Komsomol, this should be its important concern.

The Party trusts that the Komsomol members and other young people will inscribe many more brilliant pages in the chronicle of communist construction!

When considering our people's great endeavours, one must also emphasise the important role which Soviet women play in them. In many ways, our homeland owes its achievements and victories to our women's dedication and talents. Indeed, in the fulfilment of the important tasks which our Congress is to outline for the future in every sphere of social life our fine women will undoubtedly make a great contribution. The Party considers it to be its duty to display constant concern for our women, improving their condition as participants in the labour process, as mothers and educators of children, and as housewives.

Comrades, critics abroad frequently seek to distort the meaning of the measures taken by the Soviet state for the purpose of consolidating our legality and law and order. Any reference to the need to tighten up discipline and enhance the responsibility of citizens to society is depicted over there as a violation of democracy. What can one say about this?

Indeed, in our concern for the all-round development of the individual and of the rights of citizens, we have also given due attention to the problems of strengthening social discipline and fulfilment by all citizens of their duties to society. After all, democracy is inconceivable without discipline and a sound public order. It is a responsible approach by every citizen to his duties and to the people's interests that constitutes the only reliable basis for the fullest embodiment of the principles of socialist democracy and true freedom for the individual.

Let us recall Lenin's idea that everything is moral in our society that serves the interests of communist construction. Similarly, we can say that for us the democratic is that which serves the people's interests, the interests of communist construction. We reject everything that runs counter to these interests, and no one can persuade us that this is the wrong approach. We know exactly where we are going as we improve our political system. We are fully convinced that the course we have chosen is the right one.

Today, we know not only from theory but also from long years of practice that genuine democracy is impossible without socialism, and that socialism is impossible without a steady development of democracy. We see the improvement of our socialist democracy as consisting above all in a steady effort to ensure ever fuller participation by the working people in running all the affairs of society, in further developing the democratic principles of our state system, and in creating the conditions for the all-round flourishing of the individual. This is the direction in which the Party has worked and will continue to work in the future.

Comrades, socialism is a dynamically developing society. We have not marked time for a single day, we have been constantly advancing. That is why the work done to improve the political system of our society has a profound social meaning and significance.

I repeat, a great deal has been done. And the time has now come to sum up what has been accomplished. That is our premise in preparing the draft of a *new Constitution of the USSR*. This work is being done thoroughly, without any haste, so as to consider every problem that arises with the greatest possible precision, and then to place the draft for discussion by the whole people. But here, at the Congress, I should like to say a few words about some of the important points by which we are guided in this work.

The draft of the new Constitution should evidently reflect the great victories of socialism and formalise not only the general principles of the socialist system, expressing the class substance of our state, but also the basic features of the developed socialist society and its political organisation.

The nature of the tasks connected with the building of the material and technical basis of communism makes it necessary to give a more detailed definition in the Constitution of the principles governing the management of the national economy. At the same time, it is also expedient to reflect the role of the state in the spiritual life of society and in ensuring the conditions for the development of science, public education and culture. In this way we shall emphasise the humanistic character of the socialist state, a state which sets itself the goal of building communism in the interests of the working man, in the interests of the people as a whole.

One of the basic features of the draft of the new Constitution will be the

131

further consolidation and development of socialist democracy.

The idea is to establish a stricter system of accounting by all executive agencies to the elective organs of power. Furthermore, it is envisaged that draft all-Union laws are to be submitted for discussion by the whole people; such discussion is already our practice, but it remains to be given legal expression.

Of course, this is an enumeration of only some of the basic points, but I think that what has been said gives an idea of the lines on which the work is being carried on.

We have started from the premise that the new Constitution should establish and define in precise terms the supreme goal of our state. And this supreme goal is to build a communist society.

*   *   *

Comrades, at our Congress we shall sum up the results of 5 years of intensive labour. These results are good. We shall discuss our plans for the coming 5-year period. These plans are demanding but realistic and well thought out.

Let us now approach everything that has been done and everything we intend to do with a broader historical gauge.

Soon, in another 18 months, we shall be marking the sixtieth anniversary of the Great October Socialist Revolution. Six decades is less than a man's average lifespan. But in that period our country has travelled a way equalling centuries.

We have created a new society, a society the like of which mankind has never known before. It is a society with a crisis-free, steadily growing economy, mature socialist relations and genuine freedom. It is a society governed by the scientific materialist world outlook. It is a society of firm confidence in the future, of radiant communist prospects. Before it lie boundless horizons of further all-round progress.

The Soviet way of life is another major result of the road we have traversed. The atmosphere of genuine collectivism and comradeship, cohesion and friendship of all big and small nations in the country, which gain in strength from day to day, and the moral health which makes us strong and steadfast — these are the radiant facets of our way of life, these are the great gains of socialism that have become the very lifeblood of our reality.

Finally, there is Soviet man, the most important product of the past 60 years. A man who, having won his freedom, has been able to defend it in the most trying battles. A man who has been building the future unsparing of his energy and making every sacrifice. A man who, having gone through all trials, has himself changed beyond recognition, combining ideological conviction and tremendous vital energy, culture, knowledge, and the ability to use them. This is a man who, while an ardent patriot, has been and will always remain a consistent internationalist.

In the eyes of the peoples of the whole world, the Land of Soviets is by right regarded as the bulwark, the standard-bearer of peace. We have done and will continue to do all we can to safeguard and consolidate peace, and to rid mankind of new destructive wars!

Indeed, we are aware that not all the problems have yet been solved. We have a better knowledge than all our critics of our shortcomings, and are aware of the difficulties. And we have been successfully overcoming them. We know and see the ways leading to the further development and improvement of our society.

We have not yet attained communism. But the whole world sees that our Party's activity and its aspirations are aimed to do everything necessary for the welfare of man, for the sake of man. It is this supreme and humane goal of the Party that gives it kinship with the people, creates firm and indissoluble bonds between it and all Soviet people.

The Soviet people are aware that wherever there are difficulties the Communists are always there, in the forefront. The Soviet people are aware that whatever happens, the Communists will not let them down. The Soviet people are aware that where the Party acts, success and victory are assured! The people trust the Party. The people wholeheartedly support the Party's domestic and foreign policy. This augments the Party's strength and serves as an inexhaustible source of energy.

And the Communists, for their part, are aware that the people who have entrusted them with the country's leadership are a people of exceptional industry, courage, stamina, a people of generous spirit, talent and intellect. They are a people that will not flinch in time of ordeal. They are a people that take close to heart every minor failure in their gigantic undertaking. They do not boast of their achievements, but neither do they belittle them. They are responsive to the joys and sorrows of other peoples, always prepared to help them in their struggle for justice, freedom and social progress. The Soviet people are a truly great and heroic people.

Comrades, the Soviet country and our people have travelled a difficult but glorious path. I think that every one of us Communists, asked whether he would choose any other path, would say — no. Our path is the path of truth, the path of freedom, it is the path of the people's happiness.

Report at the 25th Congress of the
CPSU. 24 February 1976

Dear comrade workers of the motor-vehicle industry,

Today is a great and joyous day for you, and it is a great pleasure for me to meet with you in order to carry out an important assignment of the Politburo of the Central Committee and the Presidium of the USSR Supreme Soviet, which is to present to the outstanding workers of the Likhachov Motor Works a high award of the country, the Order of the October Revolution.

I myself had the good fortune of starting my working life as a member of a collective of a large factory. Meeting you here reminds me of how I started and of my old fellow workers. They initiated me into my first profession, taught me the complicated science of life, and made me realise the strength and nobleness of spirit of the working person. Such 'universities' are not forgotten.

I am happier still about being able to attend this meeting because regretfully I have been unable of late to pay frequent visits to factories. Major and urgent tasks of internal development and important matters concerning foreign policy constantly require, as you can imagine, considerable time and strength from all of us in the Central Committee and in the government. But when it is possible to get away for such a meeting as ours today, to talk with workers and share with them our thoughts about our plans and affairs, our cares and hopes, we feel great inner satisfaction and get a good supply of energy and optimism.

Comrades, all our plans and the entire policy of our Party are geared to the main goal of improving the life of the Soviet people, that is you, your wives and children and those labour veterans who have retired. No matter what the Party undertakes, be it foreign-policy measures or measures of a domestic nature, we Communists always ask ourselves: how and in what way will the solution of one problem or another affect the life and the well-being of the Soviet people, the ensuring of peaceful conditions for creative work for the sake of communism and the consolidation of world peace?

We also always remember that the working people of the whole world and the peoples that are fighting for freedom and independence look towards our country, the country of Lenin, the world's first country of victorious socialism, with feelings of strong solidarity and comradely exactingness, with love and hope. And all this, comrades, imposes a great responsibility on us.

Just recently, at the 25th Congress of the CPSU, the Central Committee reported to the Party and the people on the work done over the previous 5 years. In these years our motherland became richer and more powerful and Soviet people began to live much better. We are deeply satisfied with the fact that in the past 5-year period the funds allocated for raising wages and salaries, pensions and student allowances and for carrying out other social measures equalled the amount allocated over the previous two 5-year periods taken together. As a result, in this period the wages and salaries of more than 75 million people were increased, while the incomes of about 40 million people were raised through higher pensions, other benefits and student allowances.

Much has been done, but still more remains to be done. It is not sufficient today to build housing — it must be well-built and have the necessary amenities. It is not sufficient to have goods in the stores — they should be of high quality and satisfy all the demands of our people. All this is now a matter of special concern for the Party, its Central Committee and the Politburo of the CPSU Central Committee.

Take, for instance, the question of housing. Today it remains a question that concerns many people. The Central Committee of the Party, therefore, when drawing up the Tenth Five-Year Plan, devoted special attention to this problem. As much as 550 million square metres of housing is to be built in the coming 5-year period. This means that each year approximately 10–11 million people will move into new flats. This is not bad at all.

Simultaneously there will be a steady improvement in the quality of housing, in its, so to say, soundness, in the layout and the interior of flats. The recently approved programme for the elaboration of new standard houses for the next stage of mass-scale housing construction is based precisely on this. It provides for a further increase in the average per-person housing norms. Rooms, kitchens and auxiliary premises will all be bigger.

You are certainly aware that rent in our country, in the Soviet Union, has not changed since 1928, though the earnings of the blue- and white-collar workers have multiplied several times over in this period and the technical equipment of housing has increased substantially. Rent and charges for public utilities do not cover even one-third of the cost of housing upkeep and maintenance. That is why the state annually allocates about 5000 million roubles for the maintenance of housing and public utilities. We shall continue to bear such expenses.

Can any capitalist country solve problems of vital importance to the working people in this way? Of course not! This is possible only in the conditions of our socialist and truly people's system, our Soviet way of life, where all that is created by the people's labour is used to improve the living standards of the working people . . .

As the 25th Party Congress emphasised, the cardinal task of the new 5-year plan is consistently to raise the people's living standards and cultural level on the basis of dynamic and balanced development of social production and enhancement of its efficiency, the acceleration of scientific and technological progress, the growth of labour productivity and the utmost improvement of the quality of work in every sector of the national economy.

I want to repeat once again: *the utmost improvement of the quality of work in every sector*. This, comrades, is of *key importance*.

To really effectively organise collective work is a huge task calling for great attention not only on the part of managers. Modern production demands that every worker should be perfectly aware of his place in the process of work, know what he is doing and why, what depends on him, and feel that his labour is a necessary part of the overall work.

If indeed there is such an awareness, then one develops a real interest in one's work, and then work brings joy and becomes creative. When this happens the questions occur to everyone: how wisely and thriftily are we using the equipment, materials, money and time? Well, our socialist system is such that it is not enough to be merely industrious and disciplined to qualify as a good, truly front-rank worker. What is demanded of such a worker in addition is an active and lively interest in and concern for the common cause, a desire to make things still better in the team, in the shop and at the enterprise as a whole . . .

Honest and competent work is always repaid a hundred-fold. And you ZIL workers know this well from your own experience. You know that year after year more and more funds are allocated to meet the social, cultural, housing and other needs of the ZIL work force. In the Ninth Five-Year-Plan period alone they amounted to 66 million roubles. Some 38,000 ZIL workers and members of their families have moved into better flats.

More than 20,000 ZIL workers and members of their families annually spend their holidays in the factory's sanatoriums, holiday homes and disease-prevention centres, paying only a part of the actual cost. Some 17,000 children attend ZIL's creches and kindergartens and spend their holidays in Young Pioneer camps. You have your own college, secondary technical schools, a vocational school and other training centres, where 25,000 young ZIL workers study annually. Not every town could boast such facilities in the not-so-distant past.

The most active, creative part of your life you spend at work. It is especially gratifying therefore that over the last 5 years fine well-lit production shops and other buildings with good recreational facilities and other amenities have been built at ZIL. It is also very important that the drive to reduce the amount of manual and heavy physical labour is under way on a large scale. At present the level of mechanisation of material handling and other auxiliary operations at your factory is over 90 per cent. This is a good index.

We are solving the various problems of social development in an ever more comprehensive way — at each enterprise and in each labour collective. This is a typical feature of our days, of our advanced socialist society . . .

*Speech at the Likhachov Motor
Works on presenting the workers
with the Order of the October
Revolution. 30 April 1976*

Comrades, in order to create an atmosphere of trust among states, so necessary for a lasting peace, peoples must get to know and understand each other better. This is the starting-point from which we approach all cultural exchanges and human contacts.

And how do things stand in this area? We in the Soviet Union consider it important that our people know more about other people's past and present, know more about their culture so they can respect other countries' history and achievements.

That is why the Soviet state widely encourages cultural exchanges — consolidating them by inter-governmental agreements and organising more every year. Today our country has cultural relations with 120 countries. In keeping with the Final Act of the Helsinki Conference, we have adopted additional measures that will lead to more exchanges of books, films and works of art. As is known, the other socialist countries which attended the European Conference also take the same position on these issues.

As for the capitalist countries, we have heard more than enough splendid words about exchanges of cultural values, but there has been precious little when it comes to real action.

This shows in many diverse areas. Britain and France, for instance, publish books by Soviet authors in editions one-sixth or one-seventh the size of those by British and French authors published in the USSR. The number of Soviet films shown in Western countries is only a small fraction of the number of Western films shown in the Soviet Union, and that of TV programmes is only one-third, and so on.

138

On the whole, people in socialist countries know much more about life in the West than the working people in the capitalist countries know about socialist reality. What are the reasons for this? The main reason lies in the fact that the ruling class in the bourgeois countries is not interested in having their countries' working people learn the truth about the socialist countries first hand, about their social and cultural development, about the political and moral principles of citizens in a socialist society.

To weaken socialism's appeal, to denigrate it, bourgeois propaganda has come up with the myth of a 'closed society'. They claim that socialist countries shun communications with other peoples, that they avoid information exchanges and development of contacts between people.

Let us look at a few facts. Last year, 1975, alone, over 58 million guests from abroad visited the CMEA member-states. In turn, some 35 million citizens of the socialist community countries went abroad. This alone shows what all the talk about a 'closed society' is really worth.

Or take contacts between mass organisations like trade unions. On more than one occasion the US authorities have denied visas to Soviet trade-union delegations invited by US trade unions. There were even cases of representatives of Soviet trade unions not being permitted to attend international meetings in the United States.

The USSR last year received 980 trade-union and workers' delegations from abroad, while 750 Soviet delegations visited other countries.

No, the socialist countries are not a 'closed society'. We are open to everything that is truthful and honest, and we are ready to expand contacts in every way, using the favourable conditions *détente* offers. But our doors will always be closed to publications propagandising war, violence, racism and hatred. And even more so, they will be closed to the emissaries of foreign secret services and the emigré anti-Soviet organisations they have formed. When talking about the 'freedom' of contacts, certain people in the West are sometimes after free rein to engage in underhand play. We are not suffering from any 'spy mania'. But we will not give freedom for subversion against our system, against our society. Now that there has been so much scandal over the exposure of US CIA activities, I think it will be clear to everyone that our stand in this matter is well grounded, to put it mildly.

We think that cultural exchanges and the information media should serve human ideals, the cause of peace, that they should promote

139

international trust and friendship. But in certain European countries there are notorious subversive radio stations which have assumed such names as 'Liberty' and 'Free Europe'. Their existence contaminates the international atmosphere and is a direct challenge to the spirit and letter of the Helsinki agreements. The Soviet Union resolutely demands that the use of these means of 'psychological war' be stopped.

Comrades, our Party, loyal to the great ideas of proletarian internationalism, has never separated the destinies of the Soviet Union from the destinies of other countries of Europe and the world. The USSR's foreign policy, whose aim is to promote peace and people's freedom, and our domestic policy, whose aim is to build communism, not only meet the vital interests of the Soviet people, but constitute, we are certain, our contribution to the common struggle of Communists throughout the world for a better future for mankind.

You probably know, comrades, about the results of the 25th CPSU Congress, specifically about the plans for the Soviet Union's development which this Congress outlined. The scope of our national economy is now colossal indeed. Suffice it to say that the USSR now accounts for 20 per cent of world industrial output. In absolute figures, this is more than was produced by the entire world in 1950. It is easy to see the diverse and complex problems the planning and managing of such a huge economic organism involve.

The advantages of socialism allow us to ensure the continuous growth of the country's economy and, at the same time, the constant improvement of the people's living standards. Today the Party has given priority to raising production efficiency, to improving the quality of work in all the aspects this vast concept implies. This takes tremendous effort in many directions — from a wide renovation of the basis of production technology to serious new changes in the way of instilling a conscious, communist attitude to work, in encouraging the initiative of millions of working people.

It is important to stress that we do not regard furthering production and raising our people's living standards as an end in itself, but approach these tasks in the context of the main programmatic objectives of building communism.

It is a matter, in particular, of narrowing down the gap between urban and rural living conditions, which is what the agrarian policy our Party has worked out over the last few years is largely aimed at. It is also a matter of gradually erasing the distinctions between mental and physical labour, which is assisted by introducing universal compulsory 10-year education and by the remarkable rise in the intellectual level of the workers' and collective farmers' labour. And it is also a matter of succeeding, through an unprecedentedly vast housing construction programme, in giving tens of millions of people adequate living conditions in modern apartments at a record low rent. Our work in this area will continue.

The successes of our social development are possible only as a result of the people's free and conscious creative work, of their increasingly active exercise of their civil rights, of their increasingly active participation in shaping all aspects of public life. Therefore, our further advance in building communism will inevitably mean the further advance of socialist democracy. This is our Party's principled policy, and this is our day-to-day reality.

Under socialism something truly precious has taken shape in the character of the Soviet man — the sense of being his country's master, who is well aware of the connection between his own work and the country-wide cause, and who keeps in mind and cares about common interests.

This is not some kind of an abstract feeling, but the real deeds of millions. I shall try to illustrate what I mean by several examples.

If in our country a skilful worker achieves good results in his work at a factory or in the field and is ahead of his workmates, he usually wants to pass on his experience to others, to make it theirs. There are no people more respected in our country, perhaps, than these leading workers. Many of them are famous throughout the country. They are written about in the press and are elected members of the organs of state power.

More than 2 million working people in our country are exercising state power, having been elected to the Soviets. As well, almost 30 million Soviet citizens make up the *aktiv* of the Soviets, giving voluntary and unselfish assistance to the huge and complicated work of state management. Nine million working people have been elected to organs of people's control, keeping a close eye on what the various links of management are doing and combating red tape and dishonest labour.

And here is another form of what working people are doing — standing production conferences, in which workers make up 65 per cent, have been set up at industrial enterprises. In 1975 alone more than a million proposals for raising production efficiency and improving labour conditions, which these conferences drew up, were put into effect.

Although these are only individual examples, I think they can give an idea of how the work of management bodies is combined with grassroots democracy.

Of course, there are not a few shortcomings and unsolved problems in our extensive and complicated public life. We are well aware of them, and the Party is mobilising the people in order to overcome them. But no shortcomings and difficulties will ever eclipse the main historic victory our people have won following the Great October Socialist Revolution under the leadership of the Leninist Communist Party. We have built a society free from monopolist oligarchy domination, free from the fear of crises, unemployment, free from social catastrophes. We have built a society of people who are equal in the broadest sense of the word, people who know neither class, property, race nor any other such privileges, a society which not only proclaims human rights, but guarantees the conditions under which they can be exercised. We have built up a stable, dynamic and united society.

It is safe to say, comrades, that never in our history have our working people enjoyed living standards as high as they are today. Never have their educational standards been so high, and never have cultural values been more accessible. Never have they been more confident in their own future, in the peaceful future of their country than they are now. Herein lies the basis of the Soviet people's unanimous support of the CPSU policy, the basis of the unbreakable unity of the Party and the people in our country.

Speech at the Conference of the
European Communist and Workers'
Parties, Berlin. 29 June 1976

Mourousi — (commentator for the French television network TF-1): First of all, Mr. General Secretary, I want to thank you for receiving a representative of French television in this Kremlin study, where you rarely give interviews. By doing this you are, in a way, receiving France here. I am sure the French people will hear with much interest the opinions that you will voice, especially since they have cordial remembrances of your visits to France in 1971, 1973 and again in 1974, and, I would say, they are fond of you. You are someone who is loved in France.

There are many things we should like to know. First of all, let me ask you what are your duties as General Secretary of the CPSU Central Committee and what problems are now in the field of vision of the Politburo of the Central Committee of your Party.

Brezhnev: I should like, first of all, to greet French tele-viewers as my old acquaintances. This is not our first meeting. This time, as you see, my dear friends, a French journalist has come to the Kremlin and we are now in my study, in the midst of a working day. Therefore, the question about what I do seems quite a natural one. I shall try to answer it, although it will not be easy to do so.

The type of work I do and that carried out by the Politburo of the Central Committee are determined above all by the role played by the Communist Party in this country.

The Party here unites the front-ranking, the most active and politically conscious part of the working class, farmers and members of the intelligentsia. It maps out its policy on the basis of a scientific approach to and a painstaking analysis of the real requirements of life and the needs of the people. It unites all sections of society and all nationalities, and arms the people with will-power and a readiness and an ability to fight for the ideals of communism, the most progressive and just society.

The supreme guiding principle of the Party's work is everything for the people, everything for the welfare and happiness of the people. That is why the people regard the Party's policy as their own and entrust it with the leading role in society.

As far as I know, many in the West have no clear idea of our political system. Wrong ideas about it are sometimes voiced. It is asserted, for example, that the Party replaces other bodies, both state and public ones. This is wrong, of course.

Our state organs — the Supreme Soviet of the USSR, the Council of Ministers of the USSR, governmental bodies on the republican and local level — have a clear-cut sphere of competence defined in the Constitution. These organs enact and enforce laws and are responsible for the proper functioning of the economy and the advancement of science, culture, education and health service.

Public organisations have their own field of activity: the trade unions are concerned primarily with the protection of the interests of the working people and with the organisation of their work and holidays; the Komsomol is in charge of the education of the younger generation, and so on. But, I repeat, it is the Party that is the guiding spirit in society and the political organiser of the affairs of the Soviet people.

As you see, our system is different from yours. Also different is the practice of leadership in the Soviet Union from that in the capitalist countries. The range of questions which concern the Politburo and myself, as General Secretary, is much broader than that handled by the leaders in the West. We keep in the field of vision practically all aspects of the life of the people, everything that takes place on the territory of this country. This includes the ideological life of the Party and of society, economy, social problems and the development of socialist democracy. It is impossible to list everything here. International affairs also claim no small amount of our attention.

If one speaks of the main direction of our work at present, it consists in the implementation of the decisions of the 25th CPSU Congress, above all, the ensuring of a further rise in the material and cultural standards of the people and an improvement in their working and living conditions.

Interview on French television given
in the Kremlin. 5 October 1976

1977 –9

Efficiency and quality are the key tasks of the Tenth Five-Year Plan. But care should be taken to prevent this brief and precise formula from becoming an overworked phrase, from losing its active and mobilising character. We should ask ourselves searchingly every day whether we are doing everything we can to carry out this task. Here there is great scope for the trade unions to exert themselves, there is a wide field for activity before them.

The increased scale and complexity of our national economy have urgently posed the question of improving economic planning and management, of improving the entire economic mechanism. Great work is being done in this direction. The central planning and economic bodies are busy preparing specific proposals. There must be no delay in this work: it is regarded as a task of the utmost importance by the Party.

But there are other things which we never forget. In addition to good management 'from above', as they say, socialism has another powerful force for speeding up economic growth. This is the creative activity, initiative and labour enthusiasm of millions, which surge up 'from below', or to be more exact, from the very heart of society.

Herein lies one of the great advantages of socialism. Herein lies one of its main 'secrets' which has enabled us, in the course of our history, to achieve what appeared impossible and to amaze the whole world by the high growth rates of the new society and by its vital force and dynamism.

This factor will be no less important for us in the future, too. Practice constantly brings forth new forms of mass initiative. Here a great deal depends on you, comrades, on the work of the trade unions, on their ability to encourage a creative initiative, to use it for accomplishing concrete pressing tasks at each enterprise, in every branch of our work.

The first thing that comes to my mind in this context is the role of the trade unions in developing the socialist emulation movement. It will be recalled that back in 1920 the Ninth Congress of the Party instructed the trade unions to organise socialist emulation. The responsibility for this

145

SOCIALISM, DEMOCRACY AND HUMAN RIGHTS

important matter still rests with them.

It is only to be expected that socialist emulation should acquire qualitatively new features, peculiar to it at the present stage. This emulation is inseparable from the current scientific and technological revolution. It increasingly centres around the problems of efficiency and quality. It is aimed at achieving the best end results in the national economy. It is closely linked with the upwardly revised plans in which the initiative and selfless work of millions finds such striking expression.

It is not only the front-rankers, the winners, but also those lagging behind who come to light in the course of the socialist emulation movement. Such a movement helps us in this way to concentrate our efforts on rectifying shortcomings, on improving the performance of lagging sections in order to speed up overall progress.

All this makes the organisation of emulation a complex matter which must not follow beaten paths. All this confronts the trade unions with great tasks, heightens their role in economic management and in organisational and mass political work.

The task of raising the level of socialist emulation places great obligations not only on the trade unions but also on top economic executives and factory management. The enthusiasm of the masses must not be abused. Good initiatives need something more than praise: they also need constant practical support. Not a single useful initiative must be allowed to peter out. This is how the Party sees this question.

Such an approach, while ensuring greater economic effect of the socialist emulation movement, enhances its educational value and this is something we must not forget. There is nothing like socialist emulation for educating the new man and promoting his political growth and moral development.

The clear-cut political thrust of this socialist emulation is manifested most strikingly in the movement to cultivate a communist attitude to work. This movement involves tens of millions of people. But what counts here is not numbers but quality. Therefore, in conferring the lofty titles of Communist Labour Team and Communist Labour Shock Worker one should always be guided by Lenin's injunction that 'these *vey honourable titles must be won* by prolonged and persistent effort, by *practical* achievement in genuine communist development' (*Collected Works*, Vol. 29, p. 431).

Just think over these words, comrades. They embody a political, Party approach to this matter. They raise a reliable barrier against formalism, red tape, eye-wash and all those things which we Communists must combat most vigorously, I repeat, most vigorously.

There is one more aspect of work in which the trade unions have a very important part to play. This is the strengthening of labour discipline.

The Soviet man is the master of his country. He is the sole architect of the might and wealth of his society. No one except the people in this country can use the results of social labour, but we have no one to work for us either. This means that everyone must work in such a way that he need not be ashamed of himself and is able to look his comrades in the eye with a clear conscience.

It is quite natural therefore that front-ranking workers, veteran workers, and whole labour collectives should point to the need for greater exactingness towards those who forget about the dignity of working man, who lack discipline and who do not take care of public property. It is your direct duty, comrades, the duty of all trade-union organisations, to support these honest working people in every way . . .

The Party regards the trade unions as a great force capable of giving practical help in strengthening labour discipline in all sectors of production: moreover, in strengthening it by means and methods that are characteristic of our socialist system, namely, by cultivating responsibility and a conscientious attitude, applying an effective system of material and moral incentives, by friendly criticism and self-criticism, and by everyday influence exerted on the individual by the work collective . . .

Comrades, the Party had put in the forefront the task of raising the material and cultural standards of the Soviet people. It is translating into thousands of practical deeds our programme slogan: 'Everything for the benefit of man, everything for the sake of man!'

You know how much is being done in that sphere. In the past few months alone a number of important decisions have been taken. One of them provides for higher earnings for 31 million Soviet people, another is concerned with expanding the manufacture of consumer goods and raising their quality. The work in all these directions will continue. There is no doubt that the trade unions will make a tangible contribution to the accomplishment of the tasks aimed at raising the living standard of the people. For it is in the interests of man that our Soviet trade unions are functioning.

Hence the prime importance of the constant concern for improving labour conditions, minimising manual, low-skilled and physically arduous labour, and working to eliminate occupational diseases and occupational injuries.

The Party regards the technical retooling of industry, agriculture, construction and transport, for which vast sums are allocated, as the decisive means of improving labour conditions and making all production safe and convenient for man. Our goal can be formulated as follows: from safety rules to safe technology. We have embarked on that road and will undeviatingly follow it.

However, looking into the future we should also see what surrounds us today. Can we say that the situation as regards labour conditions is satisfactory? Unfortunately not. It sometimes happens that the management and trade unions ignore serious drawbacks, regard measures to improve labour conditions and safety as of minor importance, and tolerate neglect in meeting the obligations written down in collective agreements.

Early this year a decree was adopted, at the proposal of the All-Union Central Council of Trade Unions, on further improvement of labour protection and safety conditions in the national economy. But the initiative of the trade unions must not end there. What has been planned must be carried through! This is strictly demanded of all the ministries and departments, and all economic managers. It is also a key task of the trade unions.

Much remains to be done to improve public catering and everyday services at industrial enterprises. In these matters, as indeed in all the other matters affecting the interests of the man at work, the trade union committees should be more demanding and energetic.

Concern for man does not, of course, end and cannot end at the factory gate. A vast area of social policy is connected with improving the everyday living conditions of the Soviet people, concern for their health and leisure, so that the working people and their families could dispose of their free time in a reasonable way that would benefit them and society. Technical creativity, physical culture and sports, and amateur art activities are essential to the life of millions. This offers great opportunities and a vast field of activity for the trade unions.

I think it necessary to emphasise that not only Party organisations but also the trade unions cannot afford to take a passive stand at a time when considerable allocations for the construction of housing, child-care institutions, schools, hospitals, clubs and stadiums are not being fully used in a number of republics, territories and regions from year to year.

Concern for man does not only mean meeting his material requirements. Addressing the delegates to the Congress, I would like to single out the moral and ethical aspects. This does not call for special outlays. What is indispensable is universal and daily consideration and concern for people.

How are we to make an old person happier? How to alleviate the lot of an invalid? How to heal a real or imagined insult? Such questions constantly crop up. They can only be answered by constantly perfecting the art of consideration for people. Who else but the trade unions, which are in the very thick of life, should take part in that important sphere on which the future and the happiness of all the Soviet people depend?

Comrades, the Party attaches prime importance to promoting democratic principles in production. The working man in a socialist society is not a machine carrying out certain operations or instructions. He is concerned not only with the immediate result of his personal efforts but with their place and significance in the overall labour process. The desire and opportunity to make a personal contribution to the common cause are a tremendous stimulus to work, they are conducive to thinking on a nationwide scale, and they help us to identify ourselves with the common concerns.

It is only where the working man knows that his opinion is being heeded, and his attitude taken into account in the preparation of social and economic plans, that he feels himself the genuine master of production and of his destiny. Thus political and production tasks emerge.

What is being done by the trade unions in enlisting more and more working people in the management of production is only one of the manifestations of socialist democracy. Being an influential social force, the trade unions play an important role in our entire political system and in developing socialist democracy. The central thing for us in this respect has been, and will be, what is literally expressed in the world democracy, namely, rule of the people, that is, participation of the masses in running government and social affairs, the 'genuine self-government by the people' of which Lenin spoke.

Socialism and democracy are inseparable. In building communism, we will develop democracy, meaning, of course, socialist democracy, that is, a democracy that embraces the political, social and economic spheres, a democracy that, above all, ensures social justice and social equality.

Comrades, our country now has almost 700,000 local trade union organisations, about half a million workshop trade union committees, and two and a half million trade union groups. This is a powerful force, a force which is in the forefront of the effort to fulfil the 5-year plans, to raise the efficiency of production and improve all its qualitative indicators. This force is active in all the work collectives, i.e. precisely where the ideas of high politics and economics are being translated into practical language and where the people's attitude towards life and society is moulded to a large extent.

The collective in which one works is a home, family, and school rolled into one. It is here that professional skills, experience and a conscientious attitude towards work are passed on from generation to generation, and communist dedication and loyalty to the Party, readiness to be always in the front ranks in the most difficult and crucial areas, are being implanted in the hearts of youths.

It is impossible to imagine a work collective without a trade-union group, a local trade-union committee or factory committee. Millions of trade-union activists, energetic people of initiative, are voluntarily and selflessly bringing kindness, solicitude and help to every worker and his family. May this arduous but very useful work of the activists always meet with understanding and appreciation.

One more remark, comrades. I think that the Party's course aimed at efficiency and quality has a direct bearing on the style of all our social work, including trade-union work. It is not the number of measures that one should be after. Let us ask ourselves, do we not have meetings too often and are they not too long? Do we not produce too many different papers — instructions, decisions and rulings — while sometimes forgetting to check whether these papers change anything in practical life. It is not the number of papers, nor the number and length of meetings but clear political aims, businesslike manner and practical results that are the criteria by which social work can and must be measured.

Comrades, the Soviet trade unions have at their disposal a solid material basis and vast financial resources.

At present, in accordance with the decisions of the 25th Congress of the Party, a serious change in the structure of the trade unions in production and an improvement in the forms and methods of their activity are under way. That will, undoubtedly, have a positive effect on the work of the trade unions.

The trade unions have a rich arsenal of forms and means to exercise their rights — workers' meetings, standing production conferences and collective agreements. They have the right of legislative initiative. In a word, the trade unions have many rights and opportunities. It is important to use them more fully and efficiently.

I assure you, comrades, that all the just demands of the trade unions to economic managers and the administration will get the unqualified support of the Party. Pay special attention to the word 'just' . . .

Our opponents would like to find forces of some sort opposed to socialism inside our countries. Since there are no such forces, because in socialist society there are no oppressed or exploited classes or oppressed or exploited nationalities, some sort of substitute has been invented and an ostensible 'internal opposition' in socialist countries is being fabricated by means of false publicity. That is the reason for the organised clamour about the so-called 'dissidents' and why a worldwide hullabaloo is being raised about 'violations of human rights' in socialist countries.

What can be said about this? In our country it is not forbidden 'to think differently' from the majority, to criticise different aspects of public life. We regard the comrades who come out with well-founded criticism, who strive for improvement, as well-intentioned critics, and we are grateful to them. Those who criticise wrongly we regard as people who are mistaken.

It is a different matter when a few individuals, who have estranged themselves from our society, actively oppose the socialist system, embark on the road of anti-Soviet activity, violate the laws, and, finding no support inside the country, turn for support abroad, to imperialist subversive centres — those engaged in propaganda and intelligence. Our people demand that such so-called public figures be treated as opponents of socialism, as persons acting against their own motherland, as accomplices, if not agents, of imperialism. Naturally, we take and will continue to take measures against them under Soviet law.

And in this matter let no one take offence: to protect the rights, freedoms and security of the 260-million Soviet people from the activities of such renegades is not only our right, but also our sacred duty. It is our duty to the people who, 60 years ago, under the guidance of the Party of Lenin embarked on the road of building socialism and communism, to the people who, defending their socialist motherland, their right to live the way they want, sacrificed 20 million lives in the great war against the fascist aggressors — precisely for the freedom and rights of the peoples — and who will never depart from that road!

Speech at the 16th Congress of Trade Unions of the USSR. 21 March 1977

Dear Comrades,

We shall now consider the draft of a new Constitution of the USSR. The Politburo has carefully studied this document and has endorsed it in principle. Since all of you are already familiar with the draft, I shall confine myself to a few most important points.

I

Point one: *Why has it become necessary to draw up a new Constitution?*

This has become necessary, comrades, because deep-going changes have taken place in our country, in the whole of our society in the past four decades.

The 1936 Constitution was adopted when we had, in fact, just completed the building of the foundations of socialism. The system of collective farming had just been set up and had to be consolidated. The technological level of the national economy was still far below that of the most advanced industrialised countries. The legacy of the pre-revolutionary times was still felt in various spheres of life.

What we now have in the Soviet Union is an advanced, mature socialist

152

society. *Major changes of fundamental importance have affected every aspect of the social life of the country.*

The nation's economy has changed beyond recognition. Socialist ownership reigns supreme in the country. An integrated and powerful national economic organism now exists which is functioning successfully. It is being developed on the basis of a fusion of the scientific and technological revolution with the advantages of the socialist system.

The country's social make-up has also changed.

Our working class today constitutes two-thirds of the country's population. It is formed by tens of millions of educated, technically competent and politically mature people. The work they perform is becoming increasingly similar to that carried out by engineering and technical personnel. The workers have become more active socially and the scale of their participation in administering the state has considerably broadened.

The farmers, too, have changed. The collective farmer of today was born and grew up on a collective farm and his mental outlook has been formed in socialist conditions. He works with up-to-date technical equipment, and his educational background and his mode of living often differ very little from those of city dwellers.

The intelligentsia has become truly representative of the people and socialist in outlook. As the people's cultural level rises and as science attains a role of unprecedented importance in the building of communism, the part played by the intelligentsia in the life of our society also grows.

We now have equality of nations, not only in the legal sense, but in practice. All of our republics, including those which used to lag behind economically and culturally, have now achieved a high level of development. The economies of the republics have, at the same time, become inseparable components of an integrated national economy.

Underlying all these changes is the growing social homogeneity of Soviet society. The firm alliance of the working class, the collective farmers and people's intelligentsia has become still stronger. Distinctions between the main social groups are being gradually erased. The very onward march of life brings all nations and national groups of this country ever closer together. A new historical community, that of the Soviet people, has emerged.

With the attainment of mature socialism and with the adoption of the ideological and political positions of the working class by all sections of the population, our state, which was first firmly established as a dictatorship of the proletariat, has grown into a state of the whole people.

All these processes taking place in the country's life have been and continue to be directed by the Communist Party, which has been the leading, organising and mobilising force of our society ever since the October Revolution. The problems it has to solve today have become more varied and complex. The Party now plays a still more important role in society and the guiding influence it exerts on the whole of the country's domestic life and foreign policy has grown.

Finally, the international position of the Soviet Union and the entire social and political make-up of the world have also changed drastically. The capitalist encirclement of the USSR has come to an end. Socialism has become a world system. A powerful socialist community has emerged. The positions of world capitalism have been substantially weakened. Dozens of young states opposed to imperialism have sprung up on the territories of former colonies. Our country's international prestige and influence have grown immeasurably.

As a result, the world balance of forces has been completely altered. There has arisen a real possibility of preventing a new world war; the danger of outbreak of such a war has already been considerably reduced although much hard work and struggle still lie ahead of us in this respect.

On the basis of their achievements the Soviet people, under the Party's guidance, are now carrying out new tasks: the creation of the material and technical foundations of communism, the gradual transformation of socialist social relations into communist relations, and education of the people in the spirit of communist consciousness.

Such, in brief, have been the major changes in our society and in our country's life since 1936. These are the main reasons and prerequisites for drawing up a new Constitution of the USSR.

II

Comrades,
The draft of a new Constitution is the result of a long and sustained effort. It is based on the Party's clear and concrete directives. The Central

Committee's Report to the 25th CPSU Congress said: 'The draft of a new Constitution should clearly reflect the great victories of socialism and state not only the general principles of the socialist system, expressing the class essence of our state, but also the basic features of a developed socialist society and its political organisation.' It also pointed out the necessity of reflecting the principles of national economic management, the role of the state in society's intellectual life and the further development of socialist democracy.

The present draft reflects these guidelines of the Party.

In preparing the draft *we stood firmly on the ground of continuity*. The draft retains and develops the characteristic features of a socialist Constitution outlined by Lenin.

Lenin and the Bolshevik Party believed that a Constitution is not only a legal act but also a major political document. The Party regarded the Constitution as a ratification of the gains of the revolution and also as a proclamation of the fundamental aims and objectives of building socialism.

Such was also the Constitution of the USSR of 1924, which laid down the principles of the formation of a federal socialist state.

The Constitution of 1936 proclaimed the victory of socialist social relations in the USSR and made the entire system of government and administrative bodies and the electoral procedure correspond to this. The constitutional framework of social development which was then evolved has stood the test of time.

The present draft retains many of the basic provisions of the Constitution now in force, for these continue to correspond to the essence of our system and to the pattern of our development.

Thus, the draft of a new Constitution, on the one hand, sums up all the main features of the previous Soviet Constitutions and, on the other, enriches these features with a new content corresponding to the requirements of the contemporary epoch.

The draft is also based on Soviet legislation which has been recently revised and improved, and crowns, as it were, what has been done in this respect.

A great deal has been accomplished in recent years. The fundamental legislation of the USSR and the republican codes concerning most of the areas of jurisprudence have been put into effect. We now have regulations covering industrial enterprises and production associations, and a new statute on collective farms. New laws on the health service, public education, the pension scheme and environmental protection have been adopted. The rights and duties of the local Soviets have been clearly defined. The status of deputies has been defined. All these legislative acts are taken into account in the draft Constitution and have become the building blocks, as it were, of many articles of the Constitution.

There is another factor of great importance. The draft Constitution takes into account *the experience in drawing up constitutions in the fraternal socialist countries*. In the last several years Bulgaria, the German Democratic Republic, Cuba and a number of other socialist countries adopted new constitutions. A number of provisions in these constitutions are of interest for us and they have not been ignored.

Thus, comrades, the draft of a new Constitution rests on a firm practical and theoretical foundation. The Politburo believes that this assures its soundness and active influence on the further development of Soviet society.

III

Now I would like to describe *the main features of the draft Constitution*.

First, it should be noted that the draft Constitution gives *a detailed description of the leading and guiding role of the Communist Party* and clearly defines its place in Soviet society and the state. Unlike the Constitution of 1936, the draft Constitution treats this subject in greater detail in a separate article.

The draft Constitution also says that *a developed socialist society has been built in the USSR and that the ultimate goal of the Soviet Union is to build communism*.

The draft Constitution emphasises that *our state is a state of the whole people*, expressing the will and interests of the working class, the farmers and the intelligentsia, of all the nations and nationalities in the country. It is thus proposed to rename our Soviets the *Soviets of People's Deputies*.

The draft Constitution retains the important principle that the foundation of the economic system of the USSR is socialist property in the means of production. At the same time it is proposed to introduce certain amendments that have been prompted by life itself. Alongside state

156

property and the property of collective farms and co-operative societies the draft Constitution refers to the property of trade unions and other public organisations.

Generally speaking, *the main tendency of what is new in the draft Constitution consists in broadening and deepening socialist democracy.*

Above all the democratic principles of the formation and work of the Soviets have been further developed. The role of the Soviets in deciding major questions of the life of society has been enhanced.

Article 106 says that the Supreme Soviet of the USSR is empowered to deal with all matters placed within the jurisdiction of the Union of Soviet Socialist Republics. The local Soviets not only deal with all matters of local relevance but also control and co-ordinate, within the bounds of their authority, the activities of all organisations on their territories. The draft Constitution lays special emphasis on the systematic control by the Soviets over executive and administrative bodies and over the activities of organisations and officials.

The term of office of the Supreme Soviet has been extended to 5 years and that of the local Soviets to 2½ years. Courts will be elected for the same terms.

The draft Constitution defines major ways of strengthening the ties linking the Soviets and their deputies with the masses. The former must regularly report to the people concerning their activities, report to the electorate and carefully consider every proposal made by working people.

You know, comrades, that 5 years ago we adopted an important law on the status of deputies to the Soviets. To further enhance the role of deputies, the basic powers conferred on them under that law have been stated in the draft Constitution.

A new feature has been introduced in the electoral system. Under the present Constitution only citizens who have reached the age of 23 are eligible to the USSR Supreme Soviet and citizens who have reached the age of 21 can be elected to the Supreme Soviets of the Union republics. Now it is proposed that all Soviet citizens who have reached the age of 18 have this opportunity. This is vivid evidence of our society's concern for and confidence in young people.

The draft Constitution describes in detail the role of the trade unions, the Komsomol, the co-operative societies and other mass organisations in the life of the country. These organisations are to have the right to take part in solving political, economic, social and cultural problems and the right to initiate legislation. This shows once again that the state of the whole people takes into account the interests of all social sections and groups.

The draft Constitution also contains a provision on the role of collectives of working people. This reflects a major policy line of the Party and the importance it attaches to the development of democratic principles in managing production.

The building of developed socialism makes it possible for us to considerably improve the provisions in the Constitution — the country's fundamental law — *on the rights of Soviet citizens*. The famous words from the 'Manifesto of the Communist Party' — 'the free development of each is the condition for the free development of all' — have become a basic principle of our state. This is reflected in the draft.

A special section proclaims the general principle of equality of Soviet citizens. Apart from that, the draft defines with the utmost clarity the achievements of socialism in such important fields as guaranteeing women equal rights with men and the equality of all citizens regardless of race or nationality.

The Constitution now in force, as we know, also provides a *complex of social and economic rights* having to do with the very essentials of the life of the people. But we all know well the meaning of these rights has actually become deeper and their practical guarantees broader and more effective. All this is reflected in the draft Constitution. Whereas, for example, the right to work is merely stated in the previous Constitution, now this is complemented by the right to choose one's profession, type of occupation and employment in keeping with one's calling, talents, professional training and education and also — and this is no less important — with reference to the needs of society.

Whereas the 1936 Constitution proclaims the right to maintenance in case of sickness or disability, now the question is considered in a broader context, that is, the Soviet people are guaranteed the right to health protection. Whereas earlier the right to education was formulated in general terms, the draft Constitution envisages universal compulsory secondary education and extensive development of vocational training and higher education.

The draft also proclaims a right of Soviet citizens which is not included in the Constitution now in force. I refer to the right to housing, which will be guaranteed to an ever greater extent as the housing construction programme is fulfilled, and also through government assistance in co-operative and private housing construction. Our new Constitution will be one of the first in the world to proclaim this right which is vitally important for man.

The political rights and freedoms of Soviet citizens are far more comprehensively defined in the draft.

The right of every Soviet citizen to take part in the administration of state and public affairs is proclaimed and specific forms of such participation are defined.

Freedom of speech and the press, of assembly, mass meetings and street processions and demonstrations, proclaimed in the Constitution now in force, are reiterated in full in the draft. Constitutional guarantees of the rights of the individual will be considerably broadened by the right of citizens to submit proposals to government and non-government organs, to criticise shortcomings in work and to file complaints in court against the actions of officials, and the right of citizens to seek redress in court against infringements on life and health, on property and personal freedom, and on honour and dignity.

It goes without saying, comrades, that the draft Constitution proceeds from the assumption that the rights and freedoms of citizens cannot and must not be used against our social system and to the prejudice of the interests of the Soviet people.

For example, the draft says in no uncertain terms that exercise by citizens of their rights and freedoms should in no way damage the interests of society and the state and infringe on the rights of other citizens and that political freedoms are granted in keeping with the interests of the working people and for the purpose of consolidating the socialist system.

Every Soviet citizen should clearly realise that, when all is said and done, the main guarantee of one's rights is the strength and prosperity of one's homeland. To this end every citizen should be aware of his responsibility before society and conscientiously fulfil his duty to the state and the people.

The draft Constitution, therefore, emphasises the citizen's duty to work honestly and conscientiously and to defend his homeland. The duties to protect the interests of the Soviet state, to promote the growth of its strength and prestige, to assist in every possible way in the maintenance of public order, to combat embezzlement and the wasteful use of government and public property, to protect nature and safeguard its wealth, and to show concern for the preservation of cultural values are for the first time formulated as constitutional demands. The draft also obliges citizens to show concern for the education of children and to bring them up as worthy members of socialist society.

In a special chapter of the draft entitled 'Social Development and Culture', it is said that the state shows concern for the development of education, science and art, for improving the working conditions of citizens, for raising their incomes and for the growth and fair distribution of the public consumption funds. It is pointed out here that the state facilitates the fulfilment of such targets on our way to communism as the erasure of essential distinctions between town and countryside and between intellectual and manual labour, and promotes the social homogeneity of society.

A further strengthening of socialist legality and law and order has also found clear-cut expression in the draft Constitution. We know, comrades, that some of the years following the adoption of the Constitution now in force were darkened by unlawful repressions and violations of the principles of socialist democracy and Leninist norms of Party and state life. This was done in defiance of the constitutional provisions. The Party strongly condemned such practices and they must never be repeated.

Everyone knows the great amount of work done by our Central Committee, The USSR Supreme Soviet, and the Soviet Government in improving Soviet laws and in creating firm guarantees against any kind of infringements on the rights of citizens, abuses of power, and bureaucratic practices. Summing up these guarantees, as it were, the draft emphasises that observance of the Constitution and the laws is the duty of all state bodies and officials, of mass organisations and citizens.

Comrades, *the Soviet Union is a multinational state*. Experience has fully confirmed the soundness of the basic elements of the federal structure of the USSR. There is no need, therefore, to introduce any major changes in the forms of our Soviet socialist federation.

The draft, like the 1936 Constitution, points out that the sovereign rights of the Union Republics shall be safeguarded by the Union. The guarantees of these rights remain in force. Moreover, they are to be supplemented by further rights such as the right of participation of the republics in the settlement of matters within the competence of the Union of Soviet Socialist Republics by the organs of the Union. The constituent republics, in the person of their supreme authorities, are to have the right of initiating legislation in the USSR Supreme Soviet.

At the same time, the further drawing together of the nation and nationalities of the USSR has made it necessary to consolidate the federal principles of the state. This finds expression in the very definition of the USSR as an integral federal multinational state (Article 69). The consolidation of the federal principles is also reflected in several other provisions of the draft.

On the whole the approach to questions of the national state structure in the draft ensures a genuinely democratic combination of the common interests of the multinational Union and the interests of each of its component republics and ensures the all-round development and a further drawing together of all the nations and nationalities of our country.

The draft reflects *the new stage in the development of our national economy.* It points out that the economy of the USSR has become an integral economic complex embracing all sectors of social production, distribution and exchange on its territory.

It also proclaims such an important principle of the socialist economy as that of combining planned centralised guidance with economic independence and initiative of enterprises and associations.

The draft Constitution defines in greater detail the powers of central and local state bodies, ministries and departments. In contrast to the Constitution now in force, the draft includes no list of all-Union and Union–Republican ministries and departments. Since, as experience has shown, such lists change from time to time, it has been found more appropriate to publish a list in a special law on the Council of Ministers of the USSR to be adopted in accordance with Article 135 of the draft Constitution.

Comrades, fundamental changes in the international position of the Soviet Union, the immense growth of its influence in world politics, and the close interrelationship of the internal and external factors of our development have made it necessary to include in the draft Constitution a *special chapter on the foreign policy of the USSR*. This is the first time such a chapter has been introduced into a Constitution.

It says that the Soviet state consistently follows the Leninist policy of peace and is for a strengthening of the security of peoples and broad international co-operation. The foreign policy of the USSR is aimed at ensuring favourable international conditions for building communism in the USSR, at strengthening the positions of world socialism, rendering support to the struggles of peoples for national liberation and social progress, preventing wars of aggression and consistently implementing the principle of peaceful coexistence of states with different social systems. This will be the first Soviet Constitution to explicitly state that the Soviet Union is a component part of the world system of socialism and of the socialist community. It develops and strengthens friendship, co-operation and comradely mutual assistance with the lands of socialism on the basis of socialist internationalism.

A special *chapter on the defence of the socialist motherland* is also introduced for the first time. In addition, the powers of the Presidium of the USSR Supreme Soviet are to include the power to form a national Defence Council and approve its composition.

These are, in brief, the main features characterising the draft of a new Constitution of the USSR.

IV

Now allow me to turn to the tasks which we shall face in implementing the new Constitution and the significance that its adoption will have for the development of our country and the strengthening of the positions of the forces of socialism, peace and progress in the international arena.

First about the *significance of the new Constitution for the internal life of the country*.

Implementation of its provisions will raise all our state and economic activity and the entire work of government and economic management bodies to a qualitatively new level.

This concerns, first of all, the ever more effective use of the extensive powers of the elective bodies — the Soviets. Maximum use should be made of the tremendous possibilities open to the 2-million-strong army of deputies who represent all public strata, all trades and professions, and all nationalities. This powerful collective intellect of Soviet power is and will be tackling ever more difficult and diversified tasks. It can and should exercise the most effective control over the work of the executive bodies at all levels.

Much is to be done in the field of legislation. It will be necessary on the basis of the Constitution to elaborate all-Union legislation on elections, a statute of the Supreme Soviet, and a law on the Council of Ministers, and to define the powers of the territorial, regional and area Soviets and ministries and government departments. It will be necessary, without any delay, to prepare and adopt new constitutions of the Union and autonomous republics.

The new Constitution of the USSR will become the core of the Code of the Laws of the Soviet state, the drafting of which has begun in accordance with the decisions of the 25th Congress of the CPSU.

At the same time, the new Constitution is to bring about a considerable improvement in the work of all bodies responsible for the strict observance of Soviet laws. I have in mind the Procurator's Office, the courts, arbitration bodies, other administrative agencies and people's control bodies. The Party expects that all these organisations will display still greater initiative, adherence to principle and irreconcilability in combating all violations of Soviet law and order.

It is very important that the draft provides for the constant improvement of the socialist economic system as a whole and of the entire work of planning agencies and other bodies which direct economic and cultural activity. Their main functions are defined in the Constitution. It is necessary that these functions are discharged fully and precisely and that each body and every official display a greater sense of responsibility.

Soviets at all levels, the government, the ministries and government departments, and the executives of the local Soviets should constantly review their work in the light of the provisions of the Constitution. Party bodies, too, should more strictly require of Communists who head state and economic bodies that they properly fulfil their duties under the Constitution.

Implementation of the new Constitution will make it possible for millions upon millions of Soviet people to become involved even more actively in the management of economic affairs and in the exercise of control over the work of the state apparatus.

Centralism in economic management is both necessary and legitimate. However, it is equally necessary to take into careful consideration the complexity of the conditions in which our economy is developing. This is impossible without a further growth of initiative on the part of production collectives, without the active, and I would say interested, participation of the working people themselves in economic management. Under socialism democracy has been and remains an important instrument for developing the country's economy and all fields of economic and cultural activity.

In this way, the Constitution has been invested with a tremendous creative potential which should be used creatively. 'The Soviet Constitution . . . serves and will constantly serve the working people and is a powerful weapon in the fight for socialism', Lenin said (*Collected Works*, Vol. 42, p. 105). Today Lenin would have added: and also an instrument of communist construction.

There is no doubt, comrades, that the adoption of a new Constitution of the USSR, the constitution of developed socialism, the constitution of communism which we are building, will be not only an historic event for our country, but also an *event of tremendous international significance*. Its implementation will have a profound long-term influence that will be felt far beyond the confines of our motherland.

Our new Constitution will vividly show the whole world how the socialist state is developing and how it more deeply affirms and further strengthens socialist democracy. It will vividly show what socialist democracy means and wherein lies its essence. Our Constitution will show the diverse forms and the tremendous scope of the constantly growing effective participation of the broad masses of the people in administering the affairs of the state and society, something which is not known in the bourgeois countries where real power is exercised only by the numerically small class of capitalists.

In reading our new Constitution, people will see more clearly what extensive and diverse rights and freedoms are enjoyed by the citizens of a socialist society.

In its provisions the world will see a state which sets itself the goal of steady growth of the well-being and culture of the entire people, of all its classes and groups without exception, and which is actively working towards the attainment of this goal.

Finally, our new Constitution will show most convincingly that the first state of victorious socialism has for ever inscribed on its banner the word 'Peace' — peace as the highest principle of its foreign policy, which meets the interests of its own people and all the other peoples of our planet.

The new Constitution of the Soviet Union will no doubt enrich the common treasure-house of experience of world socialism.

The achievements of victorious socialism, reflected in it in concentrated form, will be an inspiring example for the peoples of those countries which have recently chosen the *road of socialist development*.

They will give still greater confidence to the working masses of the capitalist countries in their struggle for their rights, for emancipation from the yoke of capitalist exploitation.

In countering the wrong and vulgar interpretation of the concepts of *democracy and human rights* by bourgeois and revisionist propaganda, we offer the most complete and genuine complex of rights and duties of a citizen of a socialist society. On the scales of history we place the truly epoch-making gains of the working people, won thanks to the power of the working class under the leadership of the Communist Party.

V

Comrades, the Politburo of the Central Committee is of the opinion that the draft of the new Constitution, which has been approved by the Plenum, must, as was announced at the 25th Congress of the Party, be subject to nationwide discussion. This means that *we are to accomplish work of great scope and importance*.

For discussion by the Soviet people a document will be made public which reflects the main gains of the revolution and the path we have traversed in the building of a new society. Thus, the preparations for the celebration of the sixtieth anniversary of the October Revolution and the discussion of the draft of a new Constitution are organically linked; they are complementary undertakings.

The task before us is to *ensure the widest possible, free and genuinely businesslike discussion of the draft Constitution*, to draw the mass of the working people, representatives of all the sections of the population, into this undertaking and to use for these purposes our established forms of public activity.

It is also necessary to set up an efficient mechanism for considering observations and suggestions that will come from working people through all channels.

It should be kept in mind that in the course of the mass-scale discussion of the draft Constitution the practical activity of party, government and economic bodies at all levels will also come within the field of vision of the working people. There will be discussions of urgent questions which are of concern to people, of still outstanding problems and of shortcomings in our work. We must be prepared for this, and shall have to react quickly and concretely to criticism and suggestions, and to take measures to improve the state of affairs where necessary.

We are launching the discussion of a new Constitution at a time when the Soviet people, under the leadership of the Party, are working hard to fulfil the decisions of the 25th Congress of the CPSU. The nationwide discussion will help *further to invigorate the entire social life of the country*. It should awaken in the people new creative forces, give new scope to the socialist emulation drive and raise the sense of responsibility of each person for the task entrusted to him.

It is party organisations and party bodies that must ensure that discussion of the Constitution takes place on a large scale and give it precise and clear political direction. If they are able to do this correctly, this will definitely improve the political and economic results of this year, the year of the adoption of a new Constitution of the USSR and the sixtieth anniversary of the Great October Revolution.

The discussion of the draft Constitution is of vital concern to the Soviets. In organising this work they must reach out practically to the entire adult population of the country. Preparations for the elections to the local Soviets are currently in progress in all the republics. It is important to use the occasion efficiently. Perhaps it will be useful to discuss the draft Constitution at sessions of the newly elected local Soviets.

We expect active participation in the discussion of the draft Constitution on the part of our mass public organisations, and above all of the trade unions, the Komsomol, the unions and organisations of the creative professions and scientific institutions.

The mass information media have a special role to play in this. Efficient and full coverage of the course of the discussion and a respectful attitude toward the opinion of working people will be expected of our press, radio and television.

In short, comrades, the discussion of the draft of the new Constitution must become a matter of primary importance for all our organisations and for all our cadres.

In concluding my speech I would like, comrades, once again to stress that the adoption of a new Constitution of the USSR will be an important landmark in the political life of the country. It will be yet another historic contribution of our Leninist party and the entire Soviet people to the great cause of building communism and, at the same time, to the international cause of the struggle of all working people of the world for freedom, for human progress and for lasting peace on Earth.

Report on the draft Constitution of the USSR at the Plenary Meeting of the Central Committee. 24 May 1977

Before we start to examine the items on the agenda, I should like to say a few words about the work of the Supreme Soviet and its Presidium mainly with reference to the decisions of the May Plenary Meeting of the CPSU Central Committee and the immediate tasks we are to tackle together in the near future.

First of all, I should like to thank once again the Central Committee of our Party, the Supreme Soviet of the USSR and all Deputies, and you, members of the Presidium, for the great confidence you have placed in me.

The post of Chairman of the Presidium of the Supreme Soviet of the USSR is an extremely responsible one. The Presidium is indeed the nerve centre of Soviet government, linked with more than 50,000 local Soviets. Thousands of people apply to the Presidium on a great variety of questions.

You comrades are of course well aware that the Central Committee's decision in May to combine the posts of General Secretary of the CPSU Central Committee and Chairman of the Presidium of the Supreme

Soviet of the USSR was not a mere formality but an act of profound political significance.

First of all, it demonstrated the sustained growth of the leading role of the Communist Party, the core of the Soviet political system, of all state and public organisations of working people. Acting within the framework of the Soviet Constitution, the CPSU, as a ruling party, has defined and will continue to define the policy line on all key questions of national life.

The decisions of the May Meeting have also reflected the fact that in their everyday work many Politburo members have to deal with state affairs both at home and abroad. As General Secretary of the Central Committee, I too have had to represent the Soviet Union on many occasions — on your instructions as well — in relations between states, in talks on cardinal questions of strengthening international peace and security. This practice will now be carried to its logical conclusion.

Being fully aware of all this, I clearly realise the great additional responsibility that the decision of the USSR Supreme Soviet has placed on me. It is, frankly speaking, no easy job, and I count on your help, understanding and support.

As one-time Chairman of the Presidium of the USSR Supreme Soviet and a Presidium member for many years, I am firmly convinced that the strength of this body lies in our pulling together. The principle of collective leadership which is followed by the Party and the state must be applied here as fully as possible.

At the same time, any party or state body functions well only when everyone of its members pulls his weight, throws himself body and soul into the common cause. I believe, comrades, you all agree on this.

If we turn to questions which come within the purview of the Supreme Soviet, we shall see that while paying unflagging attention to legislation, planning and the Budget, it increasingly takes up questions relating to the state of affairs in the various spheres of the economy and culture and hears reports from the government on these matters. The session of the Supreme Soviet which ended today provides convincing proof of that. The control exercised by the USSR Supreme Soviet over the administrative bodies has been growing in efficiency and scope. An exceptional role in this belongs to the thirty standing committees in which more than two-thirds of the Supreme Soviet deputies work.

Naturally, comrades, in order that the decision of the Party on the further development of every aspect of the work of the USSR Supreme Soviet be implemented, its Presidium should step up its activity. I think that the active stance and initiative shown by the Presidium of the Supreme Soviet of the USSR in its work is particularly important now that a new Constitution of the USSR is to be adopted. It gives the Supreme Soviet still more opportunities for improving its work. And together, we shall use these opportunities to the best advantage.

What do I have in mind?

Above all, I have in mind the fact that the new Constitution will express still more clearly the comprehensive powers vested in the Supreme Soviet. The latter can consider and pass decisions on any matter within the jurisdiction of the USSR.

A large part of these powers are exercised by the Presidium of the Supreme Soviet, which makes it the organiser of all the work conducted by the USSR Supreme Soviet. This includes the sessions, the standing committees, and the deputies' work in their constituencies. Each of these forms of the work conducted by the country's supreme body of power should function at full capacity, so to speak, should serve still better to step up the work of the Supreme Soviet along each of its main lines.

The new Constitution will provide the base from which to carry on Soviet law-making. Suffice it to recall that the draft Constitution itself mentions about a dozen laws which will have to be adopted soon. They include Supreme Soviet rules, a law on the Council of Ministers of the USSR, the election laws, a law on people's control and other major enactments.

But I should like to draw attention here to another side of the matter. The more we develop Soviet legislation, the better must we see to it that it is strictly carried out. As an old saying goes, a law which is not obeyed need never have been made. It appears that the Supreme Soviet, its Presidium and its standing committees will have to step up their supervision over the execution of laws, and the implementation of the national economic plans and the State Budget approved by the Supreme Soviet.

In conformity with the new Constitution, guidance of the Soviets of People's Deputies will undoubtedly emerge as a major area of activity of the USSR Supreme Soviet and its Presidium.

The draft Constitution emphasises once again that all Soviets, Supreme and local, present a single system of bodies of state authority as they are the political basis of the state of the whole people.

The Communist Party has always proceeded from the fact that each Soviet is a segment of the supreme authority, that it not only enjoys the power to make decisions on all matters under its jurisdiction, but is also the vehicle of centrally made decisions. This, comrades, is an exceptionally important principle. This unity of supreme and local authority and the reliance of supreme authority on local initiative reflect the essence of the Soviets, namely, the indissoluble bond between them and the masses.

Now that it will be written down in the Constitution that the USSR establishes the common principles of the organisation and activity of the republican and local government bodies, the Supreme Soviet and its Presidium will have to step up their efforts in that direction.

Lenin stressed more than once that nothing could be sillier than to transform the Soviets into something rigid and self-contained. Indeed, comrades, the Soviets are a living and mobile organisation of the people constantly renewing themselves. Just as they succeeded in the past in uniting the revolutionary movement of the masses and the efforts of the masses to build a socialist society, so now too, in conditions of mature socialism, the work of the Soviets should increasingly be aimed at raising the efficiency of production, at carrying out the extensive social programme mapped out by the Party, and at developing every aspect of Soviet socialist democracy, that is, at carrying out the tasks involved in the building of communism.

Foreign relations constitute of course an important area of the work of the USSR Supreme Soviet and its Presidium.

The Communist Party and the Soviet state are working persistently to strengthen peace, reduce the menace of another world war, curb the arms race, and build up the positions of socialism and all forces coming out for people's freedom and social progress, and for mutually profitable co-operation of all countries. These efforts rest on the determined stand of the Soviet people and meet with support and understanding from millions of people of goodwill in every corner of the globe.

The fundamental principles of Soviet foreign policy are clearly defined in the draft Constitution. The USSR Supreme Soviet, its Presidium, the standing committees and deputies are called upon to make a substantial contribution to the implementation of these principles and promotion of contacts with other countries.

Now that the Soviet people are preparing to celebrate the sixtieth anniversary of the October Revolution and are discussing the draft of the Fundamental Law, their active and creative involvement in carrying out the plans drawn up by the CPSU and in building communism is more tangible than ever.

The people's confidence in the party and the government imposes a deep obligation on them. We must work better and pay still more attention to the growing requirements of the Soviet people . . .

Speech at a session of the Presidium of the USSR Supreme Soviet. 17 June 1977

Esteemed comrade deputies,

The present session of the Supreme Soviet has before it a task that is historic in the fullest sense of the word: the adoption of a new Constitution for the Union of Soviet Socialist Republics.

We are about to adopt the new Constitution on the eve of the sixtieth anniversary of the Great October Socialist Revolution. This is not a mere coincidence in time of two major events in the life of our country. The connection between them goes much deeper. The new Constitution, one might say, epitomises the whole 60 years' development of the Soviet state. It is striking evidence of the fact that the ideas proclaimed by the October Revolution and Lenin's precepts are being successfully put into practice.

The draft Constitution, placed before the Supreme Soviet for its consideration, is the result of many years of intensive work by a large group of people. The Constitution Commission, set up by the USSR Supreme Soviet, includes experienced Party and government workers, and representatives of the working class, the collective farmers and the people's intelligentsia — representatives of our country's numerous peoples. Eminent scientists, specialists, and men and women working in state agencies and public organisations have been involved in the pre-

171

paration of the draft. It has been twice considered by Plenary Meetings of the CPSU Central Committee.

I think that we have every right to say that the important tasks with which we have been faced in connection with the preparation, discussion and adoption of the Constitution have been fulfilled in the most conscientious way and with the most consistent observance of all the principles of socialist democracy.

I

The discussion of the draft Constitution by the whole people has been the crucial test of the quality of all the preparatory work. The discussion took place over a period of nearly 4 months and was nationwide in the true sense of the word. Altogether it involved *more than 140,000,000 men and women, that is, over 80 per cent of the adult population of the country. Never before has our country known active participation by the public on such a scale.*

The main political result of the nationwide discussion consists in the fact that the Soviet people have said: yes, this is the Fundamental Law we looked forward to. It truly reflects our gains and our aspirations and hopes, and correctly defines our rights and duties. While formalising what has been achieved, it opens up prospects for further advance in the building of communism.

The draft was discussed at some 1½ million meetings of working people at enterprises and collective farms, in military units and in residential areas. It was discussed at plenary meetings, at meetings of activists, and at general meetings of trade unions and the Komsomol organisation, and by co-operative associations and artists', writers', musicians' and other unions. The whole Party was involved in its discussion. Some 450,000 open Party meetings were held for this purpose, and these were addressed by more than 3 million men and women. The draft was considered by all the Soviets, from the rural Soviets to the Supreme Soviets of the Union Republics, that is by more than 2 million deputies, representing the whole of our people. Each of these forums approved the draft Constitution.

Finally, an unending flow of letters was received from the Soviet people.

The vast majority of these letters are marked by patriotism, whole-hearted approval of the policy of our Party and the Soviet government, breadth of vision and maturity of judgement, and by the high and exacting standards set by the authors for themselves and their comrades. The writers, like those who took part in the discussion at meetings, are men and women from all walks of life and different age groups, representing all our nations and nationalities. Party members or not, and all of them, as masters of the country, have thoroughly examined the draft Constitution, making proposals for improving the text and expressing other considerations bearing on various aspects of life in our society.

Pondering such statements and letters one comes to the conclusion that they are a reflection of that tremendous achievement of socialism — the emergence of the new man, who does not separate himself from the state but who regards the interests of the state and of the whole people as his own vital concern.

Let us recall that soon after the victory of the October Revolution Lenin said that the exploitative system had left us a legacy of deep distrust on the part of the masses for anything that had to do with the state. 'It is very difficult to overcome this, and only a Soviet government can do it', he said. 'Even a Soviet government, however, will require plenty of time and enormous perseverance to accomplish it (*Collected Works*, Vol. 27, p. 253).

The Soviet government has coped with this task. The most striking confirmation of this is the tremendous extent of the active participation of the working people in discussing the draft of the new Constitution. We can say with confidence and pride that *it is the whole Soviet people who have in fact become the true creators of the Fundamental Law of their state*.

Allow me, comrades, on behalf of the USSR Supreme Soviet, whole-heartedly to thank all the participants in the nationwide discussion of the draft Constitution and to wish them new successes in their labour for the benefit of our great motherland and further and ever more active partici-pation in the affairs of our socialist state.

The Constitution Commission reports that *the nationwide discussion has made it possible to improve the draft Constitution significantly and to write into it a number of useful additions, clarifications and amend-ments*.

Altogether some 400,000 proposals for amendments to individual articles have been made for the purpose of clarifying, improving and supplementing the wording of the draft. Having made a careful study of these proposals — many of which, of course, recur — the Constitution Commission recommends that 110 articles of the draft should be amended and one new article added. The Commission's recommendations have been circulated among all deputies. My task is to substantiate the Commission's proposals on the most essential matters.

Let me start by saying that the greatest number of proposals that have come in bear on the vital question of *the role of labour under socialism*. The comrades suggest that the character of our society as a society of working people should be described in much more explicit terms in the Constitution.

I believe that this proposal has deep significance. Soviet society consists only of working classes and social groups. In view of this it is proposed that Article 1 of the Constitution should state that the Soviet state of the whole people shall express the will and interests of the workers, peasants and intelligentsia, of the *working people* of all the nations and nationalities of the country. At the same time, we should presumably also accept this proposal: to define in the Constitution not only the political foundation of the USSR, not only the foundation of our economic system, but also the *social foundation of our state*. We now have as such a foundation the unbreakable alliance of the working class, the collective-farm peasantry and people's intelligentsia, and this needs to be clearly stated.

The comrades have also proposed more precise wording of the article dealing with the foundation of the economic system of the USSR, in order *to make clearer the fact that this foundation consists of both state property and collective-farm and co-operative property*. That is quite correct. After all, it is these two forms of socialist ownership of the means of production that determine the character of our national economy and the division of Soviet society into the two friendly classes of workers and peasants. Such clarification has been provided for.

Several thousand proposals deal with the article *on the role and importance of work collectives*. Their authors have expressed the desire to have the Constitution reflect more broadly the functions and rights of work collectives, especially in such spheres as the planning of production

174

and social development, the training and appointment of personnel, the improving of working and living conditions for the working people, the raising of their skills and qualifications and the fostering of the communist attitude to work. This should be accepted.

The work collective and the work of the Party, trade union and Komsomol organisations reflect the whole life of our society — political and spiritual. Indeed, this is the primary cell of the whole of our organism, both economic and political. That is why we regard as correct the suggestions of those who feel that the article on the work collective would be better written into Chapter I of the Constitution, which describes our political system.

Thousands of proposals have been received suggesting that the Constitution state that *any evasion of socially useful labour is incompatible with the principles of socialist society*. People want stricter penalties for absenteeism and for those who seek unearned income. One cannot but support these just observations.

Very many comrades have written to say that the Constitution should lay special emphasis on the duty of citizens *to take proper care of the people's wealth*, of our socialist property, which is the product of the people's collective labour and the foundation for the development of our society as a whole. The Constitution Commission shares the working people's view on this matter and proposes that an addition should be made to the relevant article of the Fundamental Law.

Bearing in mind the remarks received, it is proposed to clarify the wording of some other articles in the section entitled 'The State and the Individual'. Thus, in response to the wishes of many people the article on the right to housing states that *it shall be the duty of citizens to take proper care of the housing allocated to them*. The article dealing with the citizen's duty to show concern for the upbringing of children now states that *children* also *are obliged to care for their parents and help them*. I should like to note that the proposals for such an addition have come not only from older people but also from many young people, and this is especially gratifying.

The nationwide discussion has made it possible to improve a number of provisions in the draft aimed *at the further development of socialist democracy*.

Many comrades, including deputies to local Soviets, have proposed the inclusion in the Constitution of an article covering *electors' mandates*. These mandates are an expression of the most diverse requirements of the population, reflecting the specific interests of individual groups of working people and of society as a whole. Fulfilment of these mandates is therefore an important part of the work of the Soviets and of their deputies. Suffice it to say that in the past 2 years alone more than 700,000 electors' mandates have been fulfilled. That is one of the real expressions of socialist democracy. It is important that not only deputies but also the heads of enterprises, collective farms, construction projects and offices should give due attention to the carrying out of mandates.

Account should be taken also of a number of other reasonable and appropriate proposals made by the working people on the further development of the democratic principles underlying the life in our state. Thus, it would presumably be in place to stipulate, as many have suggested, that, as a rule, *no citizen may be concurrently elected to more than two Soviets*. This will help facilitate the influx of fresh forces into state bodies and help to increase the number of people taking part in the administration of the affairs of state.

As you are aware from press reports, a lively debate developed during the nationwide discussion as regards *the age at which citizens should become eligible for election to the Soviet*. There has been broad support for the article of the draft which states that citizens who have reached the age of 18 should have the right to be elected to all the Soviets. But there have been proposals to set the age at 21, 23 and even 30.

The Constitution Commission, in considering this matter, acted on the assumption that work collectives and public organisations when nominating candidates for election as deputies thoroughly discuss their qualities and make high demands on them. This is a reliable guarantee that only the most worthy comrades capable of fulfilling the difficult duties of a deputy effectively will be elected to the Soviets. There are, of course, many such men and women among our young people. Hence the minimum age for election to all the Soviets, with the exception of the USSR Supreme Soviet, can be set at 18. Considering that the USSR Supreme Soviet has to take the most responsible decisions bearing on the interests of the whole state, the right to be elected to it can be granted to citizens at the age of 21.

A great many speeches and letters voice the opinion that the *principle of responsibility and accountability of government agencies and officials to the Soviets and to the people should be enforced more strictly*. This can fully be taken care of in the relevant articles by recording the duty of executive committees, deputies and other elected officers to report systematically to *their respective Soviets and to work collectives and meetings of citizens in their neighbourhoods*.

Lastly, many believe that the articles on the procedures governing the consideration of deputies' inquiries and citizens' proposals and on the responsibility of officials for any breach of the law and for taking an incorrect attitude to criticisms voiced by the working people should be formulated even more specifically. The Commission feels that this can be taken care of in the relevant articles of the Constitution.

Now, concerning some amendments relating to *the organisation and activity of state bodies*.

Some comrades would like to have made more explicit the provision dealing with *the powers of the Union and Autonomous Republics and local Soviets to ensure comprehensive economic and social development on their territory*. This can be accepted. The Constitution defines in sufficiently clear terms the responsibility of ministries and departments for the state of their respective sectors. It would presumably be appropriate to define as clearly the functions of those local bodies which ensure the smooth co-ordination of the work and comprehensive development of enterprises and social and cultural institutions in a given territory, no matter whose jurisdiction they are under.

Citizens' wishes are also being taken into account in making some other articles more specific, notably those on the competence of ministries and state committees and local bodies of state power, and those on the courts, arbitration bodies and the Procurator's Office.

The participants in the discussion have unanimously welcomed the inclusion in the draft Constitution of a special chapter on the aims and principles of the Leninist foreign policy of the USSR. In the context of this chapter, it has been proposed to add that the Soviet Union is striving for *general and complete disarmament*. This is, of course, quite right.

On the whole, the Constitution Commission recommends the Supreme Soviet to adopt, apart from the purely editorial changes, *some 150 amendments and clarifications to the text of the Constitution*. These actually reflect the views of a far greater number of citizens. Suffice it

177

to say that tens of thousands of proposals, similar in content, were made for one amendment to the article dealing with the citizens' duty to work.

On the other hand, comrades, among the submitted proposals there are some which *the Commission was unable to accept.*

For instance, very many citizens have proposed the inclusion in the Fundamental Law of various provisions which are already to be found in our legislation, thereby raising them to a constitutional level. Among these are proposals for setting definite dates for sessions of local Soviets and reporting schedules for deputies, for defining powers of certain administrative bodies, and for specifying penalties for various offences.

Many believe that their sector of work should be reflected in the new Constitution in greater detail. Hence, the mass of proposals for including in the text specific measures, for example, for improving legislation governing economic life and environmental protection, for improving the operation of the railways, for developing the material and technical facilities in the public health and education systems, and so on.

All these proposals, comrades, are understandable and most of them are doubtless correct in themselves. But the Constitution is the Fundamental Law of the state. It is a record only of the basic, fundamental provisions, which, while having direct force, are expressed and spelled out in other legislative acts. On the basis and in pursuance of these provisions various laws and prescriptions, i.e. current legislation, will be drafted and improved as necessary. In the course of this work the numerous concrete suggestions made during the discussion of the draft Constitution should be thoroughly considered and taken into account. Incidentally, regarding the question of public health, a draft decree is now being considered in the Central Committee on a comprehensive programme of measures to improve the protection of the people's health.

Let me also tell you about *the proposals which the Constitution Commission has found to be incorrect in substance.*

Some proposals have clearly run ahead of our time, failing to take account of the fact that the new Constitution is the Fundamental Law of a state of developed socialism and not of communism. We live according to the socialist principle 'From each according to his abilities, to each according to his work'. To by-pass this principle at the present level of economic development and the people's consciousness is impossible. That is why it is not possible, for instance, to accept proposals for the introduction of equal wages and pensions for everyone, or for determining their size solely on the basis of one's seniority at work, without taking account of standards of skill and the quality of workmanship.

There have also been proposals either to abolish or sharply limit subsidiary smallholdings. However, it is well known that the form of labour involved here, in which there is no exploitation, has a useful role to play in our economy at the present stage. That is why, in our opinion, the comrades are right who propose that the Constitution should emphasise that the state and the collective farms shall assist citizens in running their subsidiary smallholdings. Besides, those who oppose subsidiary small-holdings are clearly worried not so much by their existence as by their abuse for the purpose of profiteering, instances of which, regrettably, still occur. It is here that the state agencies concerned should firmly exercise the right of control given them by the Constitution, and see to it that the plots of land made available to citizens are used rationally, for the benefit of society, and that the incomes from subsidiary smallholdings and personal labour conform to the principles of socialism.

A new historical community — the Soviet people — has, as we know, taken shape in the USSR. Some comrades — it is true that they are not many — have drawn incorrect conclusions from this. They propose introducing in the Constitution the concept of an integral Soviet *nation*, eliminating the Union and Autonomous Republics or drastically curtailing the sovereignty of the Union Republics, depriving them of the right to secede from the USSR and of the right to maintain external relations. The proposals to do away with the Soviet of Nationalities and to set up a unicameral Supreme Soviet are along the same lines. I think that the erroneousness of the proposals is quite clear. The Soviet people's social and political unity does not at all imply the disappearance of national distinctions. Thanks to the consistent pursuance of the Leninist nationalities policy we have, simultaneously with the building of socialism, successfully solved the nationalities question, for the first time in history. The friendship of the Soviet peoples is indissoluble, and in the process of building communism they are steadily drawing ever closer together and their spiritual life is being mutually enriched. But we would be taking a dangerous path if we were artificially to step up this objective process of national integration. That is something Lenin persistently warned against, and we shall not depart from his precepts.

179

There has been a lively discussion of the article stipulating that the local Soviets are elected for a term of 2½ years. Many proposals would have it extended to 5 years, to enable deputies to acquire greater proficiency in the performance of their duties. But this would markedly reduce the number of working people going through the school of government in the Soviets. If a deputy elected for 2½ years has worked well, what is there to prevent his nomination for a second term? This, incidentally, is what is being done: more than 50 per cent of deputies are elected for a second term, and this helps to maintain continuity in the work of the Soviets. We feel, therefore, that this article should not be altered.

The Constitution Commission has also received letters proposing that state functions should be vested directly in Party bodies, that the Politburo of the CPSU Central Committee should be vested with legislative power, and so on. These proposals are profoundly erroneous because they introduce confusion into the understanding of the Party's role in our society and tend to obscure the importance and functions of the bodies of Soviet power.

When our Party became the ruling party, it firmly declared at its Eighth Congress, which was directed by Lenin, that it implemented its decisions 'through the Soviet bodies, *within the framework of the Soviet Constitution*'* and that, while guiding the Soviets, it did not supersede them, that it drew a line between the functions of Party and state bodies. This Leninist principle is recorded in the CPSU Rules, and was re-emphasised in the decisions of the latest Party congresses. We also propose to have it reflected in the new Constitution.

The Party conducts its policy on state matters primarily through the Communists elected by the people to the Soviets and those working in state bodies. It believes that one of its most important tasks is to do its utmost to consolidate and perfect the power of the Soviets and to further develop socialist democracy. This is a policy of principle to which we have adhered and to which we shall always adhere.

Comrades, the discussion of the Draft Constitution has in many respects gone well beyond the framework of an analysis of the text itself. It has developed into a frank commentary, truly by the whole people, on the key aspects of our life which are of immediate concern to all Soviet people.

* *The CPSU in Resolutions and Decisions of Its Congresses, Conferences and Plenary Meetings of the Central Committee*, Vol. 2, 8th ed., p. 77, in Russian.

Collectives of working people and individual citizens have made just and — not infrequently — sharply critical remarks on various aspects of the activity of state bodies and public organisations, proposing measures for improving their work and eliminating existing shortcomings.

Many letters call for a stronger drive against parasitism, habitual breaches of labour discipline, drunkenness and other anti-social phenomena which cut across the very substance of our socialist way of life. From this persistent demand voiced by the working people, definite conclusions should be drawn by all state organisations and public organisations.

Some letters report disgraceful instances of abuse by some persons in office of their position, instances of defrauding the state by means of falsifying records and cheating, of bribe-taking, of indifference and a formal approach to the requirements of working people, instances of persecution for criticism.

I should like to stress, comrades, that all reports of this kind are being thoroughly investigated for the purpose of taking the necessary measures, including punishment of the guilty persons with the full severity of the law. In general, I must say that the establishment of due order wherever it is violated in this country — in production, government or social life — would constitute a big step forward in the development of our society. By putting an end to such things as sloppy work, waste of socialist property, red tape and bureaucratic attitude to one's work and to people, we shall considerably accelerate the country's advance and improve the life of the whole people.

Many letters and speeches suggest the further strengthening and improvement of the people's control. That is right. And it will be promoted, in particular, by the Law on People's Control in the USSR, whose adoption is provided for by the new Constitution.

A number of letters recommend the introduction of a system of incentives in the form of longer holidays for those who have long worked honestly and efficiently for the benefit of society, for the front-rankers in production. And conversely, shorter holidays for those who wilfully take time out from their working hours, that is, to put it plainly, who loaf about and absent themselves from their work. The Committee on Labour and Social Questions, other departments, and the All-Union Central Council of Trade Unions should take account of these considerations when formulating measures to improve the system of holidays, drawing also on the relevant experience of the fraternal countries.

We believe that attention should be given to proposals on measures for further improving living conditions for Great Patriotic War veterans who saw active service, including those who are now retired on pension. The Party and the Soviet state, displaying constant concern for those who fought in the Great Patriotic War, have already done much in this area. Can additional funds be found to provide further benefits to those who secured the freedom and independence of our motherland in the most arduous of wars? I believe they can.

Some suggest additional benefits to mothers, and suggestions have been made to improve the system of medical care, to introduce stricter procedures for the allocation of housing, and some others. I think that the USSR Council of Ministers, together with the All-Union Central Council of Trade Unions, should make a thorough examination of our present resources and potentialities for meeting these wishes and report on the results to the Presidium of the USSR Supreme Soviet.

Such, comrades, are the main points which the Constitution Commission deemed it necessary to report in connection with the nationwide discussion of the draft Constitution of the USSR.

II

Comrade deputies,

The draft of our new Constitution and its nationwide discussion have long been in the focus of world attention. We might even say that the discussion has virtually assumed an international scale. We regard this as fresh evidence of the immense role of socialism in the world today.

Our friends in the fraternal socialist countries have widely discussed and enthusiastically supported the draft of the new Soviet Constitution. They have studied it closely and carefully, in a comradely and businesslike spirit. They have analysed it in detail and shared their experience with us. For this we are sincerely grateful to them.

The press in the socialist countries has given the draft wide coverage. It has assessed it as a document telling the world 'the truth about socialism and mankind's future', as 'a manifesto of the epoch of building communism'. Our comrades-in-arms — the leaders of the socialist community countries — have emphasised the great importance of the draft in outlining the development prospects for their countries.

It is acknowledged with satisfaction in socialist countries that the draft of the new Constitution of the USSR reflects in various forms elements characteristic of the constitutions of the fraternal countries just as the latter have drawn on the previous experience of Soviet legislation. In this way collective experience is gained in the building of the socialist state.

The new Soviet draft Constitution has been studied with keen interest *in the young states newly liberated from colonial bondage* and now choosing the path of their further development. Prominent leaders of these states have told representatives that they hope to benefit substantially by this draft, which sums up the 60-year experience of the world's first socialist country in developing its statehood. The press in many African, Asian and Latin American countries has widely commented on the draft and underscored in particular that the Soviet Union's accomplishments which it reflects are an inspiring example to all the peoples taking the socialist road.

The working people in the capitalist countries and above all their vanguard — the Communist and Workers' Parties — have shown an exceptional interest in the draft Constitution. The communist press has published detailed accounts of the draft, analysed it and highly assessed its significance. The fraternal parties have emphasised that it is a document of great importance showing what contemporary developed socialism is and what objectives it sets itself. The Soviet Union has made a giant step forward in its democratic development; the Soviet people have proved in practice the truth of the great ideas of Marx, Engels and Lenin: the draft Constitution contains extensive material for study, reflection and debate — such are the comments of Communists in the capitalist world for whom the new Constitution of the land of the October Revolution means assistance in their just struggle for the working people's cause.

On the whole, comrades, the lively comments, the great and sincere interest and warm approval of the draft of our Constitution by the working masses of the world fill our hearts with pride in the Soviet people's achievements and illustrate even more strikingly their great international significance.

Nor has the draft Constitution been ignored by *the bourgeois press and other mass media in the capitalist world.* Some of them have given more or less objective coverage of its content.

A number of Western newspapers have pointed out that the new Fundamental Law of the USSR signifies further development of democracy in the Soviet Union, broader rights for citizens and public organisations, and an increase in their influence on state policy. The American *Baltimore Sun* has frankly acknowledged that the draft guarantees Soviet citizens broader rights as compared with any Western Constitution: the right to work, rest, choice of occupation, social security, housing, education, free medical aid. State and political leaders and the press in the capitalist countries have admitted the importance of the fact that in the foreign-policy chapter of the Constitution, the Soviet Union has reaffirmed by statutory law its dedication to the cause of peace and international co-operation. The British *Financial Times* has described the draft Constitution as an 'historic document'. The West German *Süddeutsche Zeitung* has acknowledged the 'tremendous importance' of the draft.

The masterminds of imperialist propaganda, however, obviously became worried when the discussion of our Consititution assumed a broad international scale. On 13 June the West German *General-Anzeiger* frankly expressed its dissatisfaction over the fact that 'the West is now paying too much attention to the new Soviet draft Consititution'.

This is a repetition of what we have seen time and time again in the history of the Soviet state: a striking picture of the methods of imperialist propaganda. It is blind to the achievements of our great country, with its heroic history, vivid and many-sided culture, one of the world's highest educational standards, the vigorous joint creative activity of its numerous nations and peoples. All this has very little interest for 'psychological warfare' experts. Their sole object is to obstruct the growth of the influence of socialism on people's minds, to sow distrust and hostility towards it by whatever means. Hence the stereotyped inventions, shameless fabrications and blatant lies about the Soviet Union intended for ill-informed audiences, gullible readers, listeners and spectators. Hence the tendency not so much to give information about the new Soviet Constitution as to distort its content, minimise its importance and, whenever possible, ignore its major provisions altogether.

The clauses on the rights, freedoms and duties of Soviet citizens have been attacked with especial vehemence.

This has, of course, its own logic: indeed, it is precisely the idea of 'concern' for human rights that prominent leaders of the capitalist world have lately chosen as the main thrust of their ideological crusade against the socialist countries. The critics of the Soviet Constitution, however, have found themselves in an unenviable position. They cannot escape the fact that our draft Constitution defines the social, economic and political rights and freedoms of citizens and the specific guarantees of these rights more widely, clearly and fully than ever before and anywhere else.

What, indeed, can the apologists of the capitalist system oppose to these real achievements of developed socialism? What real rights and freedoms are guaranteed to the masses in present-day imperialist society?

The 'right' of tens of millions to unemployment? Or the 'right' of sick people to do without medical aid, the cost of which is enormous? Or the 'right' of ethnic minorities to humiliating discrimination in employment and education, in political and everyday life? Or is it the 'right' to live in perpetual fear of the omnipotent underworld of organised crime and to see how the press, cinema, TV and radio services are going out of their way to educate the younger generation in a spirit of selfishness, cruelty and violence?

Propagandists and ideologists of capitalism cannot deny that socialism has long since cured these social sores. They have resorted, therefore, to another manoeuvre. They have concentrated their attacks on those provisions of the draft of our Constitution which say that the exercise by citizens of their rights and freedoms must not injure the interests of society and the state, or the rights of other citizens, and that the exercise of one's rights and freedoms is inseparable from the performance of one's duties and obligations.

According to the draft Constitution, the rights of citizens may not be used to the detriment of socialist society and the state, which means, according to the Austrian newspaper *Salzburger Volksblatt*, that 'Soviet citizens have no rights at all'. That is logic for you!

The Italian *Corriere della Sera* does not like the fact that the draft speaks of the duty of Soviet citizens to observe the USSR Constitution, Soviet laws, and comply with the code of socialist conduct. 'All these restrictions', this mouthpiece of the Italian monopolies declares, 'practically nullify civil rights, at any rate as we understand them.' It follows that the exercise of civil rights in the USSR must consist in violations of the law!

Speaking in general, it seems that from the standpoint of our class adversaries Soviet citizens should evidently be granted one and only one 'right' — to fight against the Soviet state, against the socialist system so as to gladden the hearts of the imperialists. However, we must disappoint such 'critics' of our Constitution: the Soviet people will never comply with their wishes.

Our 'critics' pretend to be unaware of the fact that the provisions in the draft Constitution which evoke their dissatisfaction fully conform to fundamental international documents. Let us remind them of this fact: the UN Universal Declaration of Human Rights clearly states that 'everyone has duties to the community in which alone the free and full development of his personality is possible', and that the exercise of rights and freedoms by citizens requires 'due recognition and respect for the rights and freedoms of others and . . . meeting the just requirements of morality, public order and the general welfare in a democratic society'.

This is the principle of life in a democratic society recognised through-out the world. It is precisely this principle that is contained in the provisions of the new Constitution of the USSR, which have aroused the hypocritical indignation of our 'critics'.

Most bourgeois analysts have also criticised the provisions defining the role of the CPSU in the life of Soviet society. They have made much of the alleged 'proclamation of the dictatorship of the Communist Party', 'the primacy of the Party over the state', 'a dangerous intertwining of the Party and government institutions', 'the obliteration of the boundaries between the Party and the state'.

What can one say on this score? The motives for this attack are clear enough. The Communist Party is the vanguard of the Soviet people, their most conscious and progressive section inseparably united with the people as a whole. The Party has no interests other than the interests of the people. To try to counterpose the party to the people by talking about the 'dictatorship of the Party' is tantamount to trying to separate, say, the heart from the whole of the body.

As I have already said, the Communist Party operates within the framework of the USSR Constitution. Bourgeois critics, however, ignore this fact. They would like to weaken the role of the Party in Soviet society, since in general they hope to weaken our country, our socialist system and to extinguish our communist ideals. Fortunately, this is beyond their power. As the Soviet people tackle the increasingly complex and responsible tasks of building communism, the Communist Party will have a growing role to play. This leads not to restriction but to the increasingly profound development of socialist democracy in full conformity with our Party's Programme.

Here is another point. Some Western critics of our new Constitution try to attack it from the 'left', as it were, advancing theoretical arguments about the authors of the draft being inconsistent in their adherence to the Marxist doctrine of the withering away of the state under communism. The Italian *Il Messaggero* laments the fact that the Soviet Constitution has 'unconditionally discarded' the communist principle of 'the withering away of the state', whose role was to be taken over by public organisations. The *New York Times* complains that the Soviet state is unable and unwilling to wither away. It is seconded by the London *Times*, which says that there is no sign of any withering away of the state.

This concern of the ideologists of capitalism for our socialist state's development in accordance with the Marxist–Leninist doctrine is certainly touching. However, their anxiety is groundless. Developments are running the precise course predicted by the classics of Marxism and formulated by our Party in its policy statements.

Our critics from the bourgeois camp (and, frankly speaking, some comrades in the ranks of the international working class movement along with them) are unable or unwilling to see the main thing — the dialectics of the development of our state and society, namely that with the development and advancement of the socialist state millions of citizens are increasingly involved in the activities of government and people's control bodies, in the management of production and distribution, in social and cultural policies and in the administration of justice. In short, along with the development of socialist democracy our statehood is gradually being transformed into communist social self-government. This is, of course, a long process, but it is proceeding steadily. We are convinced that the new Soviet Constitution will contribute effectively to the attainment of this important goal of communist construction.

III

Comrades,

The new Constitution is justly called the law of life of developed socialist society. This is the society that has been built in the Soviet Union. Such a developed, mature socialist society is also being built successfully in a number of other countries of the socialist community. And it is very important to have a clear idea of its characteristic features and its place in the historical process of the establishment of the communist system.

It will be recalled that in the early Soviet years Lenin, looking into the future, spoke and wrote of 'complete', 'full', 'developed' socialism as a prospect, a goal of socialist construction.

This goal has now been attained. The experience of the Soviet Union and of the fraternal countries has demonstrated that laying the foundations of socialism, that is, abolishing the exploiter classes and establishing public ownership in all sectors of the national economy, does not yet allow direct transition to communism. Victorious socialism has to pass through definite stages in the process of maturing, and only developed socialist society makes it possible to embark on communist construction. What is more, as we know today, the development, the advancement of socialism is a task no less complicated, no less responsible, than the laying of its foundations.

A few figures give an idea of the distance separating the present and the initial stages in the development of socialism in our country.

In this year of 1977 it takes less than a month to produce the gross social product turned out during the whole of 1936. Since then the assets-to-man ratio in material production has grown 14-fold, the power-to-man ratio in industry almost 8-fold, and in agriculture more than 15-fold.

Not only technology but also the people who operate it have changed beyond recognition. Today, 73.2 per cent of the workers have a higher or secondary (complete or incomplete) education, whereas the respective figure 40 years ago was less than 8 per cent. Over this period the number of specialists with a higher or specialised secondary education has grown 34 times in industry and 47 times in agriculture.

The living standards of the Soviet people have improved spectacularly. Here are just two examples. In 1936 we built 14.9 million square metres of housing, whereas the figure for 1977 will be over 110 million. In 1936, payments and benefits from the social consumption funds *per capita* were 21 roubles, while the respective figure for this year is 382 roubles.

As you see, the distance covered is tremendous. However, not everything can be expressed in figures. Material and cultural progress on this scale has led to a considerable evening up of the conditions of work and life in town and country, in the spheres of mental and physical labour. New generations of Soviet people have grown up under socialism, have been educated, and have formed a socialist consciousness.

These are the processes the results of which entitle us to say that developed socialism has been built in the USSR — that stage of maturity of the new society at which the restructuring of the entire system of social relations on the collectivist principles intrinsic to socialism is being completed. Hence the full scope for the operation of the laws of socialism, for bringing to the fore its advantages in all spheres of the life of society. Hence the organic integrity and dynamic force of the social system, its political stability, its indestructible inner unity. Hence the drawing ever closer together of all the classes and social groups, all the nations and nationalities, and the formation of a historically new social and international community, the Soviet people. Hence the emergence of a new, socialist culture, the establishment of a new, socialist way of life.

Of course, only that socialist society can be described as developed which is based on a powerful, advanced industry and a large-scale, highly mechanised agriculture, for this in practice makes it possible for the ever fuller satisfaction of the multiform requirements of citizens to become the central and direct goal of social development. In the conditions of our country the task of building such a material and technological base, indispensible for mature socialism, had to be tackled after the foundations of the new system had been laid. Other countries which have taken the path of socialism with an underdeveloped or moderately developed economy will evidently have to follow the same road.

In countries which already have highly developed productive forces at the time of their victorious socialist revolution the situation will be different. But they too will have to solve such complicated problems in the building of mature socialism as mastering the difficult art of organising the entire life of society along socialist lines, and, in particular, the science of planning and managing the national economy, and developing a socialist consciousness in their citizens.

In short, whatever specific conditions may prevail in a country building socialism, the stage of its advancement on its own basis, the stage of mature, developed socialist society is an indispensable link in the chain of social transformations, a relatively long stage of development on the path from capitalism to communism. Moreover, to discern and make use of all the potentialities of developed socialism means at the same time a transition to building communism. The future does not lie beyond the limits of the present. The future has its roots in the present. And by fulfilling the tasks of the present day, of the socialist present, we are gradually approaching the morrow, the communist future.

As our experience has shown, the gradual development of the state of proletarian dictatorship into a state of the whole people is one of the results of the complete triumph of socialist social relations. The Soviet Union today is a natural, inevitable stage in the development of the state born of the October Revolution — a stage characteristic of mature socialism. Consequently, the tasks of the state institutions, their structure, functions and work procedure should conform to the stage attained in the development of society.

The new Constitution of the USSR guarantees such conformity. By adopting it we shall have every right to say that another important step has been taken to bring our country nearer to the great goals of our Party and our people.

Comrades, exactly 20 years ago, on 4 October, mankind took its first step into outer space. This was heralded by the artificial earth satellite created by the genius and hands of Soviet people. The whole world could see what an 'alliance of the scientists, the proletariat and the technologists' about which Lenin dreamed at the dawn of the Soviet period was capable of. This alliance has found its embodiment in the practice of socialist construction in our country and has become a mainspring of the spectacular accomplishments of developed socialism.

The discussion of the draft Constitution has once again demonstrated the strength and vitality of the unity of all classes and social groups, of all nations and nationalities, all generations of Soviet society rallied around the Communist Party.

Millions upon millions of working people in town and country have supported the new Fundamental Law by word and by deed. They checked every line in the draft against their own practical work, against the work of their work collectives. They made further socialist pledges, amended production plans, searched for new reserves for raising production efficiency and improving work performance, and welcomed their new Constitution with signal labour accomplishments. In short, our people have again shown themselves to be the full masters of their socialist homeland. Honour and glory to the heroic Soviet people, the builders of communism!

Comrade deputies, permit me to express my confidence that the Supreme Soviet, after having discussed the draft Constitution of the USSR, will approve it, thereby equipping the Soviet people with a new powerful instrument for building communism.

Report on the draft Constitution of the USSR at the Seventh (Special) Session of the USSR Supreme Soviet. (The proposed Constitution was adopted and came into force on 7 October 1977.) 4 October 1977

Comrades,

Both chambers of the USSR Supreme Soviet have completed the discussion of the draft Constitution of the USSR. A total of ninety-two deputies spoke, representing all sections of the people, all the Union Republics and many of the Autonomous Republics.

The Editorial Commission, formed in accordance with your decision, is glad to note that all the speakers, as well as the deputies who submitted their proposals in writing, have expressed wholehearted support for the draft Constitution. Speaking on behalf of millions of their electors, they have clearly and firmly come out in favour of its adoption. This is the main outcome of our thorough discussion.

At the same time, a number of deputies have suggested certain amendments and additions. Having carefully considered their suggestions, the

Editorial Commission has come to the conclusion that most of them should be accepted. Our Constitution will only benefit from this.

For example, Deputy V. D. Postnikov, a steelworker from the Moscow Region, suggests that the Constitution should not confine itself to listing the types of property that may be personally owned by citizens, but should emphasise that the *basis of personal property consists in earned incomes*. We believe that this is a good point. It expresses our attitude to the nature and origin of personal property under socialism, where socially useful work is the source of the increasing well-being of the people and of every individual.

Deputies V. G. Meunargia, a machine operator on a farm in Georgia, and I. Y. Prokofiev, a rolling mill operator from Leningrad, suggest that it should be said in the Constitution that the Soviet state *encourages innovation and a creative attitude to work*, and that it *organises the introduction in the economy of inventions and innovations*. We are all aware of the tremendous importance of a creative attitude to work and of technical innovations by the masses for the development of the country's economy and the communist education of the people. Therefore the suggestions are acceptable, and the appropriate additions are being introduced in Articles 14 and 47.

Deputy P. F. Lomako, Minister of Non-Ferrous Metallurgy, suggests that it should be said in the Constitution that the Soviet state is continuously *improving the forms and methods of economic management*. Deputy D. P. Galkin, director of the Magnitogorsk Iron and Steel Mills, thinks it could be stated that our economy is developing with the active use, not only of cost accounting, profit and cost, but also of *other economic levers and forms of economic stimulation*.

These proposals correctly reflect the substance of the Party's economic strategy, aimed at increasing the effectiveness of production and improving the quality of work, and they deserve to be included in the Constitution.

Deputy A. V. Gitalov, leader of a tractor team in the Kirovograd Region, suggests that it should be stated in the Constitution in clear-cut terms that *collective farms and other land users have an obligation to use the land effectively, to treat it with care, and to increase its fertility*. I believe that we should support the proposal of this famous Ukrainian tractor driver. Land is a most valuable possession of ours, but it must be skilfully used. Land, as they say, is a mother to the diligent and a stepmother to the idle.

An important question has been raised by Deputy V. V. Nikolayeva-Tereshkova, Chairman of the Soviet Women's Committee, and Deputy Z. P. Pukhova, director of the Ivanovo Weaving Mill. They suggest adding to Article 35 that *the working time of women who have small children will be gradually reduced*. We consider that this proposal can be accepted. It is in keeping with the aim of the Party and the Soviet state to consistently improve woman's status as a worker, mother and home-maker in keeping with the development of the requisite economic conditions.

The Editorial Commission considers that we should also accept the proposal of Deputy M. K. Andrievsky, the head of a boarding school in the Poltava Region, that it should be specified in Article 42 that the ban on child labour is meant to protect the health of children, but on no account rules out training and education in work, which have always been and always will be a most important task of ours.

Deputies A. B. Chakovsky and R. G. Gamzatov suggest in their speeches that the Soviet citizen's right to the use of cultural gains and to creative freedom should be shown more fully. These writers suggest that it should be said that this right is secured by *the development of television and radio, book publishing and the periodical press, and the network of free libraries*, while making special mention of the role of *literature*. These specific points seem to be correct.

A related proposal has been made by Deputy M. T. Amantayeva, a schoolteacher in Kazakhstan, who suggests that it should be stated that cultural values must be used for *the ethical and aesthetic education of Soviet people*. The inclusion of these provisions in the Constitution will give a fuller idea of the tasks of the state in the cultural field and in the communist education of the people.

The Editorial Commission considers that it should also accept the suggestions of Deputy Grigory Vasilyevich Romanov and of Deputy K. I. Lushnevsky, Chairman of the Executive Committee of a District Soviet in Byelorussia, to add the provision that *the Soviets of People's Deputies and the organs they set up must systematically inform the general public about their work and about the decisions taken*. This will emphasise an important principle in the work of the Soviets, which, to use Lenin's words, were 'an authority open to all, carrying out all their functions before the eyes of the masses'.

Deputy M. S. Gorbachov, First Secretary of the Party Committee of the Stavropol Territory, considers that the relationship between the commission of the USSR Supreme Soviet and its chambers, and other public organisations should be defined in greater detail, describing more clearly the procedure for implementing the recommendations of the commissions. Accordingly, it should be pointed out in Article 125 that *recommendations of the commissions of the USSR Supreme Soviet and its chambers are subject to consideration by state and public organs, institutions and organisations.*

Comrades, the above is a summing-up by the Editorial Commission of the main suggestions made by deputies during the discussion on the draft Constitution of the USSR in the Supreme Soviet. The Commission has submitted to you the text of the draft, including all the suggested amendments.

I believe that now the USSR Supreme Soviet could begin the work endorsing the new Fundamental Law of our state.

> *Report to the USSR Supreme Soviet*
> *on the Editorial Commission's work*
> *in preparing the draft Constitution of*
> *the USSR. 7 October 1977*

Comrade deputies,

Expressing the will of the Soviet people, and in fulfilment of its mandate, the USSR Supreme Soviet has adopted the new Constitution of the Union of Soviet Socialist Republics. The Fundamental Law of the world's first socialist state of the whole people has been approved. A new historical frontier in our advance towards communism — the construction of a developed socialist society — has been constitutionally established.

Years and decades will pass, but this day in October will always remain in the people's memory as vivid evidence of the genuine triumph of the Leninist principles of the exercise of power by the people. The further our society advances along the path towards communism, the more fully will the tremendous creative potentialities of socialist democracy, power in the hands of the people, and power exercised in the interests of the people, as reflected in the new Constitution, be revealed.

The Central Committee of the CPSU and the Presidium of the USSR Supreme Soviet believe that there is good reason to mark the day of the adoption of the Soviet Union's new Constitution as one of the major events in the life of the Soviet people. Accordingly, a draft law declaring 7 October to be a holiday of the whole people — USSR Constitution Day — is being submitted for your consideration.

Now that the Constitution has been approved, it is necessary to define clearly in a special Law the procedure for putting it into effect. A draft Law has been put before you for your consideration. It provides that all legislative acts adopted before the entry into force of the Constitution shall remain in effect, in so far as they do not conflict with the new Constitution of the USSR.

In addition, subject to the provisions of the adopted Constitution, it is proposed to extend the powers of the USSR Supreme Soviet of the 9th convocation, and accordingly alter the terms of office of Republic and local bodies of state power elected before the adoption of the new Constitution.

Further, it is intended to authorise the Presidium of the USSR Supreme Soviet and the USSR Council of Ministers to draft the necessary legislative acts pursuant to the text of the Constitution, and also to authorise Soviets of People's Deputies, ministries and departments, and the heads of other state and public bodies to consider the proposals and remarks submitted by citizens in the course of the nationwide discussion of the draft Constitution of the USSR on matters relating to the activity of these bodies, and to take action to implement them.

With the adoption of this Law, that is, from today, the Constitution takes effect, and begins to live and to work.

What does this mean?

It means that its every article and provision must enter fully into the living, practical day-to-day activity of all state bodies, all persons in office, and all Soviet citizens everywhere. We have not created the

Constitution as a stage prop. It has to be fulfilled, and will be fulfilled in all its parts. It has to become and will become a powerful instrument in the further development and deepening of socialist democracy.

All of us, comrades, have witnessed the great upsurge of creative initiative and labour and political activity generated by the discussion of the new Constitution. We must not let this activity subside, but must see to it that it is developed further, assuming the concrete forms of ever broader participation by citizens in the affairs of state of the whole people. Our Party has displayed and will continue to display constant concern to ensure that the working people not merely possess the opportunities afforded by the Constitution for taking part in the administration of society, but are actually able to take part in it.

The great Lenin taught Communists to give the working people the assistance necessary for them to exercise their very broad socialist rights and freedoms. And the Party, mindful of this precept of Lenin's as well, has been consistently working to implement it.

We want the citizens of the USSR to know well their rights and freedoms, and the ways and methods of exercising them; we want them to be able to apply these rights and freedoms in the interests of the building of communism, and to have a clear understanding of their close connection with honest fulfilment of their civic duties. It is an important task of the Party and state bodies and public organisations responsible for the communist education of the working people to promote this and to help every citizen achieve a high level of political awareness.

Furthermore, the coming into force of the Constitution entails fulfilment of an extensive programme of legislative work. This includes, as I have already mentioned, the preparation of a number of new legislative acts, whose adoption is directly provided for in the Constitution or follows from it. These are key acts such as the Rules and Regulations of the Supreme Soviet, the election law, the laws on citizenship, and on the procedures governing the conclusion, execution and abrogation of international treaties, and also a number of other acts which are to be drafted in the Presidium of the Supreme Soviet and in the Standing Commissions of the Chambers.

Much work will have to be done in developing the legislation governing administrative bodies. One important act of this nature to be formulated is the Law on the USSR Council of Ministers. There is need to give general thought as to how best to reflect in legislation the measures mapped out by the 25th Congress of the CPSU for perfecting the methods employed in the administration of the economy, for the comprehensive solution of large-scale nationwide, intersectoral and territorial problems, and for setting up systems for administering groups of homogeneous sectors of the economy.

The adoption of the Constitution makes it necessary to introduce a number of amendments and additions to current legislation. This work will take time, but it should not be delayed. And here, comrades, use can and should be made of the many concrete remarks and wishes expressed by the working people in the course of the discussion of the draft Constitution.

Attention should be given, in particular, to the proposals for adopting Union fundamentals on housing legislation and Republic housing codes, and for establishing in normative acts the rights of work collectives, the duties of parents in bringing up and educating their children, and so on.

Of course, improvement of the legislation will involve not only Union but also Republic legislation. This work will be based on the new Constitutions of the Union and Autonomous Republics, which are already in the drafting stage.

The increasing social, political and labour activity of Soviet citizens and further development and renovation of our legislation make new and higher demands on all bodies of power. From this stems the need for a considerable improvement in the style and methods of work of all our state bodies, both central and local, of all ministries and departments, offices and organisations.

Here special attention should be given to enhancing the responsibility and initiative of every link and of every person working in the state apparatus, to the most scrupulous observance of discipline in planning and finance and state affairs in general, and to displaying greater attention to the creative initiatives of the working people, and to their needs and problems.

The whole sense of our Constitution, every letter, aim at ensuring that the history-making activity of the masses of the people is supported in every way and that it will steadily grow. The greater creative activity of the masses is inseparably connected with the development of socialist democracy. A sure sign of this is the many reports received by this session of the Supreme Soviet in recent days about the new victories on the labour front in factories, building projects and collective farms. Nothing could be more convincing as an expression of the support of the working people for their new Constitution. Honour and glory to the foremost workers of this 5-year-plan period!

Finally, comrades, the coming into force of the new Constitution imposes an even greater responsibility on our Leninist Party, the leading and guiding force of Soviet society. The constitutional consolidation of this role of the Party does not impart any privileges to its members. On the contrary, it imposes even greater duties upon them. Allow me, on behalf of the CPSU Central Committee and of our whole Party, to assure you, comrade deputies, that the Soviet Communists will always bear this in mind, wherever they may work.

The whole experience of the 60 years of our development along the path of the October Revolution confirms that our strength lies in the unbreakable unity of the Party and the people. This is the source of the further flourishing of socialist democracy and of all our victories. This is the guarantee of the full triumph of communism. Let us, therefore, do our utmost to strengthen and consolidate this great unity!

Closing speech at the Seventh
(Special) Session of the USSR
Supreme Soviet. 7 October 1977

Dear comrades,

Esteemed foreign guests,

The Soviet people, Communists of all countries and all progressive mankind are now celebrating a great anniversary. Sixty years ago, led by the Party founded by Lenin, the workers and peasants of Russia over-threw the power of the capitalists and landowners. That was the first victorious socialist revolution in world history.

Those unforgettable days in October shook the entire world. A new epoch, the epoch of the world's revolutionary rebirth, the epoch of transition to socialism and communism, was ushered in. It opened the road along which hundreds of millions of people are marching today and upon which the whole of mankind is destined to embark.

We were the first. And things had not been easy for us. We had to stand firm while being encircled by hostile forces. We had to break the shackles of centuries-old backwardness. We had to overcome the enormous force of historical inertia and learn to live in accordance with new principles — the principles of collectivism.

And today, as we sum up the main result of six decades of struggle and work, we can say with pride: We have held our ground; we have stood fast and won . . .

I. THE SOVIET UNION IN THE VANGUARD OF SOCIAL PROGRESS

Comrades, every time we celebrate the anniversary of the October Revolution we perceive anew its significance and its great impact on the course of history, on the destiny of the world.

Understandably, the problems solved by the October Revolution were primarily Russia's problems, posed by its history, by the concrete conditions existing in it. But basically, these were not local but general problems, posed before the whole of mankind by social development. The epochal significance of the October Revolution lies precisely in the fact that it opened the road to the solution of these problems and thereby to the creation of a new type of civilisation on earth.

The October Revolution proved that a radical change of society's political foundations was possible. The proletariat of Russia gave the answer to the most urgent, the most important political question, namely, whether the exploiters' monopoly of power was unchangeable or whether it could and should be replaced by the power of the working people.

The six decades of socialist construction most vividly demonstrate what can be achieved by working people who have taken over political guidance of society and have assumed responsibility for their country's destiny. These decades have proved that there is no way, nor can there be a way to socialism without the working people taking over power, without socialist statehood.

The victory of the October Revolution gave working people their first opportunity to put an end to exploitation and free themselves from the bondage of economic anarchy. This key problem of social progress was resolved through the abolition of private property and its replacement with public property. Anarchy of production gave way to scientific, planned economic management.

Within an historically short period of time, a huge backward country was turned into a state with a highly developed industry and collectivised agriculture. It now takes only 2½ working days for our industry to produce as much as was produced in the whole year of 1913. Today the Soviet Union's industrial output is greater than that of the whole world a quarter of a century ago. The gigantic economic growth of history's first socialist country is the result of labour freed from exploitation, the result of the labour of people who are aware that they are working for themselves, for the common good.

The October Revolution and socialism have also enriched the history of mankind by bringing about the intellectual and cultural emancipation of working people. One of the 'secrets' of the oppressors' rule has always consisted in reinforcing direct physical oppression of the masses with spiritual oppression. The ruling classes did all they could to make it difficult for the working people to gain access to education and cultural values, to make them captives of false ideas and concepts. That is why the cultural revolution was a natural continuation of the political revolution in our country.

Within the lifetime of a single generation, the Soviet land liberated itself completely and for ever from the onerous burden of illiteracy. The working people began to take an active part in cultural life; they became the creators of cultural values. A new, socialist intelligentsia has emerged from the midst of the people, and has brought fame and glory to their country with outstanding achievements in science, technology, literature and art. A union which the best minds in history had dreamed of, the historic union of labour and culture, has taken place. In the history of our country, in the history of world culture, this marks an event of tremendous significance.

Among the notable achievements of the October Revolution is the solution of the nationality question, one of the most poignant and sensitive questions in the history of human society.

While calling for a militant alliance of the working people of all nations and nationalities of our country, the Party and Lenin had always upheld the right of nations to self-determination, to complete and unconditional equality. The victory of the October Revolution was thus also a victory in the struggle for national liberation. The peoples of former tsarist Russia, for the first time, had the possibility of making an historical choice, the right to determine their own destiny.

They made their choice. They united voluntarily to form a powerful federal state and, relying on the disinterested assistance of the Russian people, they resolutely embarked upon the building of a new life.

The unity of the nations and their mutual assistance accelerated the development of all the republics at unprecedented rates. Hostility and mistrust in the relations between nations gave way to friendship and mutual respect. Internationalism was firmly established in place of the psychology of national arrogance that had been implanted for ages. Mutually enriched national cultures, forming an integral Soviet socialist culture, shone forth with fresh, vivid colours.

The equality, fraternity and unbreakable unity of the Soviet peoples became a fact. A new historical community, the Soviet people, emerged. The increasing process of the drawing together of nations is seen in every sphere of life in our society. Such, comrades, is the outstanding result of the Leninist nationality policy; such is our experience, the epochal significance of which is indisputable.

The establishment of the principles of social equality and justice is one of the greatest achievements of the October Revolution. We have every right to say that no other society in the world has done or could have done as much for the masses, for the working people, as has been done by socialism. Every Soviet citizen enjoys in full the rights and freedoms enabling him to participate actively in political life. Every Soviet citizen has the possibility to choose a road in life that conforms to his intentions and abilities, and to do work that is useful to his country and people.

The conditions under which Soviet people live and work are steadily improving. Soviet citizens do not know the humiliating feeling of uncertainty about the morrow, the fear of being left without work, without medical care and without a roof over their heads. Society safeguards their rights and interests and upholds their civic and human dignity.

Conscientiousness in work, a high sense of civic duty and high ideological and moral qualities are what determine a person's standing and prestige in our country. Herein lies an inexhaustible source of the creative initiative and intellectual growth of the individual. This is the most convincing proof of social justice and social equality.

A new Constitution of the Soviet Union was adopted recently. It reaffirms that in our country the prime purpose of all transformations, of all changes is to provide every person with conditions of living that are worthy of man. It gives further convincing proof that concepts of freedom, of human rights, democracy and social justice become truly meaningful only under socialism.

Comrades, the victory of the Great October Socialist Revolution has put our country and our people in the vanguard of social progress. Today, 60 years later, we hold a worthy place in its most advanced areas. We have been the first in the world to build a developed socialist society, and we are the first to have embarked upon the building of communism.

In accordance with the Party's policy economic development is being more and more oriented towards carrying out the many tasks that are directly linked with improving the conditions of life and work of the Soviet people.

There has also been noteworthy progress in the solution of such a different problem as housing, which requires huge outlays. One-third of all the housing built in the years of Soviet power has been constructed during the past decade. In those 10 years, 110 million Soviet people have experienced the joy of moving into new apartments.

Large resources have been allocated for the expansion of the consumer goods industry. During the past 10 years this industry has nearly doubled its output and has considerably improved the quality and assortment of goods. The retail trade turnover has also doubled. The Soviet people's need for many durables that were only recently regarded as being in short supply is now being satisfied.

Economic growth has made it possible substantially to raise wages and build up social consumption funds. During the past 10 years the real incomes of Soviet people have grown by 60 per cent. I should like to call attention to the fact that the living standards and the conditions of everyday life in rural communities have improved appreciably.

When looking into the future, we have to draw yet another conclusion. The Soviet people's level of political consciousness, culture and civic responsibility will have an ever greater part to play in every sphere of life and in the development of our society. One of the primary tasks is to foster in our citizens a desire to attain great social goals, ideological conviction and a truly creative attitude to work. This is a very important area of struggle for communism, and the course of economic construction and the country's socio-political development will be increasingly dependent on our successes in this area.

As you see, we have many problems ahead, and these are big problems. But the strength of socialism lies precisely in the fact that the new social system makes it possible not only to anticipate such problems but also to draw up plans in advance for their solution.

Comrades, the Soviet people look confidently to the future. They are sure that life will continue to improve, and become more beautiful and more meaningful. An earnest of this is the dedicated work of millions of men and women inspired by the ideals of communism. An earnest of this is the Communist Party's Leninist, scientifically substantiated policy.

For each of us Leninist Communists, it is a source of the highest satisfaction that the Soviet people link all their achievements and victories with the Party. That is quite natural because the Party is inseparable from the people. In its ranks are the finest representatives of the working class, the collective-farm peasantry and the people's intelligentsia. It enjoys the people's complete confidence.

But comrades, the confidence of the people places great responsibility on us. That is why every decision of the Party, every step it takes in the political, organisational and ideological and educational fields has to be such as to strengthen still further the unity of the Party and the people, and to ensure that the people's trust in the Party will remain strong in the future as well.

Our Party has everything needed to carry out its historical responsibility. We are inspired by the noble goal of promoting the people's well-being. We have many years of experience in building a new life. Our actions are guided by Marxism–Leninism, a science which incorporates within it all the achievements of the human mind. We are confident of our strength.

The great march begun in October 1917 and the great struggle for communism continue. Lenin wrote that 'since we are out to fight, we must desire victory and be able to point out the right road to it'. (*Collected*

Works, Vol. 9, p. 57) We do desire victory. We do know the road to it. And we shall attain victory and reach communism!

Report at a joint celebration meeting of the Central Committee and the Supreme Soviets of the USSR and the RSFSR. 2 November 1977

The sixtieth year of the Great October Socialist Revolution will command a special place in the history of the Soviet Union. It is the year of the new Constitution of the USSR, which reflects all that has been achieved by the revolutionary transforming activity of the Party and the people since the victory of October and gives a clear perspective of further communist construction.

The new Fundamental Law of the USSR is a result of the creative endeavour of great masses of the working people. It embodies their experience, knowledge and will, their concern for the prosperity of their socialist motherland, for the growth of its international prestige.

The great Lenin, defining the basic principles of construction of the socialist state, said that its Constitution 'embodies what experience has already given, and will be corrected and supplemented as it is being put into effect' (*Collected Works*, Vol. 28, p. 36). The main thing that life has given our people in the more than 40 years that have passed since the adoption of the previous Soviet Constitution is the building of a developed socialist society, the creation of the world's first state of the whole people.

I

A developed socialist society is a natural stage in the socio-economic maturing of the new system in the framework of the first phase of the communist formation. This, to use Lenin's words, is the fully established socialism from which the gradual transition to communism begins. This is precisely the stage in the development of socialism that has been achieved in our country.

When the Marxist–Leninist classics, lifting the curtain of time, charted the contours of socialism and communism they were extremely careful. Not a grain of utopia. No flights of fantasy. Only what could be scientifically proved: the basic trends of development, the main, fundamental characteristics. Theoretically it was clear that the transition from capitalism to communism would embrace a long historical period, that the new society would rise from one stage of maturity to the next. But no one could tell in advance what concretely these stages would be. Engels wrote that the question of the stages of transition to communist society 'is the most difficult of any that exist . . . '*

Lenin and the Communists of Russia were the first who had to answer that question. It is understandable that Lenin's attention was focused mainly on the immediate tasks of that period, on creating the foundations of the new social system. But genius always anticipates its age. Already at the dawn of Soviet power Lenin spoke of 'accomplished', 'full' and 'developed' socialism as the perspective, the goal of the socialist construction that had been launched. It was these ideas of Lenin's that formed the basis of the conception of developed socialist society evolved by the collective efforts of the CPSU and other fraternal parties.

The experience of the USSR, of other countries of the socialist community, testifies to the fact that laying the foundations of socialism, that is, abolishing the exploiting classes and establishing public ownership of the means of production in all sectors of the national economy, does not yet make it possible to launch the direct transition to communism. Before this certain stages in the development of socialism on its own basis must be traversed. Moreover, practice has shown that the development, the perfecting of socialism is a task no less complex, no less responsible than the laying of its foundations.

It is self-evident that a mature socialist society must rest *on highly developed productive forces, on a powerful, advanced industry, on a large-scale, highly mechanised agriculture built on collectivist principles.* Such today is the Soviet economy which, both in scale and technical capability, differs fundamentally from what we had four decades ago,

*Letter to Konrad Schmidt, Zürich, 1 July 1891.

when socialist production relations had already prevailed in town and country.

In this period the gross social product increased 18-fold, the power-to-man ratio in industry nearly 8-fold, and in agriculture more than 15-fold. Our economy today is inconceivable without nuclear power, electronics, computers, transistors and many other industries that in 1936 we did not possess. The share of the industries determining technological progress and economic efficiency in the total volume of industrial output has more than tripled.

In the initial stages of socialist construction Soviet people had to concentrate their resources and efforts on the most urgent tasks, on things that the very existence of our state depended on. Today, in the conditions of developed socialism, on the basis of the constant growth of the whole national economy, the combination of the scientific and technological revolution with the advantages of the socialist organisation of society, it has been possible to achieve a perceptible swing of the economy towards ever fuller satisfaction of the people's many and diverse material and cultural requirements. In other words, the supreme goal of socialist production today is becoming directly central to the Party's practical policy. The historical advantages of socialism as a mode of production and way of life, its genuinely humane essence are thus more fully and dramatically revealed.

The Soviet people's material and spiritual life has risen to a new, incomparably higher level. Their real incomes have increased more than 5-fold in comparison with 1936. The general culture and education of the Soviet person, who, not for nothing, is known as 'the world's biggest reader', have substantially increased. Nearly 10 million people — over seven times more than 40 years ago — are at present studying in our higher and specialised secondary schools; the transition to universal secondary education has been accomplished in the main. The labour of industrial and agricultural workers, of all Soviet people has become more creative and meaningful. Several generations of working people have already grown up and been nurtured in the spirit of collectivism and comradely mutual assistance in the condition of victorious socialism, never having experienced the oppressive, traumatic atmosphere of an exploitative society. The scientific materialist world-view has become firmly established in the social consciousness.

At the stage of developed socialism, as our experience has shown, there is a considerable *rise in the level of socialisation of the economy and a steady drawing together of state (the whole people's) and collective farm–co-operative forms of socialist property.* In recent years this has been actively promoted by the Party's line of deepening specialisation and concentration of agricultural production on the basis of interfarm co-operation and agro-industrial integration, a line developing the ideas of Lenin's co-operative plan in their application to present-day conditions. More than 7000 interfarm organisations and amalgamations set up by the joint efforts of state enterprises and collective farms are functioning in the country today. This is a new phenomenon in our socio-economic practice.

Profound changes have also taken place in the social structure of Soviet society. The Soviet working class, which is its leading force, today totals more than 70 million people, or two-thirds of the gainfully employed population (whereas in 1936 it was only one-third). The workers' social activity and political maturity, their participation in government are constantly growing. The proportion of workers among deputies of the Soviets at all levels has increased five-fold over the past 40 years and now stands at more than 42 per cent. Their general educational and professional training is constantly improving. Today 73.2 per cent of workers have a higher or secondary (not less than 8 years) education, whereas 40 years ago the figure was less than 8 per cent. A production worker of a new type, harmoniously combining physical and mental work, is growing up in the conditions of developed socialism and under the influence of the scientific and technological revolution.

Our collective-farm peasantry has also changed considerably. In social status it is coming steadily closer to the working class and its educational level and way of life now differ little from those of the urban population. A collectivist psychology, a high ideological level and dedication to the cause of socialism and communism are the characteristic features of today's peasant, born and brought up in the collective farm.

Our intelligentsia, replenished mainly by workers and peasants, gives all its creative energy to the building of the new society. This is the fastest growing contingent of the Soviet working people. The past four decades have seen a 34-fold increase in the number of people with a higher or specialised secondary education in industry, and a 47-fold increase in agriculture.

Socialism has developed in Soviet people a sense of being the true masters of their country, it has fostered in them an urge to master the Leninist science and art of managing all social life on socialist principles. The broad masses of the working people have become an unfailing source of the formation of socialist cadres. These are people who organically combine party spirit and thorough knowledge, keen political awareness and a well-developed feeling for the new, an ability to assess their own activities critically and listen attentively to the voice of the masses.

In the process of building developed socialism the social basis of the socialist system in our country has expanded. The alliance of the working class and the collective-farm peasantry has developed in the solid political and ideological unity of these classes with the people's intelligentsia, which has now fully adopted the positions of socialism. The unbreakable alliance of workers, peasants and intellectuals, of all who are engaged in either physical or mental labour, is the prime source and guarantee of further success in communist construction.

The formation of a historically new social and international community — the Soviet people — has become an important symbol of developed socialism in our country, an indicator of the growing homogeneity of Soviet society, the triumph of the nationalities policy of the CPSU. This means that the common features of Soviet people's behaviour, character and world-view, which do not depend on social and national distinctions, are gradually assuming importance in our country.

Thanks to the convergence of the diverse forms of socialist property, the gradual obliteration of any essential distinctions between town and country, between mental and physical labour, and adoption by all working people of the ideological and political positions of the working class, the interests and goals, the social ideals and psychology of all strata of the population have drawn closer together than ever before. On this basis substantial changes have also occurred in the political system. Essentially they consist of *the growing of the state of the dictatorship of the proletariat into a socialist state of all the people.*

Such are the objective processes that led our Party to the conclusion that *developed socialism has now been built in the USSR, that is to say, a degree, a stage in the maturing of the new society has been reached when the repatterning of the totality of social relations on the collectivist principles intrinsically inherent in socialism is completed.* Full scope for the functioning of the laws of socialism, for the manifestation of its advantages in all spheres of social life, the organic integrity and dynamism of the social systems, its political stability and indestructible intrinsic unity — such are the major distinguishing features of the developed socialist society. It stands to reason that the principle of distribution according to labour still holds good even at this stage of the development of the new system, and will continue to do so for some time.

We proceed from the fact that cognition and use of all the opportunities offered by developed socialism mark, simultaneously, transition to the building of communism. In other words, the dialectics of development are such that as the mature socialist society perfects itself it gradually grows into a communist society. It is impossible to divide these two processes, to draw a line between them.

We are profoundly convinced that *no matter what the specific conditions in the countries building socialism may be, the stage of its perfection on its own basis, the stage of mature, developed socialism is the essential link between social transformations, a relatively long period of development on the road from capitalism to communism.* It stands to reason that this necessity, this regularity will be embodied in their own way in the conditions of the various socialist countries.

In the USSR the task of building a suitable material and technical basis for developed socialism had to be accomplished after the foundations of the new system had been laid. Evidently this is the common road for all countries that initiate socialist transformations with a weak or medium developed economy. In countries that by the time their socialist revolution is victorious will have highly developed productive forces, the position will, of course, be different in many ways. But even they, undoubtedly, will have to solve such complex problems of building and perfecting mature socialism as, for example, mastering the difficult science of organising all social life on socialist principles, including the science of economic planning and management, the bringing together of all classes and social groups on the basis of the socialist interests and communist ideals of the working class, fostering the socialist consciousness, perfecting and developing socialist statehood and democracy.

II

Socialist democracy is one of the world-historic gains of the Great October. Democracy has revealed itself for the first time in its true meaning, that is, as the power of the people. For the first time real civil and political equality of rights has been won by those who never experienced it under any exploitative system — the working people. For the first time the principles of democracy have been extended to all spheres of the life of society, including its basis — production relations.

Democracy, which is natural and necessary in the conditions of socialism, is not something that is fixed and static in its forms, functions and manifestations. It develops as society develops as a whole. It is possible, of course, to assess the level of development of socialist democracy only if one has a clear criterion for doing so. Marxist–Leninists have such a criterion. Under socialism, Lenin observed, 'for the first time in the history of civilised society, *the mass* of the population will rise to taking an *independent* part, not only in voting and elections, *but also in the everyday administraion of the state*' (*Collected Works*, Vol. 25, pp. 487–8). This was and remains for us the main criterion, the criterion which we take for assessing the successes of our democracy, determining the paths of its further development and improvement.

On the basis of this criterion we can say quite justifiably that our society of developed socialism has also become a society of developed socialist democracy. *At the stage of mature socialism, in the conditions of the state of the whole people the increasingly broad and active participation of the working people in administering the life of the country has firmly established itself as the central trend of the political development of Soviet society.*

The most representative organs of our state power, *the Soviets,* are working more effectively today. The democratic principles of their formation and activity have been further developed. The prestige, the powers of the deputies have grown and their ties with the masses have strengthened.

At the present time we have more than 2.2 million people's deputies. And if we take into account those previously elected to the Soviets, the country has many millions of people who have been through the great school of government, of political leadership. Twice as many questions are considered and decided in the Soviets today than 10 years ago. Most of these questions are studied in advance by standing commissions of which there are at present 330,000. Beside the 1.8 million deputies, 2.6 million other citizens, activists, take part in their work.

The working people's demands on those whom they elect as their representatives have become stricter. It is well known that the voters' right to recall their deputy is an important element in our democracy. In the past 10 years about 4000 deputies who, in one way or another, had not justified the trust of their constituency, were recalled from Soviets at various levels, including the Supreme Soviet. So this democratic right is not merely proclaimed, but carried out in practice and serves as a good means of raising deputies' sense of responsibility for their activities.

The deputies report back more regularly to their constituents. At the suggestion of deputies of the USSR Supreme Soviet a clause has been introduced into the new Constitution specially emphasising the obligation of the Soviets and the organs which they set up to keep the population well informed about their work and the decisions they take. This promotes a more consistent realisation of the principle of publicity — the key principle of the activities of the Soviets, of which Lenin said that they are 'an authority open to all, they carry out all their functions before the eyes of the masses, are accessible to the masses, spring directly from the masses, and are a direct and immediate instrument of the popular masses, of their will' (*Collected Works*, Vol. 10, p. 245).

The Soviets, which form the basis of the political system of the USSR, are the major instrument for the exercise of genuine people's power. But socialist democracy also has a good many other, constantly improving forms of participation of the working people in the administration of the state and public affairs. Some of these forms of people's power were not previously formalised in the Constitution. But they arose and developed in life. And it is about them that I should like to speak in somewhat greater detail.

Nationwide discussions have become an established feature of the practice of our democratic life. Not a single state plan for the development of the national economy, not a single major act of legislation — on marriage and the family, on pensions, on questions of protecting nature, for example — has been passed in recent years without nationwide discussion of the draft.

211

Clearly, the question of the new Constitution, of what kind of Constitution it should be, could be posed only at such a nationwide forum. The Constitutional Commission set up by the USSR Supreme Soviet prepared, with the help of a large number of scientists, legal experts, experienced officials of the state apparatus and public organisations, the draft of the Fundamental Law, which was then discussed by more than 140 million people, more than four-fifths of the adult population. They spoke at meetings of workers, of Party, trade union and Komsomol organisations, at sessions of the Soviets, on radio and television. They wrote to the newspapers and the Constitutional Commission. The 180,000 letters from working people are living, genuine documents of our democracy.

Those who were in close touch with the life of our country in those days know that this was a time of a tremendous upsurge in creative energy, a time of heated discussions, of arguments between people deeply concerned with the subject. Soviet people put forward nearly 400,000 proposals on specific amendments to the draft of the Fundamental Law. Many of them had to do with key questions of our life — the role of labour under socialism, the definition of the social basis of the Soviet state, the taking into consideration of voters' mandates in the work of the Soviets, the citizens' duties to protect socialist property, the right to practise small, subsidiary farming, etc.

The Constitutional Commission had to work hard to analyse and classify the proposals submitted before presenting its recommendation for endorsement by the Supreme Soviet, which, taking into account all opinions expressed in the course of these nationwide discussions, introduced amendments to 118 (of the 173) articles and added one new article.

So, when we say that the actual maker of the Constitution is the whole Soviet people, it is not an exaggeration, not just a fine-sounding phrase. It is a fact. And it shows that in our country we do not have alienation of the working people from political power, that the masses' distrust of everything to do with the state, that eternal feature of exploitative society, has been completely overcome.

During the discussion of the draft Constitution Soviet people showed in full measure their exacting, proprietary attitude to all matters concerning society. Many sharply critical remarks were addressed to various institutions, enterprises, organisations and their administrations. We pay all due attention to the criticisms voiced by the public and seek to remove the shortcomings that they reveal. In freedom of criticism our Party sees an effective instrument for the development of democratic society, an indispensable condition for the normal functioning of all its institutions.

Participation in nationwide discussions helps Soviet people to become more clearly aware of the close connection between their daily affairs and the wide horizon of social development. The connection between the working people's interests and aspirations and the key objectives of communist construction also manifests itself vividly in the socio-political activity of the *production teams.*

Questions concerning the role of the production team in our society figured prominently in the discussion of the draft Constitution. This is understandable. After all, it is in this primary unit of our social organism that the initiatives affecting the life of the whole country are born and developed.

Suffice it to say that the drawing up of the state plan begins from the production team. And it is natural that its fulfilment and overfulfilment also depend, to a decisive degree, on the efficiency and initiative of the production teams. Take, for example, the Moscow No. 1 Car-and-Tractor Electrical Equipment Plant. Its production team, when discussing the Tenth Five-Year Plan, made more than 200 proposals, most of which were put into effect. The result was that the factory produced additional output worth 2.1 million roubles.

Many questions going beyond narrow production interests are decided in the production teams. These questions range over the organisation of socialist competition, distribution of the material incentive funds, improving of professional skills, deployment of personnel, and concern for the rest and leisure, for the everyday life of the working people, the satisfaction of their spiritual needs. Raising the quality of medical care, further defining the principles of the use of the growing housing fund, more energetically combating red tape, devoting more attention to the moral upbringing of the young people, these are only a few of the highly significant social problems raised by the production teams in connection with the discussion of the draft Constitution.

In accordance with numerous proposals made by the working people, broad rights in the discussion and deciding of state and public affairs, in administering enterprises and institutions have been formally assigned to the production team in the new Fundamental Law; the very article on the role of the production team has been transferred to the chapter on the political system of the USSR.

The deepening of socialist democracy has become one of the driving forces of the country's economic progress. In its turn, the multiplication of the production resources and national wealth of Soviet society has become an important factor in strengthening and developing its democratic principles.

In the conditions of mature socialism the economic basis of socialist democracy has expanded, the rights of citizens have acquired a more substantial material content, and the guarantee of these rights has become more effective. Anyone who compares the new Fundamental Law of the USSR with the previous Constitution can be sure that it reflects qualitative changes in the extent of the rights and freedoms of the Soviet person.

The new Fundamental Law, it goes without saying, fully confirms the freedoms written down in the previous Constitution — freedom of speech, the press, assembly, meetings, processions and demonstrations. At the same time other political rights that have long since become common practice in public life have been formalised in the Constitution. Of fundamental importance is the new article proclaiming that a citizen of the USSR has the right to participate in government, in administering public affairs. Compared with the previous Constitution, the new Fundamental Law grants Soviet people more rights in the protection of their personal interests. The safeguards of citizens' political rights have also been strengthened. For example, it is obvious that the right to criticise becomes more meaningful when, as has been done in the Soviet Union, it is backed up by a constitutional clause forbidding any persecution for criticism and the stipulation that anyone guilty of violating this clause shall be punishable by law.

Now about the socio-economic rights concerning the very foundations of people's life. I will cite only a few examples by which the advances in this sphere may be assessed. The right to work has for decades been regarded as a matter of course in our country. Today it incorporates the right to choose a profession, the kind of occupation and activity corresponding to one's vocation, professional qualifications and so on. We can now give our citizens this guarantee because we have created an economy which has not only a steadily growing, but also a more varied demand for labour power, for specialists. We can also guarantee this right because we have evolved a highly developed system of general and special education, of professional training and improving skills.

The new Constitution endorses the vitally important right to housing. This was not mentioned in the previous Constitution. Today a reliable material base has been created for this right. Seven times more housing is built annually than in 1936. The right to material security in old age was also written down in the previous Constitution. But today, in comparison with 1936, there are dozens of times more people in advanced age who enjoy this right. And the average state pension has increased almost 3-fold.

The fact that socialist democracy proclaims not only political but also socio-economic rights, that it not only proclaims them but guarantees them, constitutes one of the fundamental features distinguishing it from bourgeois democracy. In a society of mature socialism with its highly developed economic potential this distinguishing feature of socialist democracy stands out in bold relief.

Providing wide scope for the political, economic and spiritual activity of citizens, their representatives and organisations, our democracy guides this activity towards goals that the whole people, all of society are interested in attaining. At the same time it must ensure expression of the multiform specific interests of various groups, dovetailing and co-ordinating them with the interests of society as a whole. A big part in this work is played by public organisations.

Thus it is one of the indispensable concerns of the trade unions to protect the interests of labour. They act resolutely and unhesitatingly when any manager of an enterprise forgets the standards laid down in labour legislation or the social needs of the working people. Last year, nearly 10,000 such administrators were removed from their posts at the demand of trade union committees. But we do not have the conflict between labour and capital, between workers and employers, that is intrinsic in bourgeois society. In such conditions the trade unions give best expression to the interests of the working people by organising their participation in the management of production, in administering all public affairs. A result of this, for example, is the activity of the standing production committee. There are 130,000 of these in the USSR today and

64 per cent of their members are workers. Every year 1.5 million proposals for increasing production efficiency are submitted by these
committees. Obviously this brings considerable benefit to the national
economy. But at the same time the material possibilities for better
satisfaction of the social and everyday needs of the working people
themselves are expanded.

Or, let us take the Komsomol — our youth organisation. Young people
have an urge for the romantic. And when the Komsomol, for example,
attracts hundreds of thousands of young men and women to the construction of the Baikal-Amur Railway, it combines the young people's specific
interests with a great nationwide interest — the building of a new transport artery in Siberia.

In short, socialist democracy ensures a sensitive response to the
growing diversity of social interests and opens up a broad field for the
initiative and socio-political activity of the masses.

*The development of socialist statehood and socialist democracy is a
process in which the key role belongs to the Communist Party.* The CPSU
has been promoted to the role of leading and guiding force of our society
by the victory of the October Revolution, by the whole 60-year history of
the Land of Soviets. This role of the Party is clearly reflected in the
Fundamental Law of the Soviet state.

In guiding the activities of the Soviets, the CPSU does not take their
place; it strictly delimits the functions of Party and state organs and
pursues its line primarily through the Communists working in them. The
essence of this Leninist principle is clearly expressed in the Fundamental
Law, which stresses that all Party organisations function within the
framework of the Constitution of the USSR. Like all the Soviet people,
Soviet Communists are fully aware that no privileges accrue to the Party
from the constitutional formalisation of the leading role of the CPSU in
our state and our society. On the contrary, this places additional responsibility on the Party because its guiding role is carried out not by the force of
authority but thanks to its high political prestige and ideological influence
among the masses.

The efforts that the Party constantly makes to strengthen socialist
legality and law and order help to extend the democracy inherent in the
nature of our social system.

As we know, one of the standard methods of present-day anti-communist propaganda trying to discredit the Soviet system is to cite the illegal repressions, the violations of the principles of democracy and socialist legality that occurred during the years of the personality cult. Of course, they prefer to ignore the fact that it was the CPSU that openly and uncompromisingly condemned such practices committed in contravention of the principles of the Constitution, carried out extensive work to establish Leninist standards of Party and state life, and created firm safeguards aganst the abuse of power and violations of citizens' rights.

The Communists have always regarded the realisation of democratic rights and freedoms as an effective weapon of the working people in the struggle for socialism and communism. Knowledge of one's rights, the ability to apply them in the interests of building the new society is a most important feature of the Soviet person's active, life-asserting position, his high level of political culture, the formation and development of which have always been and remain as the focus of our Party's attention. It goes without saying that the citizen's understanding of his responsibility to society, his high patriotic duty to work honestly and conscientiously for the benefit of the people, to be always ready to defend the revolutionary gains of the motherland of October, forms an indispensable element of political culture. The idea that performance of civic duties is just as much a necessary element of democracy as the exercise of rights and freedoms was expressed by very many participants in the discussions of the draft Constitution. And this idea is clearly expressed in the appropriate articles of our Fundamental Law.

We stand firm by the position that the democracy of socialism is incompatible with any barracks-type bureaucratic order or any anarchistic libertarianism in relation to socialist principles, standards and laws. As we know, the banner of the First International, founded by Marx and Engels, bore the words: 'No rights without duties, no duties without rights'. Today this slogan of the Working Men's International Association has become one of the important principles of the life and work of Soviet working people.

The rise and development of socialist democracy is a complex process. We are well aware that in this sphere we also have unsolved problems and difficulties. There is much work to be done in bringing all the standards of our legislation into accord with the new Constitution. We believe that

217

considerable reserves lie in improving the work of all departments of the state apparatus, which should take a more responsive attitude to creative initiative, to the needs and anxieties of the working people. We also demand more, expect more effectiveness from the agencies of people's control, whose importance and authority have been raised by the Constitution that has come into force.

We are doing everything necessary to perfect Soviet democracy, to develop our statehood in the direction of communist social self-government. The adoption of the new Constitution of the USSR is another big step along the road to this great goal of the Communists of all countries.

III

The establishing and development of the world's first socialist state has always aroused great interest beyond the borders of our country, leaving neither the supporters of socialism nor its class adversaries indifferent. It is quite natural therefore that the major advances in the development of the political system of Soviet society formalised in the new Constitution of the USSR, and the actual process of its discussion and adoption, have attracted the attention of the whole planet. A number of trends indicating the international significance of this major event in the life of the Soviet people may be singled out.

Above all, our country's new Constitution contributes to the theory and international practice of the construction of socialism, enriching them with the experience gained in organising the first ever socialist state of the whole people.

Revealing the fundamental importance of internationalising revolutionary experience and creatively assimilating everything valuable produced by the struggle of the working people throughout the world, Lenin noted that each attempt, taken by itself, to build a new society might be one-sided and suffer from certain inconsistencies, that 'complete socialism' is created 'by the revolutionary co-operation of the proletarians of all countries' (*Collected Works*, Vol. 27, p. 346).

It is known that in working out their own Constitutions the fraternal countries which embarked upon the road of socialism later than us, took into consideration the achievements of Soviet legislation, which was then the only source of practical experience of socialist state construction. Today, in many of these countries the task of building a developed socialist society is being posed and successfully accomplished. And, as the leaders and the press of these states have noticed, the new Soviet Constitution is a useful document for defining the perspectives of their own development.

In drawing up the new Fundamental Law of the USSR we, in our turn, relied not only on the constitutional experience of Soviet history but also paid great attention to the practice of other socialist countries. This helped us, in particular, to enrich the content of certain articles of the Constitution concerning citizen's rights and duties and to improve its general structure.

Taken as a whole it is nothing else but an accumulation of collective experience of socialist state construction. And the richer this experience the more clearly the general patterns of formation and development of socialism's political system emerge, the more fully their international importance is revealed. The essence of the matter, of course, is not that certain stereotypes take shape which have only to be copied. The essential point is that scientifically grounded and practically tested guidelines are evolved that in the specific conditions of various countries help them to find the correct solutions to the complex problems of asserting and developing socialist statehood and socialist democracy.

Life has proved that such guidelines can be of use not only directly in the building of socialism, but also on the roads towards it. This is shown, for example, by the character of many of the comments on the new Soviet Constitution in the countries of Asia, Africa and Latin America. Prominent figures and the press of these countries note that the experience of socialist construction reflected in our Constitution contains a great deal that is of value to peoples who, after liberating themselves from colonial dependence, are confronted with the choice of a path of further development, with the problems of strengthening their national statehood.

The international importance of the new Constitution of the USSR is determined also by its indisputable *influence on the course of the contemporary contest between the two world systems.*

By the very fact of its existence, its example, socialism has always exerted a positive influence on the internal life of the capitalist countries and helped in the just struggle of the progressive forces. The new Constitution, incorporating all the 60-year experience of our country's development along the path of October, multiplies the magnetic force of the socialist example. It patently reveals the practical paths towards effective and truly democratic solutions of the problems of social development in the interests of the working people.

The truth about socialism, about its democracy, embodied in the Constitution, gives the Communists of the world an effective ideological weapon in the struggle with our common class enemy — imperialism. This is pointed out by the representatives of many Communist and Workers' parties.

It stands to reason that the Constitution of a developed socialist society has proved unpalatable to those who are fighting against socialism, who spare neither effort nor resources to prevent the victory of the new system. In the report at the Session of the USSR Supreme Soviet on 4 October 1977, I spoke of the most characteristic attacks that our bourgeois opponents delivered at the draft Constitution. Since its adoption the picture has not changed in this respect. So I am not going to repeat myself here. Readers can study our position on this question from the text of the report, which examines the arguments of bourgeois propaganda and shows their contrived and hypocritical character.

We know that there are still a good many people in the world who take at face value the inventions of propaganda that denigrates the Soviet state and socialist democracy. I am confident that their numbers will be reduced as the world learns more about the new Constitution of the USSR and the life of our people. In this connection I should like to express my gratitude to the Communist and Workers' parties of the non-socialist part of the world who, often in the difficult circumstances of rampant anti-Soviet campaigns, do so much to give a true picture of life in the Land of Soviets, to provide an objective analysis of the problems of developed socialist society. The more people learn about the achievements of socialism and the more clearly they visualise the scale and complexity of the problems that it had to solve and has solved, the more convinced supporters there will be of the new social system and the firmer will be the political and ideological positions of world socialism, of all the Marxist–Leninist parties — the leading force in the fight against imperialism, and for peace, democracy and social progress.

Yet another aspect of the international importance of the new Soviet Constitution is that in both spirit and letter it serves the cause of peace, the security of the peoples, the strengthening of the anti-imperialist solidarity of all progressive forces.

All the aims and thoughts of our people revolve around peaceful, creative endeavour. In the USSR and other socialist countries, as distinct from the imperialist states, there are no classes or social groups that have any interest in the arms race, in military preparations. By including in the new Constitution a special chapter formalising the peaceful character of the foreign policy of the Soviet Union, our people have once again stressed their determination to follow the Leninist course of peace, the course of ridding humanity of the horrors of war, of the material hardships and mortal dangers implicit in the arms race. This chapter contains clauses corresponding to the fundamental obligations that the Soviet Union has undertaken as a participant in vital international agreements, including the Final Act of the Helsinki Conference. Indisputably this imparts additional weight to the efforts that are being made in the world for a further normalisation of the international situation, for the development of *détente*.

The Soviet Union is a component of the world system of socialism. A profound and consistent international solidarity unites our Party, the whole people with the progressive, liberation forces of the world, with the international Communist movement. It is natural therefore that the Constitution should clearly reflect the class character of the Soviet state's foreign policy, its social ideals and political sympathies, its traditional support of the people's struggle for national liberation and social progress. It also reflects the positions that have been worked out by the CPSU on a collective basis together with the other Communist parties and have been recorded in their joint documents, for example, at the Berlin Conference of Communist and Workers' Parties of Europe.

In short, our Constitution elevates to the rank of a state law of the USSR that which constitutes the very essence of the foreign policy of the socialist state — its concern for peace, for the creation of international conditions consonant with the struggle for national freedom and social progress, for socialism and communism.

In making the new Constitution we worked on the assumption that it would become an important means for the further development and deepening of socialist democracy, a powerful instrument for building communism.

The discussion and adoption of the new Fundamental Law of the USSR have evoked a powerful upswing in the labour and socio-political activity of our people directed towards accomplishing the great tasks posed by the 25th Congress of the CPSU, towards the building of communist society. In fulfilling these tasks the Soviet people, rallied closely around their Leninist Communist Party, see not only their great patriotic duty, but also their internationalist duty to the world's working class, to all humankind.

Article: 'A Historic Stage on the Road to Communism', published in World Marxist Review, *no. 12. December 1977*

Comrade delegates,
Esteemed guests of the Congress.

On behalf of the Central Committee of the CPSU and all members of our Party of Lenin, I extend warm greetings to the participants in our highest Komsomol assembly, and through you to all Komsomol members and all Soviet youth.

Fifty-eight years ago, speaking at the 3rd Congress of the then still very young Komsomol, Vladimir Ilyich Lenin singled out as most important the question of 'what we should teach the youth and how the youth should learn if it really wants to justify the name of communist youth, and how it should be trained so as to be able to complete and consummate what we have started' (*Collected Works*. Vol. 31, p. 284).

Lenin's approach to the matter has retained all its relevance today. What we should teach the youth and how the youth should learn (not only in the sense of learning at school, of course, but also in the broader sense of learning life) so as to be able to become true builders of communism —

this is still the main thing in the work of the Komsomol and in the Party's guidance of this work.

By and large, I think, Communists of the older generation can be pleased with Soviet youth of the present day. They are growing up with communist convictions, and are deeply faithful to the cause of the Party and the great Lenin. Millions of young men and women are models of courage, tenacity and fidelity to the ideals of the October Revolution. They are working with great enthusiasm in all sectors of the front of communist construction, and are actively furthering the fulfilment of the country's strenuous development plans. They inject their unique, romantic spirit and, I should say, youthful fervour into every undertaking. For this we thank the Komsomol and all young people of our Soviet land.

May the pure flame of patriotism burn on in your hearts, along with a noble sense of personal responsibility for your job and for all that is happening in the country.

The 25th Congress of our Party endorsed an extensive programme for the current 5 years and the longer term. It is directed to one aim — that the Soviet people should enjoy an even better life, that they should lead fuller and happier lives, and that we should advance ever more confidently to communism, our radiant goal. Much of what the Party has set out in the 5-year plan is being successfully achieved, but much still remains to be done, and this, of course, also by you young people.

I

The striving for efficiency and quality is a most important hallmark of our country's present period. This is no passing campaign. It is a course taken by the Party, as we say, in all earnest and for a long time. It is not only the key task of the current 5-year period, but also the determining factor in our economic and social development for many years ahead. If you like, it is also an educational programme for a whole generation of Soviet people.

Our country has colossal natural riches. The exertions of several generations have created a powerful economic potential in both our industry and agriculture. We have raised and trained large numbers of educated and qualified cadres and have secured fairly good conditions of life for our people.

It is now more important than ever to use all this wealth thriftily and sensibly, to make it serve the people profitably and to use it with the maximum benefit.

Certainly, efficiency and quality are very broad concepts. They include such basic elements as the most rational distribution of the productive forces, the improvement of nationwide planning and a comprehensive approach to major economic problems. In this respect the Party has — specifically at last year's December plenary meeting of the Central Committee — set clear-cut tasks for our government bodies, notably for State Planning Committee and the ministries concerned. But in solving them much depends on each enterprise, each workshop and team and each worker.

What does this mean?

It means that you must work not simply with discipline and diligence but also conscientiously, skilfully, efficiently and work well, so that others should respect you for your work and you, too, should have self-respect.

It means that work must be organised sensibly at every work place, with an effective system of incentives for stable and high-quality production and for its further improvement.

This means making thrifty use of the nation's material wealth, the prime law in the life and labour of Soviet people, and searching perseveringly for new ways of eliminating unproductive expenditure.

This means that in our work collectives we must create such a moral atmosphere and mentality that everyone will consider it his natural duty — and will have the opportunity — to work at maximum efficiency and to maximum effect, an atmosphere in which the position of idlers, truants, burglars and pilferers of public property will be truly intolerable.

These are our tasks, comrades. The Party has set them out clearly and persuasively. Millions of working people have approved the Party's call and responded to it in their work.

You probably know from press reports of the extensive, systematic and painstaking work done in this connection at enterprises in Moscow, Leningrad, Minsk, Lvov, the Urals, the Kuznetsk basin, Tashkent and Karaganda, and in many other work collectives across the country.

Youth are actively involved in these efforts. You have advanced the slogan, 'Youthful enthusiasm and creativity for the 5-year plan of efficiency and quality'. This is a splendid slogan. And it is a point of honour for the Komsomol to secure its daily application by all young workers, collective farmers, technicians and engineers.

Useful experience has been gained at our leading enterprises, such as the Volga motor works, in tackling the problem of higher production efficiency and higher-quality labour in a comprehensive manner. We have a right to expect that such experience will spread far and wide. And it is also up to the Komsomol to promote this.

Or take the Shchekino method. It enables a considerable rise in production with a drop in the number of workers. One would think everything is clear. But the method has not so far won the following it deserves. Some managers and officials do not seem able to shake off long-established canons, to revise and alter certain principles of management and forms of organising production.

It is high time, comrades, that we should learn to introduce advanced experience effectively and carry every useful undertaking through to the end.

What are the decisive sectors in the campaign for efficiency and quality in our economy today? There are several. But I would again give pride of place to capital construction and transport. Our success along the entire economic front depends in many ways on improving the state of affairs in these sectors. These matters were closely studied at the December plenary meeting of the Central Committee last year and, as you know, I had occasion to refer to them again during my recent visit to the country's Eastern regions.

As I have already stressed, we shall be very critical of economic managers who show inefficiency, an inability to deploy energy and resources correctly and who freeze national resources in uncompleted construction. But the matter concerns not only managers. It also depends on the work and sense of responsibility of millions of people employed in construction and transport, and among them millions of young men and women, including members of the Komsomol. Special importance attaches here to creative initiative, to dedicated work in all sectors and to the emulation movement, whose main purpose is to secure the ultimate economic results for the country as a whole.

It would be useful, for example, to take up on a broad scale the initiative of emulation among related trades on the principle of a 'work relay', which is a competition between building workers, designers and industrial, transport and agricultural workers for the prompt or pre-schedule commissioning of the most important plants and projects in the 5-year plan.

As concerns transport, here we can point to the valuable Leningrad workers' initiative — the experience of co-operation between seamen, railwaymen and road transport and river fleet workers in the Leningrad transport zone.

These and similar undertakings need your support, dear friends; they need your energy and youthful enthusiasm.

The Komsomol has always been a reliable steward of great Soviet building projects. This splendid tradition continues. But the projects have changed in many ways. Today they constitute not only separate giant building sites but embrace vast geographical areas.

Let me here take just one such area. Its importance for the country's future is increasing from day to day. I mean Western Siberia or, more precisely, the Tyumen region.

In a matter of 10 years we have turned this taiga land into our country's chief supplier of petroleum. A powerful gas and chemicals industry is being built there. No longer are forest or deer paths typical of the Tyumen landscape, but rising cities, oil and gas fields, factories, railways and roads. And on what a scale! Think of it, comrades: one million square kilometres on the Ob River are being economically developed and settled. This equals approximately the combined area of Spain, Italy and Britain.

Yes, we did not hesitate to invest huge resources there. And we were not mistaken. The expenditure was justified. Today, Tyumen supplies nearly half of Soviet oil and a large amount of gas. Several days ago our Party's Central Committee congratulated the oil workers of Western Siberia on their 1000-millionth ton of oil. This is a big labour victory. Glory and honour to those who get the northern black gold for us!

We will live with the Tyumen deposits for many years to come. And in the next 10 years we expect to get the bulk of the increase in oil and gas output and of the output of valuable chemical raw materials made from them there in Tyumen. In this connection we are entering or, more precisely, have already entered a new and more complicated stage in the development of Western Siberia. The work there is to be doubled or trebled. This will call for new material and technical outlays and for an influx of people.

What could the Komsomol do to help Western Siberia? I am aware that thirteen Komsomol priority projects are already under construction there. Still, I would ask you to redouble attention to this area.

What the building projects need is not simply hands. A definite number of building workers, assemblymen, drivers, drillers, teachers and people of other professions must be sent there — that is the need.

When the 'offensive' on Western Siberia was just beginning, a slogan was advanced to take its wealth not by number but by skill, that is, by means of up-to-date technology and techniques. And much has been accomplished there.

Take the prefabricated unit method of building which, incidentally, was developed and introduced by young, enthusiastic workers and engineers of *Tyumen Gasmontazh* (a construction trust). What the method amounts to in substance is that many of the oilfield facilities are manufactured complete in factory shops far from the building site, and are then delivered in units to any remote place, where it only remains to assemble them.

It is estimated that this method makes it possible to quadruple the productivity of labour in fitting out the Siberian oilfields. And that means a reduction of thousands, even tens of thousands, in the number of workers needed.

As you see, the development of Western Siberia can also be helped by those who are working elsewhere. For this those who are filling Tyumen orders — whether in the Ukraine, Azerbaijan, the Volga lands, Moscow, or any other part of the country — should assume Komsomol stewardship over them and help develop the spaces and mineral resources of Tyumen with the minimum manpower.

I believe that this principle can also be applied to other large building projects. Experience of this kind already exists. There is the Leningraders' pledge, for example, to fill orders for building projects ahead of schedule. Involve the youth everywhere in this undertaking, comrades, and keep the orders for the country's building projects under constant supervision. Let the 'Komsomol Spotlight' give no rest to those who fall behind.

Now about agriculture.

Undoubtedly, we have accomplished much in carrying out our agricultural policy. But much has still to be done in order effectively to meet the growing demands of Soviet people and the needs of industry. Our current plans as well as new projects on which the Party is working at present are oriented towards these aims. Raising the efficiency of agriculture, notably that of animal husbandry, is a primary task.

Let me be frank: it will be hard to accomplish it without the active involvement of youth.

Of course, this applies first of all to youth in the countryside. They personify the future and in many ways determine the present of Soviet agriculture. Nowadays our farming is inconceivable without machinery. That is why we attach fundamental importance to the Komsomol motto, 'If you live in the country you must know farming machinery'. The technical training of young men and women in country areas must proceed on a truly mass scale.

Our countryside is changing. Houses built there in the past 13 years total 450 million square metres. This is no trifle, comrades; it matches the total of prewar housing in Soviet cities. Villages boast houses of culture, shopping centres and cafés — many of them not inferior to those in cities. It is up to the youth, the Komsomol, to be the chief driving force behind these changes, to operate the new machinery, to build the modern villages and introduce a high level of culture there.

Certainly, people cannot be made to stay in the countryside by edict. Creating good working and living conditions, cultivating a respect for farm work and a love of nature and of the land, the ability and desire to turn one's hands to it — that is our method of attracting the rising generation to working in the fields and on livestock farms.

Let me recall the initiative of school-leavers in Kostroma region. They wanted to stay and work on the land. And as I was preparing for this meeting with you, I inquired how they were making out now. I was informed that these schoolchildren of yesterday have turned out to be good tillers of the soil, livestock farmers and machine operators and have found their vocation in this fine and noble work. They have formed youth collectives on farms and have learned new trades. Many are continuing their education. And by now their example is being followed by tens of thousands in different parts of our great motherland.

The Party thanks the young men and women who have chosen to

devote themselves to the grand programme of developing agriculture and it highly esteems their initiative. It sets youth a good example. I think it will continue to find many followers.

Tremendous significance attaches to the Komsomol's helping to carry out the Party decision on transforming agriculture in the non-black-earth zone of the Russian Federation. Keep it up, friends, and hold aloft the banner of the Leninist Komsomol on this youth priority project!

Springtime field work is at its height just now throughout the country. Allow me to wish youth in the countryside and everybody working on collective and state farms to do their job well, to wish them success, and, the main thing, to gladden our hearts with a good harvest.

Speaking of agricultural problems, I wish to address myself to city youth too. The basis for good harvests and high productivity on livestock farms is nowadays laid in the city too. The end result of a farmer's or stockbreeder's work depends in many ways on the city worker. This means that young people in cities can play an important part here. They would do well to launch an emulation movement for the prompt supply to farms of everything they need — machinery, fertilisers, building materials and equipment for stockbreeding, and also to help on rural building projects.

And there is yet another important task, comrades. As our economy grows and the well-being of Soviet people rises, working in such fields as retail trade and the public services gains in significance. I have already had occasion to refer to the tremendous bearing they have on the mood and health of people and, consequently, on their good work. Everybody probably knows this from his own experience. Yet, as you surely know, it is precisely in these spheres that we still have shortcomings, sometimes glaring ones. There are many reasons for this — material, organisational and moral. But one thing is clear: order must be established.

And I think the Komsomol should make trade and the public services the object of its constant and unflagging concern. Put them under your effective stewardship. Make a thorough study of the state of affairs, help with fresh people and by educating those already employed there, and by rallying public opinion, and with initiatives addressed to economic and administrative bodies. In my view this would be useful. So, friends, tackle the matter!

So, comrades, there is a lot to do, work enough for all. Perhaps some of you think that I am setting you too many tasks. But, after all, there are nearly 38 million of you Komsomol members. A tremendous force! You should be equal to any task.

And today the most urgent task is not only to fulfil but also to overfulfil this year's plan. This is exceedingly important for the fulfilment of the 5-year plan as a whole. It is upon this that Party, government and economic bodies, trade union and Komsomol organisations and all working people must concentrate their efforts at the present time. Here very much depends on you, on youth. And we are sure you will not let us down!

II

Dear comrades, in the final count the fulfilment of all our plans depends on people, on their knowledge, culture, and political awareness.

Our main compass along the road to Communism is the Marxist–Leninist teaching on the laws of social development. It is impossible to overestimate the importance of a profound and systematic study of this revolutionary science; conscientious and thorough study, not mechanical learning by rote of particular truths and formulas. Knowledge of theory is of no value unless it becomes conviction and is followed up by deeds. In other words, every young Leninist must be an active political fighter able to carry out the Party's policy in practice and irreconcilably to combat hostile ideology.

The Party and Komsomol devote great attention to the moral upbringing of youth. One cannot affirm the norms and principles of Communist morality without waging a continuous hard struggle against anti-social behaviour and spiritual poverty, and its inevitable concomitants — drunkenness, hooliganism and breaches of labour discipline. Immorality, which is not always noticeable at first glance, presents no less a danger. Indifference, parasitism, cynicism and claims to take from society more than one gives to society — these moral flaws must not escape the view of the Komsomol and, for that matter, of our public as a whole.

Concern for raising the people's standard of living is the pivot of the Party's home policy. By this we mean both a higher material and higher cultural level of life. The one cannot be divorced from the other.

We reject both the cult of poverty and asceticism and the consumer cult, the mentality of the philistine for whom a kopeck, in Gorky's apt phrase, is the sun in his sky. For us material blessings are not an aim in itself, but a precondition for the all-round development of the personality. It is important, therefore, that our rising well-being should be accompanied by an enrichment of the purpose and meaning of life.

The fact that the Soviet people, including youth, of course, are highly educated and very well informed sets much higher demands on the manner of educational work.

Manifestations of indifference and formalism are especially intolerable in this area. It is time all workers on the ideological front should end the mechanical and thoughtless repetition of axiomatic truths and the verbose gabbling that still survives here and there. It is time to make it a rule to talk to people in plain and comprehensible terms, and to put live thought and feeling into every phrase you write. This, too, is a question of quality and efficiency, moreover in such an important sector of communist construction as the education of the new man.

The Party and Komsomol are bringing up the young citizens of our society to be loyal sons and daughters of the Soviet motherland and firm fighters for the communist cause. These qualities are translated into the great deeds of millions of people, they multiply the power of our motherland and raise the well-being of the people.

Recently, during my visit to the Urals, Siberia and the Far East, I was deeply gratified again to see for myself what splendid people and what magnificent youth we have in these wealthy but in many ways still severe regions. One might say that youth are making the climate there warmer with the warmth of their devoted hearts.

Especially memorable were the meetings with a group of young Baikal–Amur Railway builders at one of the stations and with young people in the city of Komsomolsk-on-Amur. They were splendid young men and women. They spoke of their life and work with responsibility and competence, and also with enthusiasm. Their eyes are set on the future. As I listened to them the line of the well-known song came to mind: 'We young masters of the earth are conquering space and time.'

The magnificent qualities of Soviet people are also in evidence in the ranks of our glorious Armed Forces. Here young people get a real steeling. Here they not only learn organisation and discipline but also display a high degree of awareness, self-sacrifice and on occasions true

231

heroism.

During my visit to the East I also acquainted myself with how our borders are being guarded and with those who are performing their far from easy duty there — the fine men of our Army, Navy and border troops. I can say one thing, comrades: the borders of our motherland are dependably protected against all emergencies; its defence is in experienced and loyal hands. And I can assure you that the young people of the Soviet land guarding its peace and tranquility have everything they need to perform their lofty mission.

Comrades, Soviet people who have grown up in a fraternal family of nations and have been reared on the ideas of Marxism–Leninism are internationalists by their very nature. Internationalist traditions are embodied in their deeds today more broadly and diversely perhaps than ever before. And here, as in many other things, youth are to the fore.

Young people sent by the Leninist Komsomol are working in more than a hundred countries abroad. Thousands of our country's sons and daughters are doing noble work in the socialist countries of Europe and in distant Cuba, in the hot sands of the Sahara, in the jungles of South-East Asia, in India, the Arab East and other parts of the world — building factories and power stations, helping to develop natural resources, treating the sick and teaching children. Often enough their labour is a real, unassuming and unpublicised, disinterested and self-sacrificing feat. A feat for the sake of peace and progress, the fraternity and friendship of nations. A feat that adds to the prestige of our motherland and helps people to understand the truth about our socialist system and the communist morality and ideals of Soviet people.

Let us, comrades, express our sincere thanks to these splendid representatives of our people. They are helping to carry out the peaceful Leninist policy of our Party and the Soviet state and they are daily displaying that internationalism in action which Vladimir Ilyich Lenin valued so highly.

Proletarian, socialist internationalism — this is our great strength. It is the fruit of our convictions and the fervour of our hearts. It is our banner. Be ever faithful to it, dear friends!

Speech to the 18th Congress of Komsomols. 25 April 1978

Baku itself has changed beyond recognition in conditions of socialism. Mayakovsky once wrote that there was pitifully little verdure in the city: '. . . only about 18 meagre leaves or so.' It is even difficult now to imagine that that was really the case.

The sombre old 'black city' is long gone. In its place is beautiful Baku, broad, high and spacious with a population of almost 1,500,000. It is a pleasure to see the greenery of its parks and the bright hues of the flowers, the modern enterprises, the streets lined with bright beautiful houses, and your latest acquisition, the metro.

The working pulse of Baku is beating strongly. All the economic regions of our country and many countries in the world receive its industrial products.

In short, Baku is the worthy capital of a Republic which has under the sun of socialism in a brief period of history become a flourishing land of modern industry, developed agriculture and advanced culture.

When I spoke here in Baku in the autumn of 1970, I drew the attention of Party, government and economic bodies of the Republic to the lag in the rate of increase in industrial production, to the shortcomings in the development of agriculture and to the inadequate use of hidden reserves. I can say today that you drew the proper conclusions from this criticism.

The state of affairs has clearly improved. This is the result of the purposeful organisational, political, ideological and educational work of the Central Committee of the Communist Party of Azerbaijan and the Party organisation of the Republic; it is the outcome of the vigorous labour efforts of the entire people of Azerbaijan. It reflects a healthier situation and an improved moral and psychological atmosphere which had an immediate effect on the results of your economic activity.

Azerbaijan is making great strides ahead. In the Ninth Five-Year Plan period and in the first 2 years of the Tenth Five-Year-Plan period, your industry has produced almost as much as it did in the previous 15 years. As for the growth rate of overall production, it has reached the level envisaged for the first 3 years of the Tenth Five-Year-Plan period. This is not bad at all, comrades. This is a practical response to the decisions of the 25th Congress of the Party and the December 1977 Plenary Meeting of the CPSU Central Committee.

What you are doing in the field of agriculture also gives us cause to rejoice.

In the period from 1971 to 1977 you have raised the average annual output of raw cotton by nearly one-half in comparison with the Eighth Five-Year-Plan period. The annual production of grain has in recent times been raised from the previous level of 600,000–700,000 tons to approximately 1,130,000 tons. Grape- and vegetable-growing is developing very well. In the period from 1971 to 1977 you sold more vegetables to the state than you did in the whole of the preceding 30 years.

Livestock productivity is also rising, though the achievements here are more modest.

Permit me to express confidence that, in fulfilling the decisions of the July (1978) Plenary Meeting of the CPSU Central Committee, you will achieve fresh successes in developing all sectors of agriculture.

The example of development shown by your Republic, comrades, graphically demonstrates what fruits are borne by persevering work and the consistent application of the social policy worked out by the Party. This is also shown by the rise in the well-being of the people, by the scale of housing construction and the impressive development of culture and science.

The successes of the working people of Azerbaijan are receiving the recognition they deserve. Your Republic has held the Red Banner for 8 years in a row. This makes you duty-bound to do many things, comrades. We hope you will continue to be faithful to your fine traditions.

In brief, you do have something to be praised for. However, I believe that our celebration will not be spoiled if we also talk about shortcomings and unresolved tasks. Such is the communist businesslike style of work, and we will not depart from it.

Soviet people do not reconcile themselves to obstacles in the way of their advance, to all forms of deception of the people and the state. It is good that they react so sharply to such things. It is necessary to attach great importance to criticisms coming from the working people.

There is nothing more harmful for the Party and the people than attempts to hush up shortcomings, to avoid justified criticism, to silence it, not to speak of suppressing criticism and persecuting those who criticise.

Regrettably, we still come across such things.

Workers in ministries and administrative departments, as well as in leading bodies of republics and regions, do not always deem it necessary to respond in the proper way to criticism, including criticism in the press. There have even been cases of pressure being brought to bear upon those who criticise.

There have also been cases when issues of the satirical newsreel *Fitil'* ('Time Fuse'), dealing with a particular region of the country, have not been shown there on the instructions of local leaders. Who gave them the right to issue such orders?

The suppression of criticism, comrades, violates the norms of communist morality and the Fundamental Law of the USSR. This is an evil which should not be left unpunished. We highly value the people's initiative and no one will be allowed to undermine this source of our strength!

> *Speech on presenting the city of Baku*
> *with the Order of Lenin.*
> *22 September 1978*

Dear comrades,

Dear Muscovites, . . .

I regard your trust as trust in the Communist Party of the Soviet Union and in the political line which the Party adopted at its 25th Congress.

This line is aimed at promoting our economic development and improving the life of the working people, at perfecting socialist democracy and strengthening the fraternal friendship of all the big and small nations of our country, at building up the defence strength of the Land of the Soviets and safeguarding lastng peace and international security. It is this political line, combined with the dedicated labour of the Soviet people, that is the basis of all the achievements of our society. It is precisely this political line that shapes the substance of all the work of the Supreme Soviet of the USSR.

I think I would be right in saying that the main event in the activities of the Supreme Soviet of the Ninth Convocation was to debate and adopt the new Constitution of the USSR. Together with the new Constitutions of the Union and Autonomous Republics, this Constitution reflects the most characteristic and stable attributes of the statehood and entire system of social relations of developed socialism.

In accordance with the requirements of the Constitution, the highest organ of state power in the USSR has set about implementing a vast programme of reforms further updating Soviet legislation. Along with this, the USSR Supreme Soviet and its Presidium have intensified their efforts in guiding the Soviets and supervising observance of the law. It is my firm belief that these trends of activity will play an increasing role in the work of the Supreme Soviet of the Tenth Convocation. A good and well-thought-out system of laws coupled with their strict observance constitute legality, the legal order without which the socialist way of life and socialist democracy are inconceivable.

The achievements of socialist democracy are beyond doubt. And it is just as indubitable that the potentialities of the Soviet people's rule are still far from exhausted.

The CPSU Central Committee is giving foremost attention to increasing the activity of Party organisations, the Soviets of People's Deputies, trade unions and the Komsomol. The Party is going to the polls with a broad programme of improving the forms and methods of their multiple activities. The essence of this programme is that everyone, I repeat, every Soviet person, should feel himself or herself involved in the affairs of state and be certain that his or her views and remarks will be heeded and taken into account in major or minor decision-making.

This is what makes it necessary to continue and even further intensify determined and uncompromising action against all instances of law-breaking, the suppression of criticism, red tape, formalism and bureaucracy. There must be more publicity. More attention must be paid to the needs and views of people. There must be more direct and interested communication with the masses. That is how the Party poses the question. That must be the style of work of all the Soviets of People's Deputies, from the Supreme Soviet down to the village and settlement Soviets . . .

All-round economic growth has laid a good basis for raising the people's standard of living. Approximately four-fifths of the national income, that is, 1½ trillion roubles, were allocated directly to public welfare in 1974-8. This was nearly one-third more than in the previous

5-year-plan period.

In working to secure strict fulfilment of the social programme adopted by its 25th Congress, the Party will continue to give paramount attention to improving the life of Soviet people: boosting the wages and real incomes of the working people, expanding public funds and building housing.

It is important to emphasise that the achievements of the Soviet Union as a whole are also achievements of each Republic. I shall cite just one fact. The industrial output of Kazakhstan is now five times greater than that of the whole of pre-revolutionary Russia. Only the combined efforts of the working people of that Republic and of the working people of the whole Soviet Union made it possible to raise Kazakhstan to such heights. The same may be said about any other Republic. Such is the result of the Leninist nationalities policy and of the friendship and brotherhood of the Soviet peoples.

. . . The new USSR Supreme Soviet, the government and central economic bodies will have to work in a very important period — when the current Five-Year Plan is being completed and the next is in preparation. The Eleventh Five-Year Plan must in full measure embody the Party's economic policy and incorporate the latest achievements of economic, scientific and technical thought, all our experience.

Lenin attached tremendous significance to the economic activities of the Soviets. His library in the Kremlin contains a review of the activities of the Moscow City Soviet Executive Committee. At the place where it was said that in 3½ months in 1920 the Executive Committee discussed forty-six organisational and only eight economic questions, Vladimir Ilyich underlined the figures and wrote in the margin: 'It should be the other way round.'

The new Constitution has extended the rights of the Soviets in the economic field. They must learn how to use these rights. All the more so since in building up the economy there are tasks which no one can tackle better than the Soviets.

It is common knowledge that a great deal has been done in recent years to specialise and concentrate production and to enhance branch factors in management. But all the more active should the Supreme and local Soviets and their executive bodies be in their work to ensure comprehensive economic and social development in their territories. Only a reasonable combination of branch and territorial factors can guarantee efficient economic management.

Our Soviets and Soviet democracy have a vast latent vitality. It should be used ever more fully to disclose existing reserves, to criticise short-comings, to compare views and formulate sound decisions. Soviet democracy can and must serve economic progress still better, while economic progress has been and will remain the foundation, the material basis for more fully guaranteeing the rights and freedoms of Soviet people and further developing socialist democracy.

To tackle the economic tasks facing us will require a creative approach, a high sense of responsibility and the strictest discipline in all units of the economy. This applies both to economic executives at all levels and to those directly participating in production. Let everyone at his lathe, in the field or at his drawing board ask himself if he has done everything possible to improve the productivity and quality of his work, to save materials and not to waste time. Judging by the letters reaching the Party Central Committee and the Presidium of the Supreme Soviet and by the character of working people's speeches in the course of the election campaign, Soviet people are clearly aware of the importance of this question for the development of our country at the present juncture.

The requirement to improve the degree of organisation and increase responsibility and discipline in every area of work is one of the main mandates of the voters. So comrades, let us do everything to see that this mandate is carried out — not in words but in deeds!

Report at a meeting with the
Baumansky District electorate,
Moscow. 2 March 1979

At the first session of the USSR Supreme Soviet of the Tenth Convocation that took place on this day Leonid Brezhnev spoke about the tasks to be accomplished by the Supreme Soviet Deputies in improving the people's well-being, ensuring socialist law and order, and in preserving peace in the world.

Dear comrade deputies,

First of all, allow me on behalf of those who have been elected members of the Presidium of the USSR Supreme Soviet and on my own behalf to thank cordially the Central Committee of the Communist Party and the deputies to the Supreme Soviet for the great trust placed in us. I am sure that every one of us will spare no efforts to justify this trust.

It is a great honour and a great responsibility to be a deputy to the highest body of state authority. It is a still greater honour and a still greater responsibility to work in the Presidium, the permanently functioning organ of the Supreme Soviet.

The new Constitution has created the most favourable conditions for the Supreme Soviet of the USSR to exercise actively its broad powers. In following the Party's political line, the Supreme Soviet is tackling with ever greater energy and sense of purpose the major problems of the country's development. The most essential prerequisite for this is the activity of each deputy.

The very composition of the deputies indicates that those who have assembled here in the Kremlin Hall represent the best thoughts and the rich experience of the people. The deputies to the USSR Supreme Soviet are working people, representatives of labour collectives. They know from their own experience how the decisions of the highest body of state authority are translated into practice and what questions are thrust to the forefront by life today.

First among these is the question of steadily enhancing the efficiency of the national economy, of unfurling and using all its vast potentialities. Therein lies the main condition for raising still further the people's prosperity and for the all-round strengthening of the might of our homeland.

In accordance with the Constitution, the USSR Supreme Soviet is accomplishing these tasks directly or through bodies which it forms.

The most important role in conducting our economic and social policy is played by the government, ministries and state committees. The stage of mature socialism and the scientific and technological revolution place even higher demands on the mechanism of economic management, presuppose its further improvement and require ever greater and more purposeful organisational work.

We need the smooth and efficient functioning of the entire apparatus of management, real responsibility on the part of each person for the task entrusted to him, a persistent struggle against violations of state discipline and against all forms of extravagance, bad management and abuses. The primary role must be played in this by the 9 million members of the People's Control movement and the People's Control Committee of the USSR which heads it and which will be formed at this session.

A great role in the life of our society is played by the enforcement of socialist law and strict observance of Soviet legality elsewhere.

The USSR Supreme Soviet holds the most important levers for exerting the state's influence on public life. And the Constitution demands that these levers should operate faultlessly, that the guiding, co-ordinating and controlling activity of the Supreme Soviet should be developed in every way.

The Supreme Soviet of the Tenth Convocation is to discuss the questions connected with the conclusion of the current Five-Year-Plan period and the drawing up and implementation of the Eleventh Five-Year Plan of the country's development. Guiding ourselves by the directives of the Congresses of the Party and the Plenary Meetings of its Central Committee, we shall tackle a wide range of problems in the sphere of the economy and culture, planning and the material stimulation of production. We shall be constantly concentrating our attention on questions concerned with raising the living standards of the Soviet people and with the further advance of our people along the road of communist construction.

The improvement of legislation remains, as before, an important element of the activity of the Supreme Soviet. Vast and, I would say, intensive work lies ahead in this respect. It will require from the appropriate bodies a serious creative approach and a high level of responsibility.

Our policy aimed at ensuring that each of our laws and each decision that is adopted should be implemented without deviation and should have real effect remains unchanged.

With the adoption of the new Constitution considerable progress has been made in increasing the control of the USSR Supreme Soviet over the observance of laws, over meeting plan assignments and over the work of management bodies. We have already accumulated useful experience in discussing the reports of the government, ministries and departments at sessions of the Supreme Soviet, at its Presidium and at meetings of Standing Commissions. This practice should be continued in future, too, and, moreover, should become more purposeful.

A special place here belongs to the Standing Commissions. They must act more vigorously, must discuss the most vital, burning questions, must be persistent in ensuring the implementation of their recommendations and must exercise better control over their implementation. I believe that the regulations of the Supreme Soviet and the renewed statute of the Standing Commissions that we are to adopt will play a positive role in solving these tasks.

The new Constitution of the USSR has created broad opportunities for stepping up the activity of the Presidium of the Supreme Soviet in different directions. One of its most important duties is a consistent improvement in directing the work of Soviets at all levels, the summing up and passing on of the experience they have accumulated, as well as control over how the voters' mandates are being implemented and how the numerous proposals of the working people are being put into practice.

Implementing steadily the programme of economic and social development worked out by the 25th Party Congress, the USSR Supreme Soviet is called upon to give constant care to ensuring peaceful external conditions for communist construction in our land and to strengthening its defence capability. Guiding itself by the Leninist principles of the Party's foreign policy, it will continue to work persistently to safeguard peace on earth.

With these aims in view we must co-operate more broadly with representative bodies of the fraternal socialist countries, with the parliaments and peaceful public organisations of all countries, while giving active support to the peoples waging a struggle for national and social liberation.

In a word, comrade deputies, we are faced with vast work, both on the domestic and foreign-policy fronts. So let us work in such a way as to live up to the profound trust of the Soviet people, those toilers and fighters forging ahead under the Leninist banner of the Communist Party.

Speech at a session of the USSR
Supreme Soviet. 18 April 1979

INDEX

243

INDEX